Small Business Taxes

2nd Edition

by Eric Tyson, MBA

for
dummies®
A Wiley Brand

Small Business Taxes For Dummies®, 2nd Edition

Published by: **John Wiley & Sons, Inc.**, 111 River Street, Hoboken, NJ 07030-5774, www.wiley.com

For general information on our other products and services, please contact our Customer Care Department within the U.S. at 877-762-2974, outside the U.S. at 317-572-3993, or fax 317-572-4002. For technical support, please visit www.wiley.com/techsupport.

Wiley publishes in a variety of print and electronic formats and by print-on-demand. Some material included with standard print versions of this book may not be included in e-books or in print-on-demand. If this book refers to media such as a CD or DVD that is not included in the version you purchased, you may download this material at http://booksupport.wiley.com. For more information about Wiley products, visit www.wiley.com.

Library of Congress Control Number: 2019931479

ISBN 978-1-119-51784-9 (pbk); ISBN 978-1-119-51781-8 (ebk); ISBN 978-1-119-51783-2 (ebk)

Manufactured in the United States of America

C10008034_020419

Contents at a Glance

Table of Contents

Introduction

Welcome to the 2nd edition of *Small Business Taxes For Dummies!*

Starting and operating a small business involves many moving parts and issues. Money is the lifeblood of any business. You need money to start a business, and you need money to keep a business going.

As you earn and spend money in your business, taxes permeate just about everything that you do. Taxes are too often maddeningly complicated. But they need not be so. Enter this book! And the Tax Cuts and Jobs Act federal income tax bill, which took effect in 2018, produced many changes that reduced and positively impacted small business taxes.

I've owned and operated numerous small businesses in my life. I love the freedom and opportunity to pursue what I believe in and what interests me. And I generally detest dealing with tax issues. But I also know how important tax issues are in terms of the financial success or lack thereof for a small business.

Handled in the best possible way, you can save yourself tens of thousands — if not hundreds of thousands — of dollars by making informed tax moves. And you can comply with the tax rules and regulations and stay out of trouble with the Internal Revenue Service and your state and local tax authorities.

But if you stick your head in the sand or give in to the complexities of the tax laws, you may end up in trouble both financially and with the law.

About This Book

For most folks, their single biggest "expense" is their tax bill. And for tens of millions of small business owners, the nation's tax laws are a complex and constantly changing web ready to trip them up and siphon off their most precious and valuable business resource — their money.

Small Business Taxes For Dummies, 2nd edition, assists both current and aspiring small business owners with important tax planning issues, filing issues, dealing with IRS audits and notices, getting help, and more.

This book provides you with a crash course on taxes and your small business. Specifically, the goal is to ensure your understanding of the myriad tax rules and incentives so you can legally minimize your tax bill, stay in compliance with the law, and maximize your company's success. You need not read this book in the order it's presented. You can use the book as a reference and selectively read material currently relevant and of greatest interest to you.

Here are the biggest changes and updates in this edition:

>> Complete coverage of the federal income tax bill that took effect in 2018 and discussion of its impact on small business owners who file Schedule C as well as its impact on other incorporated businesses

>> Expanded coverage of issues affecting incorporated small businesses, partnerships, and LLCs

>> Expanded coverage of other business taxes including payroll and sales taxes

>> Additional coverage of websites and other online tax resources

>> Information on how to use apps and software for managing your small business tax issues

>> Enhanced coverage of sideline businesses and for millennials juggling multiple gigs

I've written this book so you can efficiently find information and easily understand what you find. And although I'd like to believe that you want to pore over every last word I've written, I actually make it easy for you to identify "skippable" material. This information is the stuff that, although interesting, isn't essential for you to know. Text in sidebars: The sidebars are the shaded boxes that appear here and there. They include helpful information and observations but aren't necessary reading.

Foolish Assumptions

In writing this book, I made some assumptions about you, dear reader:

>> You want expert advice about important small business tax and financial topics — such as the best way to purchase and write off equipment and other

business expenses, establish and fund retirement accounts, and correctly complete common business tax forms — and you want answers quickly.

>> Perhaps you want a crash course in small business tax and financial issues and are looking for a book to help solidify major financial concepts and get you thinking about your small business taxes in a more comprehensive way.

This book is basic enough to help novices get their arms around thorny tax issues. But advanced readers will be challenged, as well, to think about their small business taxes in a new way and identify areas for improvement.

Icons Used in This Book

The icons in this book help you find particular kinds of information that may be of use to you.

TIP

This target flags strategy recommendations for making the most of your small business tax decisions.

ERIC'S PICKS

This icon highlights the best products and services I've come across in the small business tax arena.

REMEMBER

This icon points out information that you'll definitely want to take away from this book.

WARNING

This icon marks things to avoid and points out common mistakes people make when making small business and tax decisions.

INVESTIGATE

This icon tells you when you should consider doing some additional research. Don't worry — I explain what to look for and what to look out for.

Where to Go from Here

This book is organized so you can go wherever you want to find complete information. You can check out the table of contents to find broad categories of information and a chapter-by-chapter rundown of what this book offers, or you can look up a specific topic in the index.

If you're not sure where you want to go, you may want to turn a few pages and start at the beginning with Part 1. It gives you all the basic information you need to assess your small business tax situation and points to places where you can find more detailed information for improving it.

In addition to the material in the print or e-book you're reading right now, this product also comes with some access-anywhere goodies on the web. Go to www.dummies.com and type in "Small Business Taxes For Dummies Cheat Sheet" in the search box to discover a list of pointers that can help you think about the role of money in your life and start achieving your financial goals.

1

Understanding Small Business Taxes

Minimize your tax bill through year-round tax planning and understand the recent tax bill. Be sure to factor taxes into your small business decisions, check out common tax mistakes, and understand tax terms and rates.

Decide what business entity (corporation, LLC, sole proprietorship, and so on) to use, and consider what benefits to offer to your employees.

Investigate your small business retirement account options — such as SEP-IRAs, SIMPLE plans, 403(b) plans, and 401(k) plans — and select top-notch investments.

Handle small business real estate decisions, such as deciding whether to work out of your home, lease space, or buy property.

Plan your estate, including your small business. Determine your estate's tax concerns and reduce your expected estate taxes.

Chapter **1**

Small Business Taxes 101

E ven though I write about personal finances, including tax issues, I don't particularly enjoy dealing with taxes. I would rather cut my lawn, take care of my neighbor's dog, or even visit my dentist (for a routine cleaning). At least in all these cases, I know my time commitment is reasonably limited, and when I'm done, I'm satisfied that the job has been done well, and I can move on to something else.

Filling out state and federal tax forms is often complicated and confusing. Because I write about taxes, I feel that it's essential for me to complete my own forms and returns, which forces me to wallow in the details as much as possible so that I can more fully appreciate the challenges taxpayers face. (By contrast, prior surveys have found that the representatives in Congress who sit on committees that draft the nation's tax laws generally use paid tax preparers themselves.) A report from the National Taxpayer Advocate cited "the complexity of the tax code as the No. 1 most serious problem facing taxpayers."

Though some of this book deals with the drudgery of completing required tax forms, much of it deals with the more interesting — and dare I say, fun — part of taxes, which is planning ahead and strategizing so as to reduce and minimize your taxes. You see, if you simply view your role with taxes and your small business as jumping through the many hoops that federal, state, and local authorities require, you're missing out on something really big — saving and keeping more of your hard-earned money.

This chapter introduces the basics of small business taxes. Here, I discuss the value of tax planning all year long, and I define some important tax-related terms regarding the taxes you pay or may come across.

Valuing Year-Round Tax Planning

Taxes are a large, vital piece of your small-business and personal-financial puzzle. You're required by law to complete your tax forms each year and pay the taxes you owe. You do this because you have deadlines and don't want contact initiated by local or state authorities or the IRS, to result in fines, penalties or worse, jail time!

Nothing really forces you to plan ahead regarding your tax situation and small business. That's why the vast majority of small business owners don't take steps year-round to plan and reduce their taxes. However, tax planning all year is valuable because it enables you to stay on top of your tax and business financial situation and minimize the taxes you legally owe. In this section, I explain typical ways in which taxes enter small business decisions and some common tax mistakes folks make in this realm.

Factoring taxes into small business decisions

REMEMBER

Taxes infiltrate many areas of your small business and your personal finances. Some people make important financial decisions without considering taxes (and other important variables). Conversely, in an obsession to minimize or avoid taxes, other people make decisions that are counterproductive to achieving their long-term business and personal financial goals. Although taxes are an important component to factor into your major business and financial decisions, taxes shouldn't drive or dictate the decisions you make.

The following list shows some of the ways that tax issues are involved in making sound financial decisions throughout the year.

>> **Type of business and benefits offered:** The type of business entity you select for your business — sole proprietorship, S corporation, limited liability company (LLC), and so on — can have significant tax and other consequences. The benefits you're able to utilize and offer to your employees, if you have them, also have tax ramifications (see Chapter 2).

>> **Retirement accounts:** Taking advantage of retirement accounts can mean tens, perhaps even hundreds of thousands more dollars in your pocket come

retirement time. Offering retirement account access to your employees can also be a valuable employee benefit for recruiting and retaining good employees if they understand what they have. Refer to Chapter 3 for more on retirement accounts.

>> **Spending:** Throughout this book, I discuss myriad spending decisions you may face in your small business, such as buying equipment (Chapter 8), spending on employee benefits (Chapter 2), and so on. These decisions will often affect your taxes both now and in the future.

>> **Protecting your assets:** Some of your insurance decisions also affect the taxes you pay. You'd think that after a lifetime of tax payments, your heirs would be left alone when you pass on to the great beyond — but that's wishful thinking. Estate planning can reduce the taxes that are siphoned off from your estate. See Chapter 5 to find out more about estate planning.

>> **Tracking your business financials:** Throughout the year, you should stay on top of your business's income and expenses so that you can see your business's financial health and record the numbers you need come tax time. Chapter 6 covers these important issues.

Checking out common tax mistakes

Even if some parts of the tax system are hopelessly and unreasonably complicated, there's no reason why you can't learn from the mistakes of others to save yourself some money, no matter the time of year. With this goal in mind, this section details common tax blunders that people make when it comes to managing their money.

Seeking advice after an important decision

Too many people seek out information and hire help *after* making a decision, even though seeking preventive help ahead of time generally is wiser and more financially beneficial.

TIP

Before making major small business and financial decisions, educate yourself. This book can help answer many of your questions. You may also want to do further research on your own (see Chapter 12) and/or hire a tax advisor (refer to Chapter 13) for some advice before making your decision(s).

Failing to withhold or submit enough taxes

If you're self-employed (or earn significant taxable income from investments outside retirement accounts), you need to make estimated quarterly tax payments. You also need to withhold taxes for your employees and send those taxes along to the appropriate tax agencies. Some small business owners don't have a human resources department to withhold taxes and dig themselves into a perpetual tax hole by failing to submit estimated quarterly tax payments.

To make quarterly tax payments, complete IRS Form 1040-ES, "Estimated Tax for Individuals." This form (discussed in Chapter 10) and its accompanying instructions (and payment coupons) explain how to calculate quarterly tax payments. For more information on the requirement for employee tax withholding, see Chapter 6.

Missing legal deductions

REMEMBER

Some taxpayers miss out on legitimate tax write-offs because they just don't know about them. If you aren't going to take the time to discover the legal deductions that are available to you and that I discuss throughout this book, then you should pay for the cost of a competent tax advisor at least once. Fearing an audit, some taxpayers (and even some tax preparers) avoid taking deductions that they have every right to take. Unless you have something to hide, such behavior is foolish and costly. Note that a certain number of returns are randomly audited every year, so even when you don't take every allowable deduction, you may nevertheless get audited! And, if you read Chapter 11, you can find out how to deal with an audit like a pro.

Forsaking retirement accounts

All the tax deductions and tax deferrals that come with accounts such as 401(k)s, SEP-IRA plans, and individual retirement accounts (IRAs) were put in the tax code to encourage you to save for retirement. That's something that you as a small business owner should be doing for yourself as well as encouraging your employees to do.

Most excuses for missing out on these accounts just don't make good financial sense. Some folks underfund retirement accounts because they spend too much and because retirement seems so far away. Others mistakenly believe that retirement account money is totally inaccessible until they're old enough to qualify for senior discounts. (See Chapter 3 to find out all about your small business retirement account options.)

Not owning real estate

In the long run, owning a home should cost you less than renting. And because mortgage interest (on up to $750,000 of mortgage debt) and property taxes (up to $10,000 when combined with your state income tax payments) are deductible, the government, in effect, subsidizes the cost of homeownership.

If you have a home office, you may be able to take additional expenses on your tax return. If you need a retail or commercial space for your small business, you should compare leasing to buying and be sure to factor in the tax benefits of owning. See Chapter 4 for more about real estate and taxes.

Neglecting the timing of events you can control

TIP

As a small business owner, you should pay attention to how your net income for the year is shaping up for the current year and how things are looking for next year. For example, if you're in the early stages of your business and you can see that you'll have more income next year, then it may be in your best interest tax-wise to delay paying some expenses from late in the current year into early next year. (This works when using cash basis accounting.)

Or suppose that you operate on a cash accounting basis and think that you'll be in a lower tax bracket next year. Perhaps business has slowed of late or you plan to take time off to be with a newborn or take an extended trip. You can send out some invoices later in the year so that your customers won't pay you until January, which falls in the next tax year.

Not using tax advisors effectively

REMEMBER

If your financial situation is complicated, going it alone and relying only on the IRS publications to figure your taxes usually is a mistake. Many people find the IRS instructions tedious and not geared toward highlighting opportunities for tax reductions. Instead, you can start by reading the relevant sections of this book. When you're overwhelmed by the complexity of particular small business and tax decisions, get advice from tax and financial advisors who sell their time and nothing else. (Chapter 13 has tips on hiring help.)

As a small business owner, ask yourself how much you're worth running your business versus how much you're worth as a bookkeeper. Then ask yourself which task you enjoy more and consider hiring a bookkeeper.

Note that using a tax advisor is most beneficial when you face new tax questions or problems. If your tax situation remains complicated or if you know that you'd do a worse job on your own, by all means keep using a tax preparer. If your situation is unchanging or isn't that complicated, consider hiring and paying someone to figure out your taxes one time. After that, go ahead and try completing your own tax returns.

Noting How Corporate and Individual Tax Reform Impacts Small Business

Corporate tax reform in the United States was long, long overdue. For too many years, corporations in the United States faced a much higher corporate income tax rate than did companies based in most overseas economies. As a result, increasing numbers of U.S. companies had chosen to expand more overseas rather than in the United States and to be headquartered outside of the United States, which wasn't good for the long-term health of U.S. economy and labor market.

Congress passed the Tax Cuts and Jobs Act in late 2017, which took effect with tax year 2018. It was the most significant tax reform package passed since the Tax Reform Act of 1986. What follows are the highlights of the most significant provisions that affect (and mostly benefit) small business.

Checking out corporate income tax rate reduction and simplification

At 35 percent, the United States had had one of the highest corporate income tax rates in the world before 2018. The Tax Cuts and Jobs Act slashed the corporate income tax rate to 21 percent, which represented a 40 percent reduction.

The corporate tax rules and deductions were simplified, including eliminating the corporate alternative minimum tax and closing some loopholes. The United States also moved to a *territorial* tax structure whereby U.S. companies would no longer pay a penalty to bring their overseas profits back home. The immediate impact of this change was to enable U.S. corporations to bring back to the United States more than $2 trillion being kept overseas to avoid excessive taxation.

The vast majority of small businesses aren't operated as traditional so-called C-corps (more on those in a moment). Most small business owners operate as sole proprietorships (filing Schedule C), LLCs, partnerships, or S corporations. In those cases, the business owner's profits from the business generally flow or pass through to the owner's personal income tax return and that income is taxed at personal income tax rates (see the section "Twenty percent deduction for pass through entities" for more information).

Reducing individual income tax rates

Just as the corporate income tax rate was reduced by the Tax Cuts and Jobs Act legislation, so too were the individual income tax rates. Most of the tax bracket rates were reduced by several percentage points (see Table 1-1 later in this chapter). This, of course, is excellent news for the vast majority of U.S. small business owners who operate their businesses as pass through entities (for example, sole proprietorships, LLCs, partnerships, S-corps).

Note that at higher levels of income, the individual income tax rates begin to exceed the 21 percent corporate tax rate. Seeing this helps you to better understand the next point as to why pass-through entities are being granted a special tax deduction on their profits.

Noting 20 percent deduction for pass-through entities

In redesigning the tax code, Congress rightfully realized that the many small businesses that operate as so-called pass-through entities would be subjected to higher federal income tax rates compared with the new 21 percent corporate income tax rate. *Pass-through entities* are small business entities such as sole proprietorships, LLCs, partnerships, and S corporations and are so named because the profits of the business pass through to the owners and their personal income tax returns.

To address the concern that individual business owners that operated their business as a pass-through entity could end up paying a higher tax rate than the 21 percent rate levied on C-corporations, Congress provided a 20 percent deduction for those businesses. So, for example, if your sole proprietorship netted you $60,000 in 2018 as a single taxpayer, that would push you into the 22 percent federal income tax bracket. But, you get to deduct 20 percent of that $60,000 of income (or $12,000) for the pass-through deduction so you would only owe federal income tax on the remaining $48,000 ($60,000 – $12,000).

Another way to look at this is that the business would only pay taxes on 80 percent of its profits and would be in the 22 percent federal income tax bracket. This deduction effectively reduces the 22 percent tax bracket to 17.6 percent.

This is a major change that not surprisingly has made small business owners exceedingly optimistic about being able to grow their businesses. In fact, in a January, 2018 survey of small business owners conducted by the nonprofit National Federation of Independent Business just after the tax bill was passed and signed into law, a record percentage of those surveyed (covering the survey's 45-year history) expressed optimism about it being a good time to expand their businesses.

This 20 percent pass-through deduction gets phased out for service business owners (such as lawyers, doctors, real estate agents, consultants, and so on) at single taxpayer incomes above $157,500 (up to $207,500) and for married couples filing jointly incomes more than $315,000 (up to $415,000). For other types of businesses above these income thresholds, this deduction may be limited so consult with your tax advisor.

Enjoying better equipment expensing rules

Through so-called section 179 rules, small businesses have historically been able to immediately deduct the cost of equipment, subject to annual limits, they purchase for use and place into service in their business. But the 2017 tax bill expanded these rules.

Now, more businesses can immediately deduct up to one million dollars in such equipment expense annually (up to the limit of their annual business income). And, this deduction can also now be used for purchases on used equipment. These provisions, which don't apply to real estate businesses, remain in effect through 2022 and then gradually phase out until 2027 when the prior depreciation schedules are supposed to kick back in.

Increasing maximum depreciation deduction for automobiles

The new tax bill included a major increase in the maximum amount of auto depreciation that can be claimed. The annual amounts of auto depreciation have more than tripled. Effective with tax year 2018, the maximum amounts that can be claimed are as follows:

>> **Year 1:** $10,000 up from the prior limit of $3,160

>> **Year 2:** $16,000 up from the prior limit of $5,100

>> **Year 3:** $9,600 up from the prior limit of $3,050

>> **Year 4 and beyond:** $5,760 up from the prior limit of $1,875, until costs are fully recovered.

These annual limits will increase with inflation for cars placed into service after 2018.

Limiting interest deductions

Effective with 2018, companies with annual gross receipts of at least $25 million on average over the prior three years are limited in their deduction of interest from business debt. Net interest costs are capped at 30 percent of the business's earnings before interest, taxes, depreciation, and amortization (EBITDA). Farmers and most real estate companies are exempt.

Then, effective in 2022, this provision actually gets more restrictive and would thus effect even more businesses. At that point, the 30 percent limit will apply to earnings before interest and taxes.

Reducing meal and entertainment deductions

The tax reform bill of 2017 eliminated the entertainment expense deduction for businesses. Under prior tax law, 50 percent of those expenses were deductible for example when a business entertained customers and even employees at sporting events, fitness clubs, and restaurants.

The new rules do include some exceptions. On-site cafeterias at a company's offices and meals provided to employees as well as business meals associated with travel are 50 percent deductible. Meals provided to prospective customers as part of a seminar presentation are still fully deductible. Holiday parties and company picnics are also fully deductible as long as they are inclusive of everyone.

Eliminating the health insurance mandate

Since the Affordable Care Act (a.k.a. Obamacare) was passed by Congress in 2010, some Republicans in Congress vowed to repeal it. With the election of Republican Donald Trump in 2016, it seemed that the pieces were in place for Obamacare's successful repeal. But, Republicans fell one vote short in the Senate when the late Arizona Senator John McCain gave the repeal measure his infamous thumb down vote.

So, the 2017 tax bill included a little known or discussed measure that eliminated Obamacare's mandate effective in 2019, which required people to have or buy health insurance coverage and if they didn't, they'd face a tax penalty. So, the penalty tax also disappears in 2019.

Revising rules for using net operating losses

Net operating losses (NOLs) can no longer be carried back for two years. However, NOLs may now be carried forward indefinitely until they are used up. Previously the carry forward limit was 20 years.

NOLs are limited each year to 80 percent of taxable income.

Understanding the Different Types of Taxes You Pay and Your Tax Rates

REMEMBER

Most small business owners pay income taxes at the personal income tax rates. That's because the vast majority of small businesses are run as sole proprietorships. And many of those that aren't, such as partnerships, LLCs, and S corporations, pass through their income in such a way that the income is generally taxed to its recipients as personal income. Some small business owners pay a corporate rate if their business is incorporated as a regular so-called *C-corporation.* (The type of business entity you elect is discussed in Chapter 2.) See the later section "Corporate income tax rates" for more details.

When it comes to federal income taxes, many people remember only whether they received a refund or owed money. But you should care how much you pay in taxes and the total and marginal taxes that you pay so you can make decisions that lessen your tax load. Although some people feel happy when they get refunds, you shouldn't. A refund simply signifies that you overpaid your taxes during the previous year. When you file your income tax return, you settle up with tax authorities regarding the amount of taxes you paid during the past year versus the total tax that you're actually required to pay, based on your income and deductions.

In this section, I define important tax terms such as total taxes, taxable income, marginal tax rates, and corporate tax rates, and I also discuss the federal and state income tax systems.

Defining total taxes and taxable income

The only way to determine the total amount of income taxes you pay is to get out your federal and state tax returns. On each of those returns, about one-third of the way before the end, is a line that shows the total tax. Add the totals from your federal and state tax returns, and you probably have one very large expense!

Your taxable income is different from the total amount of money you earn during the tax year from employment and investments. *Taxable income* is defined as the amount of income on which you actually pay income taxes. You don't pay taxes on your total income for the following two reasons:

>> **Not all income is taxable.** For example, you pay federal income tax on the interest that you earn on a bank savings account but not on the interest from *municipal bonds* (loans that you, as a bond buyer, make to state and local governments).

>> **You get to subtract deductions from your income.** Some deductions are available just for being a living, breathing human being. And, the Tax Cuts and Jobs Act greatly increased the standard deductions. For tax year 2018, single people receive an automatic $12,000 standard deduction, heads of household qualify for $18,000, and married couples filing jointly get $24,000. (People older than 65 and those who are blind get slightly higher deductions.) Other expenses, such as mortgage interest and property taxes, are deductible to the extent that your total itemized deductions exceed the standard deductions.

Your marginal income tax rate for federal income taxes

Marginal is a word that people often use when they mean "small" or "barely acceptable." But with taxes, marginal has a different meaning. The government charges you different income tax rates for different portions of your annual income. So your *marginal tax rate* is the rate that you pay on the so-called "last dollars" you earn. You generally pay less tax on your first, or lowest, dollars of earnings and more tax on your last, or highest, dollars of earnings. This system is known as a *graduated income tax,* a system that goes back hundreds of years to other countries.

The fact that not all income is treated equally under the current tax system isn't evident to most people. When you work for an employer and have a reasonably constant salary during the course of a year, a stable amount of federal and state taxes is deducted from each paycheck. Therefore, you may have the false impression that all your earned income is taxed equally.

Table 1-1 gives the 2018 federal income tax rates for singles and for married people filing jointly.

TABLE 1-1

2018 Federal Income Tax Brackets and Rates

Federal Income Tax Rate	Individuals Taxable Income	Married Filing Jointly Taxable Income
10%	$0 to $9,525	$0 to $19,050
12%	$9,525 to $38,700	$19,050 to $77,400
22%	38,700 to $82,500	$77,400 to $165,000
24%	$82,500 to $157,500	$165,000 to $315,000
32%	$157,500 to $200,000	$315,000 to $400,000
35%	$200,000 to $500,000	$400,000 to $600,000
37%	More than $500,000	More than $600,000

REMEMBER

Your marginal tax rate is the rate of tax that you pay on your last, or so-called highest, dollars of taxable income. For example, according to Table 1-1, if you're single and your taxable income during 2018 totals $50,000, you pay federal income tax at the rate of 10 percent on the first $9,525 of taxable income. You then pay 12 percent on the amount from $9,525 to $38,700 and 22 percent on income from $38,700 up to $50,000. In other words, you effectively pay a marginal federal tax rate of 22 percent on your last dollars of income — those dollars in excess of $38,700.

After you understand the powerful concept of marginal tax rates, you can see the value of the many financial strategies that affect the amount of taxes you pay. Because you pay taxes on your employment income and your investment earnings (other than retirement accounts), you need to make many of your personal financial decisions with your marginal tax rate in mind.

>> For example, when you have the opportunity to earn some extra money, how much of that extra compensation you get to keep depends on your marginal tax rate. Your marginal income tax rate enables you to quickly calculate the additional taxes you'd pay on the additional income.

>> Conversely, you quantify the amount of taxes that you save by reducing your taxable income, either by decreasing your income — for example, with pretax contributions to retirement accounts — or by increasing your deductions.

Actually, you can make even more of your marginal taxes. In the next section, I detail the painful realities of income taxes levied by most states that add to your federal income tax burden. If you're a middle-to-higher income earner, pay close attention to the sidebar later in this chapter where I discuss the alternative minimum tax.

State income taxes

Your total marginal rate includes your federal *and* state income tax rates. As you may already be painfully aware, you don't pay only federal income taxes. You also get hit with state income taxes — that is, unless you live in Alaska, Florida, Nevada, South Dakota, Texas, Washington, or Wyoming. Those states have no state income taxes. As is true with federal income taxes, state income taxes have been around since the early 1900s.

TIP

You can look up your state tax rate by getting out your most recent year's state income tax preparation booklet. Alternatively, Figure 1-1 gives you an idea of your state tax rates; it reflects state individual income taxes. Some states impose other taxes — such as local, county, or city taxes; special taxes for nonresidents; or capital gains taxes — which aren't included in this table.

STATE INDIVIDUAL INCOME TAXES
(Tax rates for tax year 2018 -- as of January 1, 2018)

	TAX RATE RANGE (in percents) Low	High	Number of Brackets	INCOME BRACKETS Lowest	Highest	PERSONAL EXEMPTIONS Single	Married	Dependents	FEDERAL INCOME TAX DEDUCTIBLE
ALABAMA	2.0 -	5.0	3	500 (b) -	3,001 (b)	1,500	3,000	500 (e)	Yes
ALASKA	No State Income Tax								
ARIZONA (a)	2.59 -	4.54	5	10,179 (b) -	152,668 (b)	2,150	4,300	2,300	
ARKANSAS (a)	0.9 -	6.9 (f)	6	4,299 -	35,100	26 (c)	52 (c)	26 (c)	
CALIFORNIA (a)	1.0 -	12.3 (g)	9	8,223 (b) -	551,473 (b)	114 (c)	228 (c)	353 (c)	
COLORADO	4.63		1	-----Flat rate-----		4,150 (d)	8,300 (d)	4,150 (d)	
CONNECTICUT	3.0 -	6.99	7	10,000 (b) -	500,000 (b)	14,500 (h)	24,000 (h)	0	
DELAWARE	0.0 -	6.6	7	2,000 -	60,001	110 (c)	220 (c)	110 (c)	
FLORIDA	No State Income Tax								
GEORGIA	1.0 -	6.0	6	750 (i) -	7,001 (i)	2,700	7,400	3,000	
HAWAII	1.4 -	11.0	12	2,400 (b) -	200,000 (b)	1,144	2,288	1,144	
IDAHO (a)	1.6 -	7.4	7	1,472 (b) -	11,043 (b)	4,150 (d)	6,300 (d)	4,150 (d)	
ILLINOIS	4.95		1	-----Flat rate-----		2,000	4,000	2,000	
INDIANA	3.23		1	-----Flat rate-----		1,000	2,000	2,500 (j)	
IOWA (a)	0.36 -	8.98	9	1,598 -	71,910	40 (c)	80 (c)	40 (c)	Yes
KANSAS	3.1 -	5.7	3	15,000 (b) -	30,000 (b)	2,250	4,500	2,250	
KENTUCKY	2.0 -	6.0	6	3,000 -	75,001	10 (c)	20 (c)	10 (c)	
LOUISIANA	2.0 -	6.0	3	12,500 (b) -	50,001 (b)	4,500 (k)	9,000 (k)	1,000	Yes
MAINE (a)	5.8 -	7.15	3	21,450 (l) -	50,750 (l)	4,150 (d)	8,300 (d)	4,150 (d)	
MARYLAND	2.0 -	5.75	8	1,000 (m) -	250,000 (m)	3,200	6,400	3,200	
MASSACHUSETTS	5.10		1	-----Flat rate-----		4,400	8,800	1,000	
MICHIGAN (a)	4.25		1	-----Flat rate-----		4,000	8,000	4,000	
MINNESOTA (a)	5.35 -	9.85	4	25,890 (n) -	160,020 (n)	4,150 (d)	8,300 (d)	4,150 (d)	
MISSISSIPPI	3.0 -	5.0	3	5,000 -	10,001	6,000	12,000	1,500	
MISSOURI (a) (o)	1.5 -	5.9	10	1,028 -	9,253	2,100	4,200	1,200	Yes (p)
MONTANA (a)	1.0 -	6.9	7	3,000 -	17,900	2,400	4,800	2,400	Yes (p)
NEBRASKA (a)	2.46 -	6.84	4	3,150 (b) -	30,420 (b)	134 (c)	268 (c)	134 (c)	
NEVADA	No State Income Tax								
NEW HAMPSHIRE	State Income Tax of 5% on Dividends and Interest Income Only								
NEW JERSEY	1.4 -	8.97	6	20,000 (q) -	500,000 (q)	1,000	2,000	1,500	
NEW MEXICO	1.7 -	4.9	4	5,500 (r) -	16,001 (r)	4,150 (d)	8,300 (d)	4,150 (d)	
NEW YORK (a)	4.0 -	8.82	8	8,500 (b) -	1,077,550 (b)	0	0	1,000	
NORTH CAROLINA	5.499		1	-----Flat rate-----		----------None----------			
NORTH DAKOTA (a)	1.10 -	2.90	5	38,700 (s) -	424,950 (s)	4,150 (d)	8,300 (d)	4,150 (d)	
OHIO (a)	0.0 -	4.997	8	10,650 -	213,350	2,300 (t)	4,600 (t)	2,300 (t)	
OKLAHOMA	0.5 -	5.0	6	1,000 (u) -	7,200 (u)	1,000	2,000	1,000	
OREGON (a)	5.0 -	9.9	4	3,450 (b) -	125,000 (b)	201 (c)	402 (c)	201 (c)	Yes (p)
PENNSYLVANIA	3.07		1	-----Flat rate-----		----------None----------			
RHODE ISLAND (a)	3.75 -	5.99	3	62,550 -	142,150	4,000	8,000	4,000	
SOUTH CAROLINA (a)	0.0 -	7.0	6	2,970 -	14,860	4,150 (d)	8,300 (d)	4,150 (d)	
SOUTH DAKOTA	No State Income Tax								
TENNESSEE	State Income Tax of 3% on Dividends and Interest Income Only (y)					1,250	2,500	0	
TEXAS	No State Income Tax								
UTAH	5.0		1	-----Flat rate-----		(v)	(v)	(v)	
VERMONT (a)	3.55 -	8.95	5	37,950 (w) -	416,700 (w)	4,150 (d)	8,300 (d)	4,150 (d)	
VIRGINIA	2.0 -	5.75	4	3,000 -	17,001	930	1,860	930	
WASHINGTON	No State Income Tax								
WEST VIRGINIA	3.0 -	6.5	5	10,000 -	60,000	2,000	4,000	2,000	
WISCONSIN (a)	4.0 -	7.65	4	11,450 (x) -	252,150 (x)	700	1,400	700	
WYOMING	No State Income Tax								
DIST. OF COLUMBIA	4.0 -	8.95	5	10,000 -	1,000,000	1,675	3,350	1,675	

(a) 19 states have statutory provision for automatically adjusting to the rate of inflation the dollar values of the income tax brackets, standard deductions, and/or personal exemptions. Massachusetts, Michigan, and Nebraska index the personal exemption only. Oregon does not index the income brackets for $125,000 and over.

(b) For joint returns, taxes are twice the tax on half the couple's income.

(c) The personal exemption takes the form of a tax credit instead of a deduction

(d) These states use the personal exemption amounts provided in the federal Internal Revenue Code. Note, the Tax Cut and Reform Act of 2017 has eliminated personal exemptions from the IRC. These states will need to enact legislation to reinstate a personal exemption for tax year 2018. We have reported here the exemption amounts before the federal tax change.

(e) In Alabama, the per-dependent exemption is $1,000 for taxpayers with state AGI of $20,000 or less, $500 with AGI from $20,001 to $100,000, and $300 with AGI over $100,000.

(f) Arkansas has separate brackets for taxpayers with income under $75,000 and $21,000. The tax rates for lower income taxpayers are scheduled to decrease beginning in tax year 2019.

(g) California imposes an additional 1% tax on taxable income over $1 million, making the maximum rate 13.3% over $1 million.

(h) Connecticut's personal exemption incorporates a standard deduction. An additional tax credit is allowed ranging from 75% to 0% based on state adjusted gross income. Exemption amounts are phased out for higher income taxpayers until they are eliminated for households earning over $71,000.

(i) The Georgia income brackets reported are for single individuals. For married couples filing jointly, the same tax rates apply to income brackets ranging from $1,000, to $10,000.

(j) In Indiana, includes an additional exemption of $1,500 for each dependent child.

(k) The amounts reported for Louisiana are a combined personal exemption-standard deduction.

(l) The income bracket reported for Maine are for single individuals. For married couples filing jointly, the same tax rates apply to income brackets ranging from $42,900 to $101,550.

(m) The income brackets reported for Maryland are for single individuals. For married couples filing jointly, the same tax rates apply to income brackets ranging from $1,000, to $300,000.

(n) The income brackets reported for Minnesota are for single individuals. For married couples filing jointly, the same tax rates apply to income brackets ranging from $37,850 to $266,700.

(o) Beginning after tax year 2017, the top Missouri tax rate is scheduled to decrease by 0.1 each year [if revenue gain requirements are met] until it reaches 5.5%.

(p) The deduction for federal income tax is limited to $5,000 for individuals and $10,000 for joint returns in Missouri and Montana, and to $6,350 for all filers in Oregon.

(q) The New Jersey rates reported are for single individuals. For married couples filing jointly, the tax rates also range from 1.4% to 8.97%, with 7 brackets and the same high and low income ranges.

(r) The income brackets reported for New Mexico are for single individuals. For married couples filing jointly, the same tax rates apply to income brackets ranging from $8,000 to $24,000.

(s) The income brackets reported for North Dakota are for single individuals. For married couples filing jointly, the same tax rates apply to income brackets ranging from $64,650 to $424,950.

(t) Ohio provides an additional tax credit of $20 per exemption. Exemption amounts reduced for higher income taxpayers.

(u) The income brackets reported for Oklahoma are for single persons. For married persons filing jointly, the same tax rates apply to income brackets ranging from $2,000, to $12,200.

(v) Utah provides a tax credit equal to 6% of the federal personal exemption amounts (and applicable standard deduction). Note, the Tax Cut and Reform Act of 2017 has eliminated personal exemptions and increased the standard deduction in the IRC. Utah will need to enact legislation to reinstate a personal credit for tax year 2018.

(w) Vermont's income brackets reported are for single individuals. For married taxpayers filing jointly, the same tax rates apply to income brackets ranging from $63,350 to $416,700.

(x) The Wisconsin income brackets reported are for single individuals. For married taxpayers filing jointly, the same tax rates apply income brackets ranging from $15,270, to $336,200.

(y) Tennessee Hall Tax Rate on Dividends and Interest is being phased out, 1% reduction each year

Source: Federation of Tax Administrators, January 2018.

FIGURE 1-1:
State marginal tax rates.

THE ALTERNATIVE MINIMUM TAX

In 1969, Congress created a second tax system — called the alternative minimum tax (AMT) to ensure that higher-income earners with relatively high amounts of itemized deductions pay at least a minimum amount of taxes on their incomes. When it was added to the federal income tax code in 1969, the AMT affected a mere 155 high-income taxpayers; in 2017 before tax reform was passed, it hit about 5 million taxpayers! Thanks to the Tax Cuts and Jobs Act, which took effect in 2018, it's anticipated that AMT will impact "just" 200,000 taxpayers.

If you have a bunch of deductions from state income taxes, real estate taxes, certain types of mortgage interest, large miscellaneous itemized expenses, or passive investments (such as limited partnerships or rental real estate), you may fall prey to the AMT. The AMT is a classic case of the increasing complexity of the U.S. tax code. As incentives were placed in the tax code, people took advantage of them. Then the government said, "Whoa! We can't have people taking that many write-offs." Rather than doing the sensible thing and limiting some of those deductions, Congress created the AMT instead.

The AMT restricts you from claiming certain deductions and requires you to increase your taxable income. So you must figure the tax you owe both under and out of the AMT system, and then pay whichever amount is higher. Unfortunately, the only way to know for certain whether you're ensnared by this second tax system is by completing — you guessed it — another tax form. Form 6251, "Alternative Minimum Tax — Individuals" is a bear of a form, so if you're confronting it for the first time, you may want to enlist the support of a qualified tax advisor. Also, be aware that if you don't calculate the AMT on your return and you should have, the IRS will calculate the bill for the additional tax, interest, and possibly late payment penalties.

Corporate income tax rates

As I explain earlier in this chapter, the vast, vast majority of small business owners pay income taxes on their business earnings at the personal income tax rates. That's because most small businesses are organized as sole proprietorships, which have income taxed as personal income. Also, many other small businesses that are organized as partnerships, LLCs, and S corporations pass through their income to the business owners in such a way that it, too, is taxed as personal income.

Thus, only a small percentage of small business owners have their income taxed as regular, so-called C-corporations. The Tax Cuts and Jobs Act, which took effect in 2018, compressed the previous numerous corporate income tax brackets to just one rate – 21 percent. In the next chapter, I discuss how the tax rate a business pays along with other factors play a role in determining what's the best business entity for your business.

Employment (payroll) taxes

Business owners are responsible for the timely payment of all employee related payroll or employment taxes. Some of these are withheld from the employees' pay while others are paid by the employer. Here are the taxes I'm talking about:

>> Federal income tax withholding

>> State income tax withholding

>> Social Security and Medicare taxes (aka FICA) – half paid by employer, half paid by employees

>> Federal unemployment tax – paid by employers

>> State unemployment tax

It's imperative that you understand and properly withhold and pay all of these taxes on a timely basis. For a list of state tax authorities, visit www.taxadmin.org/state-tax-agencies. Otherwise, you and your business could be subject to stiff penalties and interest charges. Here's an overview of the frequency with which employment taxes are required:

>> Larger employers (paid more than $50,000 in employment taxes the previous calendar quarter) must submit/deposit their employment taxes every two weeks.

>> Moderate-sized employers (those that have between $2,500 and $50,000 in employment taxes) can submit their employment taxes monthly.

>> Smaller employers (have less than $2,500 in employment taxes quarterly) may submit their employment taxes with their quarterly employer tax returns. Those with $1,000 or less for income tax withholding and Social Security and Medicare tax payments or federal unemployment tax payments under $500 can pay annually.

Employers must generally deposit these taxes electronically using the Electronic Federal Tax Payment System (EFTPS), which was originally launched in 1996 and doesn't charge users. This system enables the transfer of your funds from your bank account to the U.S. Treasury.

If your annual employment taxes for your business exceed $1,000, you must file each quarter IRS Form 941, "Employer's Quarterly Federal Tax Return." You can instead file IRS Form 944, "Employer's Annual Federal Income Tax Return" if your annual employment taxes are less than or equal to $1,000.

To ensure the timely credit of your taxes, plan on submitting them at least one day before they're actually due. Alternatively, your tax advisor, payroll service, bank, or other financial institution can make the deposit on your behalf.

For more information, visit www.eftps.gov or call 800-555-4477.

Also, remember that self-employed individuals need to pay self-employment taxes, which are Social Security and Medicare taxes. See Chapter 10 for all the details.

Sales taxes

As you probably already know from your years as a consumer many towns, cities, counties, and states levy sales taxes on the purchase of particular goods and services. A related tax, known as a *use tax*, may be levied on the buyer of certain products from out of state.

As the seller of goods or services within a state with a sales tax, your business is obligated to collect and submit said tax to the relevant agency for sales tax collection in your state.

The Streamlined Sales Tax Governing Board was created by the National Governor's Association (NGA) and the National Conference of State Legislatures (NCSL) in 1999 to simplify sales tax collection. By visiting their website at www.streamlinedsalestax.org/ you can find a list of Certified Service Providers that can help you collect and remit sales tax to the state(s) in which you do business. There is no cost to your business for this service, and using it eliminates any risk of your business being audited for sales tax collections.

Chapter **2**

Making Important Business Decisions

As a small business owner, you face many important decisions. This chapter deals with two big ones that come up in the early days, months, and years of your venture.

» First is the type of business entity you'll operate under — sole proprietor, C or S corporation, limited liability company (LLC), and so on. This decision impacts the liability exposure you have, tax-reporting requirements, and income taxes you and your business will owe.

» The second is the benefits your business may consider for yourself and any employees.

SIDELINE BUSINESSES, TAX WRITE-OFFS, AND THE HOBBY LOSS RULES

Many supposed tax gurus state that you can slash your taxes simply by finding a product or service that you can sell on the side of your regular employment. The problem, they argue, is that as a regular wage earner who receives a paycheck from an employer, you can't write off many of your other (personal) expenses. Open a sideline business, they say, and you can deduct your personal expenses as business expenses.

The pitch is enticing, but the reality is something quite different. You have to spend money to get tax deductions, and the spending must be for legitimate purposes of your business in its efforts to generate income. If you think that taking tax deductions as a hobby is worth the risk because you won't get caught unless you're audited, the odds are stacked against you. The IRS audits an extraordinarily large portion of small businesses that show regular losses.

You need to operate a real business for the purpose of generating income and profits, not tax deductions. The IRS generally considers an activity a hobby (and not a business) if it shows a loss for three or more of the preceding five tax years. (***Exception:*** The IRS considers horse racing and breeding a hobby if it shows a loss for at least six of the preceding seven tax years.) Some years, a certain number of businesses lose money, but a real business can't afford to do so year after year and remain in operation. The IRS commonly views these activities as hobbies, particularly when they generate little if any income: antique collecting, crafts, creating art, photography, stamp collecting, training and showing dogs or horses, and writing.

Even if your sideline business passes this hobby test as well as other IRS requirements, deducting any expenses that aren't directly applicable to your business is illegal. Also, the Tax Cuts and Jobs Act passed in late 2017 and that took effect in 2018, eliminated the ability for those engaged in a hobby to deduct their expenses as an itemized deduction up to the limit of the income from their hobby for the calendar year. Now, those engaged in a hobby are supposed to report their revenue for tax purposes but are no longer able to claim an itemized deduction for their hobby expenses.

Choosing Your Business Entity

Many small business owners don't fully consider (or aren't even aware of) the options they have for the entity under which they conduct their business. Most entrepreneurs default into sole proprietor status for a variety of reasons. But you should be aware of all your choices — such as C corporations, S corporations, partnerships, and LLCs. That's what I discuss in this section.

Sole proprietorships

If you're interested in running your own business, odds are you'll do so as a so-called *sole proprietor.* About 70 percent of self-employed folks operate their businesses as sole proprietors because setting up a business this way is easier and generally less costly than other options. In this section I discuss the advantages and disadvantages of operating your business as a sole proprietorship.

Understanding the "solo" advantages

The pros of operating as a sole proprietor (going solo) may or may not outweigh the cons for a given small business owner. Each business (and owner) is unique and should weight the pros and cons. Consider the following advantages:

>> **Simplest tax rules and record keeping compared with other business entity options:** You report your business income and expenses on Schedule C of IRS Form 1040 (discussed in detail in Chapter 8), and the net income or loss carries over to your personal income tax return. Though no walk in the park itself, compared with corporate tax forms, Schedule C is easier to complete.

>> **Low cost to establish or discontinue:** Without incorporating, it's a relative snap to get going or shut down.

>> **High flexibility to switch to other entity forms:** You can easily switch to any of the other entities (corporation, LLC, and so on) I discuss later in this chapter.

>> **Good retirement plan options:** You can stash away a large chunk of your business earnings in a tax-advantaged retirement account (discussed in Chapter 3).

So does this mean that running your small business as a sole proprietorship is the way to go for you and your company? Not necessarily — next up are the drawbacks, which you should weigh in your case.

Weighing the disadvantages of operating "solo"

WARNING

Organizing and running your small business as a sole proprietorship has its cons, and these may outweigh the pros, depending on the type of business you're running. Here are the drawbacks you should be aware of:

>> **Liability exposure:** Unlike in a corporation, where you have some shielding from liability thanks to the corporate structure, a sole proprietorship offers no such protection. However, as I discuss in the later section "Investigating liability insurance," you may be able to buy liability insurance, depending on the type of business you operate.

- **Only one owner is permitted:** If you want to provide some small ownership stakes to key employees, you can't do that in a solo business. One exception: You can share ownership with your spouse so long as your spouse "materially participates" (that is, works) in the business. If both you and your spouse are owners, you each need to file your own Schedule C (more work), and you each need to pay Social Security tax on your share of the earnings (more tax).

- **Estate issues:** With some business entities, the business structure survives your passing, but not so with a sole proprietorship. This may have negative consequences on the tax front and if you want your survivors to be able to easily continue with the company. (Flip to Chapter 5 for an introduction to estate planning.)

- **You're taxed on all profits, even if you don't want to take them all out of the business:** If you have a big year or two, don't need all the money your business is generating, and want to leave some of it in the business, you still pay personal income tax on all those earnings as a solo. Not so with some other entities I discuss later in this chapter.

- **Increased audit risks:** The IRS knows that it finds more tax mistakes and fraud with solo businesses, so on average, it tends to audit such companies at a somewhat higher rate.

Now, in enumerating these possible drawbacks to operating a business as a sole proprietorship, I'm not trying to scare you off from doing so or talk you into, for example, incorporating. You need to consider which pros and cons may or may not apply to your situation and the type of business you're envisioning or operating. And you need to consider the alternative entities, like the ones later in this chapter.

The incorporation decision

A corporation, technically speaking, is a legal entity that's separate from its founders, managers, and employees; it's owned by shareholders. Your personal assets are protected in case the corporation is sued. C corporations (the subject of this section) provide the most financial protection to shareholders, but many small businesses choose to be S corporations because they're cheaper to start and easier to maintain and have just one level of taxation compared with the two levels of taxation for C corporations. (I discuss S corporations in more detail later in this chapter.)

Before you call a lawyer or your state government offices to figure out how to incorporate, you need to know that incorporating takes time and costs money. Corporations generally involve the highest costs and most administrative hassles among the range of business entities for you to use. There are fees to incorporate, and each state levies an annual fee that you must pay, even if you have no business income that year. You also have higher legal and accounting costs thanks to the more complex tax rules and filings required of corporations, including the dreaded IRS Form 1120, "U.S. Corporation Income Tax Return" (see the first page of the form in Figure 2-1; the complete, most recent form is located at www.irs.gov/pub/irs-pdf/f1120.pdf).

Form 1120 — Department of the Treasury, Internal Revenue Service

U.S. Corporation Income Tax Return

For calendar year 2018 or tax year beginning _____, 2018, ending _____, 20 ____

▶ Go to *www.irs.gov/Form1120* for instructions and the latest information.

OMB No. 1545-0123

2018

A Check if:
1a Consolidated return (attach Form 851)
b Life/nonlife consolidated return
2 Personal holding co. (attach Sch. PH)
3 Personal service corp. (see instructions)
4 Schedule M-3 attached

TYPE OR PRINT

Name
Number, street, and room or suite no. If a P.O. box, see instructions.
City or town, state or province, country, and ZIP or foreign postal code

B Employer identification number
C Date incorporated
D Total assets (see instructions) $

E Check if: (1) ☐ Initial return (2) ☐ Final return (3) ☐ Name change (4) ☐ Address change

Income

1a	Gross receipts or sales	1a
b	Returns and allowances	1b
c	Balance. Subtract line 1b from line 1a	1c
2	Cost of goods sold (attach Form 1125-A)	2
3	Gross profit. Subtract line 2 from line 1c	3
4	Dividends and inclusions (Schedule C, line 23, column (a))	4
5	Interest	5
6	Gross rents	6
7	Gross royalties	7
8	Capital gain net income (attach Schedule D (Form 1120))	8
9	Net gain or (loss) from Form 4797, Part II, line 17 (attach Form 4797)	9
10	Other income (see instructions—attach statement)	10
11	**Total income.** Add lines 3 through 10 ▶	11

Deductions (See instructions for limitations on deductions.)

12	Compensation of officers (see instructions—attach Form 1125-E) ▶	12
13	Salaries and wages (less employment credits)	13
14	Repairs and maintenance	14
15	Bad debts	15
16	Rents	16
17	Taxes and licenses	17
18	Interest (see instructions)	18
19	Charitable contributions	19
20	Depreciation from Form 4562 not claimed on Form 1125-A or elsewhere on return (attach Form 4562)	20
21	Depletion	21
22	Advertising	22
23	Pension, profit-sharing, etc., plans	23
24	Employee benefit programs	24
25	Reserved for future use	25
26	Other deductions (attach statement)	26
27	**Total deductions.** Add lines 12 through 26 ▶	27
28	Taxable income before net operating loss deduction and special deductions. Subtract line 27 from line 11.	28
29a	Net operating loss deduction (see instructions)	29a
b	Special deductions (Schedule C, line 24, column (c))	29b
c	Add lines 29a and 29b	29c

Tax, Refundable Credits, and Payments

30	**Taxable income.** Subtract line 29c from line 28. See instructions	30
31	Total tax (Schedule J, Part I, line 11)	31
32	2018 net 965 tax liability paid (Schedule J, Part II, line 12)	32
33	Total payments, credits, and section 965 net tax liability (Schedule J, Part III, line 23)	33
34	Estimated tax penalty. See instructions. Check if Form 2220 is attached ▶ ☐	34
35	**Amount owed.** If line 33 is smaller than the total of lines 31, 32, and 34, enter amount owed	35
36	**Overpayment.** If line 33 is larger than the total of lines 31, 32, and 34, enter amount overpaid	36
37	Enter amount from line 36 you want: **Credited to 2019 estimated tax** ▶ / **Refunded** ▶	37

Sign Here

Under penalties of perjury, I declare that I have examined this return, including accompanying schedules and statements, and to the best of my knowledge and belief, it is true, correct, and complete. Declaration of preparer (other than taxpayer) is based on all information of which preparer has any knowledge.

▶ Signature of officer — Date — ▶ Title

May the IRS discuss this return with the preparer shown below? See instructions. ☐ Yes ☐ No

Paid Preparer Use Only

Print/Type preparer's name — Preparer's signature — Date — Check ☐ if self-employed — PTIN
Firm's name ▶ — Firm's EIN ▶
Firm's address ▶ — Phone no.

For Paperwork Reduction Act Notice, see separate instructions. — Cat. No. 11450Q — Form **1120** (2018)

FIGURE 2-1: The corporate tax form — IRS Form 1120 — entails a high degree of difficulty. Shown is page one.

Courtesy of the Internal Revenue Service

In some instances, the decision to incorporate is complicated, but in most cases, it need not be a difficult choice. Taxes may be important to the decision but aren't the only consideration. This section presents an overview of the critical issues to consider. I discuss liability considerations, including whether you can obtain liability insurance for your chosen profession, as well as tax and other considerations.

TIP

If you weigh the following considerations of incorporating and you're still on the fence, my advice is to keep it simple: Don't incorporate. After you incorporate, un-incorporating takes time and money. Start as a sole proprietorship and then take it from there. Wait until the benefits of incorporating for your particular case clearly outweigh the costs and drawbacks of incorporating. Likewise, if the only benefits of incorporating can be better accomplished through some other means (such as purchasing insurance), save your money and time and don't incorporate.

Getting a handle on liability protection

The chief reason to consider incorporating your small business is for purposes of liability protection. Attorneys speak of the "protection of the corporate veil." Don't confuse this veil with insurance. You don't get any insurance when you incorporate. You may need or want to buy liability insurance instead of (or in addition to) incorporating (see the next section for details). Liability protection doesn't insulate your company from being sued, either.

When you incorporate, the protection of the corporate veil provides you with the separation of your business assets and liabilities from your personal finances in most situations (gross negligence and bad faith being notable counterexamples). (You must follow the ground rules, though, for being a corporation.) Why would you want to do that? Suppose that your business is doing well, and you take out a bank loan to expand. Over the next few years, however, your business ends up in trouble. Before you know it, your company is losing money, and you're forced to close up shop. If you can't repay the bank loan because of your business failure, the bank shouldn't be able to go after your personal assets if you're incorporated, right?

Unfortunately, many small business owners who need money find that bankers ask for personal guarantees, which negate part of the liability protection that comes with incorporation. Additionally, if you play financial games with your company (such as shifting money out of the company in preparation for defaulting on a loan), a bank may legally be able to go after your personal assets. So you must adhere to a host of ground rules and protocols to prove to the IRS that you're running a bona fide company. For example, you need to keep corporate records and hold an annual meeting — even if it's just with yourself!

A business can be sued if it mistreats an employee or if its product or service causes harm to a customer. But the owner's personal assets should generally be protected when the company is incorporated and meets the other protocols for being a legitimate business just discussed.

Investigating liability insurance

Before you incorporate, investigate and find out what actions can cause you to be sued. You can do this by asking others in your line of business or advisors who work with companies like yours. Then see whether you can purchase insurance to protect against these potential liabilities. Insurance is superior to incorporation because it pays claims.

If you belong to a professional group(s), especially if it has a national office, the group may be able to provide information on the percentage of members who are incorporated and on legal and insurance issues. Also, insurance agents may be able to advise on their experience with claims in your specific industry.

Suppose that you perform professional services but make a major mistake that costs someone a lot of money, or worse. Even if you're incorporated, if someone sues you and wins, your company may have to cough up the dough. This situation not only costs a great deal of money but also can sink your business. Only insurance can cover such financially destructive claims.

You can also be sued if someone slips and breaks a bone or two. To cover these types of claims, you can purchase a property or premises liability policy from an insurer.

Accountants, doctors, and a number of other professionals can buy liability insurance. A good place to start searching for liability insurance is through the associations that exist for your profession. Even if you aren't a current member, check out the associations anyway. You may be able to access any insurance they provide without membership or you can join the association long enough to get signed up. Incorporating, however, doesn't necessarily preclude insuring yourself. Both incorporating and covering yourself with liability insurance may make sense in your case.

Understanding corporate taxes

Corporations are taxed as entities separate from their individual owners. This situation can be both good and bad. Suppose that your business is doing well and making lots of money. If your business isn't incorporated, all your company's profits are taxed on your personal tax return in the year that you earn those profits.

If you intend to use the profits to reinvest in your business and expand, incorporating can appear to potentially save you some tax dollars. When your business is incorporated (as a regular or so-called *C corporation*), effective 2018, all of your profits are taxed at the 21 percent corporate tax rate, which is lower than most of the individual income tax brackets for moderate and higher income earners.

But, there's more to this tax rate comparison story. Unincorporated small businesses that operate as so-called pass-through entities (for example, sole proprietorships, LLCs, partnerships, and S corporations), named so because the profits of the business *pass through* to the owners and their personal income tax returns, have a new advantage. To address the fact that business owners that operated their business as a pass-through entity could face a higher personal federal income tax rate than the 21 percent rate levied on C-corporations, Congress provided a 20 percent deduction for those pass-through businesses. So, for example, if your sole proprietorship, LLC, partnership, or S-corporation netted you $80,000 in 2018 as a single taxpayer, that would push you into the 22 percent federal income tax bracket, a bit above the corporate rate of 21 percent. But, you get to deduct 20 percent of that $80,000 of income ($16,000), so you would only owe federal income tax on the remainder $64,000 ($80,000 − $16,000). Another way to look at this is that the business pass-through owner would only pay federal income taxes on 80 percent of his profits and would be in the 22 percent federal income tax bracket. This deduction effectively reduces the 22 percent federal income tax bracket to 17.6 percent, which is lower than the 21 corporate tax rate.

One caveat to the previous points: The 20 percent pass-through deduction gets phased out for service business owners (such as lawyers, doctors, real estate agents, consultants, and so on) at single taxpayer incomes above $157,500 (up to $207,500) and for married couples filing jointly incomes over $315,000 (up to $415,000). For other types of businesses above these income thresholds, this deduction may be limited so consult with your tax advisor.

WARNING

Resist the temptation to incorporate just so you can leave your money in the corporation, which may be taxed at a lower rate than you'd pay on your personal income. Don't be motivated by this seemingly short-term gain. If you want to pay yourself the profits in the future, you can end up paying more taxes. Why? Because you pay taxes first at the corporate tax rate in the year your company earns the money, and then you pay taxes again on these same profits (this time on your personal income tax return) when you pay yourself from the corporate till in the form of a dividend.

Another possible tax advantage for a corporation is that corporations can pay, on a tax-deductible basis, for employee benefits such as health insurance, long-term care insurance, disability insurance, and up to $50,000 of term life insurance. The owner usually is treated as an employee for benefits purposes. (See the later section "Benefits that are deductible for corporation owners" for details.) Sole proprietorships and other unincorporated businesses usually can take only tax deductions for these benefit expenses for employees. Benefit expenses for owners who work in the business aren't deductible, except for pension contributions and health insurance, which you can deduct on the front of IRS Form 1040.

Another reason not to incorporate, especially in the early years of a business, is that you can't claim the losses for an incorporated business on your personal tax return. On your business tax return, you have to wait to claim the losses against profits. Because most companies produce little revenue in their early years and have all sorts of start-up expenditures, losses are common.

Examining other incorporation considerations

Because corporations are legal entities distinct from their owners, corporations offer other features and benefits that a sole proprietorship or partnership doesn't. For example, corporations have shareholders who own a piece or percentage of the company. These shares can be sold or transferred to other owners, subject to any restrictions in the shareholders' agreement.

Corporations also offer *continuity of life,* which simply means that corporations can continue to exist despite the death of an owner or the owner's transfer of his or her share (stock) in the company.

REMEMBER

Don't incorporate for ego purposes. If you want to incorporate to impress friends, family, or business contacts, you need to know that few people would be impressed or even know that you're incorporated. Besides, if you operate as a sole proprietor, you can choose to operate under a different business name ("doing business as" or d.b.a.) without the cost — or the headache — of incorporating.

Knowing where to get advice

If you're totally confused about whether to incorporate because your business is undergoing major financial changes, getting competent professional help is worth the money. The hard part is knowing where to turn because finding one advisor who can put all the pieces of the puzzle together can be challenging. And be aware that you may get wrong or biased advice.

TIP

Attorneys who specialize in advising small businesses can help explain the legal issues. Tax advisors who do a lot of work with business owners can help explain the tax considerations. Also, a tax advisor should be able to prepare tax illustrations comparing the same business operated as a sole proprietorship, S corporation, and C corporation and the tax that the business would owe under different scenarios. If you find that you need two or more advisors to help make the decision, getting them together in one room with you for a meeting may help and ultimately save you time and money. Chapter 13 has details on getting help for your small business.

One step further: S corporations

Subchapter S corporations, so named for that part of the tax code that establishes them, offer some business owners the best of both worlds. You get the liability protection that comes with being incorporated as with a C corporation, and the business profit or loss passes through to the owner's personal tax returns (like in a sole proprietorship). In this section, I discuss the tax specifics of using S corporation status and the requirements for S corporations.

S corporation tax specifics

An S corporation is known as a *pass-through entity* for tax purposes. This simply means that the income that the company earns passes through to the company's owner/shareholders and is taxed at each person's individual level.

So if the business shows a loss in some years, the owners/shareholders may claim those losses in the current year of the loss on their tax returns against other income earned. This is potentially useful in the early years of a new business, a time when most companies lose money. To be able to claim losses, you must "materially participate" in the business, which generally means that you actively work in the company at least 500 hours per year, although 100 hours will suffice if that's the most among all other shareholders.

If, like most businesses, the company becomes profitable, it may actually make sense then to convert back to a regular C corporation to partake of the potential advantages of that status. That includes being able to retain earnings in the company, which you can't do with an S corporation, and being able to use tax-advantaged fringe benefits. (If you plan to take all the profits out of the company, an S corporation may make sense for you.)

Even though the corporation doesn't pay federal income tax, the company must annually complete and file IRS Form 1120S — "U.S. Income Tax Return for an S Corporation" (see the first page of the form in Figure 2-2; the complete form is located at www.irs.gov/pub/irs-pdf/f1120s.pdf). Also, some states levy a state income tax on S corporations, and many states require paying an annual fee.

TIP

One way an S corporation can save its owner/shareholders tax money is by paying them some of their compensation in the form of dividends. The reason this saves tax money is because dividends aren't subject to payroll or employment taxes. You must be careful, though, to ensure employee salaries are reasonable and not set artificially low and made up for by high dividend payments. Dividend payments shouldn't amount to more than 30 percent of a person's cash compensation when his or her salary/wages are totaled.

S corporation requirements

All corporations actually begin as so-called *C corporations,* which are the corporations discussed in the section "The Incorporation Decision" earlier in this chapter. The United States has more than twice as many S corporations today as C corporations. To become an S corporation, your business must go through an additional "tax election" step. See IRS Form 2553, "Election by a Small Business Corporation."

U.S. tax laws allow most, but not all, small businesses to be S corporations. To be an S corporation in the eyes of the almighty IRS, a company must meet all the following requirements:

>> Be a U.S. company

>> Have just one class of stock

>> Have no more than 100 shareholders who are all U.S. residents or citizens and aren't partnerships, other corporations, or, with certain exceptions, trusts

TIP

Be sure to investigate limited liability companies (LLCs), the subject of a later section, before committing to forming an S corporation. LLCs offer the passing through of income that S corporations do and are generally simpler to initiate and operate.

Form **1120S**		**U.S. Income Tax Return for an S Corporation**			OMB No. 1545-0123

Department of the Treasury
Internal Revenue Service

▶ Do not file this form unless the corporation has filed or is attaching Form 2553 to elect to be an S corporation.
▶ Go to *www.irs.gov/Form1120S* for instructions and the latest information.

20 18

For calendar year 2018 or tax year beginning _____ , 2018, ending _____ , 20 ____

A S election effective date	TYPE OR PRINT	Name	D Employer identification number
B Business activity code number (see instructions)		Number, street, and room or suite no. If a P.O. box, see instructions.	E Date incorporated
C Check if Sch. M-3 attached ☐		City or town, state or province, country, and ZIP or foreign postal code	F Total assets (see instructions) $

G Is the corporation electing to be an S corporation beginning with this tax year? ☐ Yes ☐ No If "Yes," attach Form 2553 if not already filed

H Check if: **(1)** ☐ Final return **(2)** ☐ Name change **(3)** ☐ Address change **(4)** ☐ Amended return **(5)** ☐ S election termination or revocation

I Enter the number of shareholders who were shareholders during any part of the tax year . . . . ▶

Caution: Include **only** trade or business income and expenses on lines 1a through 21. See the instructions for more information.

Income

	1a	Gross receipts or sales	1a		
	b	Returns and allowances	1b		
	c	Balance. Subtract line 1b from line 1a		1c	
	2	Cost of goods sold (attach Form 1125-A)		2	
	3	Gross profit. Subtract line 2 from line 1c		3	
	4	Net gain (loss) from Form 4797, line 17 (attach Form 4797)		4	
	5	Other income (loss) (see instructions—attach statement)		5	
	6	**Total income (loss).** Add lines 3 through 5 . . . . ▶		6	

Deductions (see instructions for limitations)

	7	Compensation of officers (see instructions—attach Form 1125-E) . .		7	
	8	Salaries and wages (less employment credits)		8	
	9	Repairs and maintenance		9	
	10	Bad debts		10	
	11	Rents		11	
	12	Taxes and licenses		12	
	13	Interest (see instructions)		13	
	14	Depreciation not claimed on Form 1125-A or elsewhere on return (attach Form 4562)		14	
	15	Depletion **(Do not deduct oil and gas depletion.)**		15	
	16	Advertising		16	
	17	Pension, profit-sharing, etc., plans		17	
	18	Employee benefit programs		18	
	19	Other deductions (attach statement)		19	
	20	**Total deductions.** Add lines 7 through 19 . . . . ▶		20	
	21	**Ordinary business income (loss).** Subtract line 20 from line 6		21	

Tax and Payments

	22a	Excess net passive income or LIFO recapture tax (see instructions) .	22a		
	b	Tax from Schedule D (Form 1120S)	22b		
	c	Add lines 22a and 22b (see instructions for additional taxes) . . .		22c	
	23a	2018 estimated tax payments and 2017 overpayment credited to 2018	23a		
	b	Tax deposited with Form 7004	23b		
	c	Credit for federal tax paid on fuels (attach Form 4136)	23c		
	d	Refundable credit from Form 8827, line 8c	23d		
	e	Add lines 23a through 23d		23e	
	24	Estimated tax penalty (see instructions). Check if Form 2220 is attached . . . . . . ▶ ☐		24	
	25	**Amount owed.** If line 23e is smaller than the total of lines 22c and 24, enter amount owed .		25	
	26	**Overpayment.** If line 23e is larger than the total of lines 22c and 24, enter amount overpaid . .		26	
	27	Enter amount from line 26: **Credited to 2019 estimated tax** ▶ _____ **Refunded** ▶		27	

Sign Here

Under penalties of perjury, I declare that I have examined this return, including accompanying schedules and statements, and to the best of my knowledge and belief, it is true, correct, and complete. Declaration of preparer (other than taxpayer) is based on all information of which preparer has any knowledge.

▲ _____ Signature of officer   Date   ▶ _____ Title

May the IRS discuss this return with the preparer shown below (see instructions)? ☐ Yes ☐ No

Paid Preparer Use Only

Print/Type preparer's name	Preparer's signature	Date	Check ☐ if self-employed	PTIN
Firm's name ▶			Firm's EIN ▶	
Firm's address ▶			Phone no.	

For Paperwork Reduction Act Notice, see separate instructions.   Cat. No. 11510H   Form **1120S** (2018)

FIGURE 2-2:
Page one of IRS Form 1120S, "U.S. Income Tax Return for an S Corporation."

Courtesy of the Internal Revenue Service

Partnerships

A *partnership* occurs in the eyes of the tax authorities when two or more people — the *general partners* (GPs) — operate a business together and divide the profits (or losses). The division need not be done equally.

The GPs are responsible for the company's debts and liabilities. A partnership may also have *limited partners* (LPs) who generally provide financing to the business and who aren't active in the company itself. Most small business partnerships don't have LPs.

A partnership is similar to a sole proprietorship and other pass-through entities for income tax purposes. Partners pay personal income taxes on their share of the partnership's income distributed to them. This is done on IRS Form 1040 Schedule E, "Supplemental Income and Loss" (see the first page of the form in Figure 2-3; the complete form is available at `www.irs.gov/pub/irs-pdf/f1040se.pdf`). As sole proprietors do, partners pay self-employment taxes on income earned.

REMEMBER

Though the partnership itself doesn't pay any federal income tax, it has plenty of federal income tax reporting requirements. In fact, the tax rules and reporting requirements of a partnership are quite extensive and challenging. The partnership must file IRS Form 1065, "U.S. Return of Partnership Income." And the partnership must complete and annually issue IRS Schedule K-1 of Form 1065 to each partner. You'd be well advised to use the services of a tax advisor if you're going to have your business function as a partnership (see Chapter 13 for the scoop on getting help).

Limited liability companies (LLCs)

In the past generation, a new type of corporation has appeared. *Limited liability companies* (LLCs) offer business owners benefits similar to those of S corporations and partnerships but are even better in some cases.

Like an S corporation, an LLC offers liability protection for the owners — hence the name limited liability company. In addition to the veil of overall liability protection for the owner's personal finances, an owner's liability for business debts is limited in an LLC to his or her percentage ownership share in the business.

LLCs also pass the business's profits through to the owner's personal income tax returns, like a sole proprietorship or partnership. You can pass through losses as well and deduct them against your other income so long as you materially participate in the business.

LLCs are generally much simpler to set up and administer than a corporation. But, to be realistic going into it, don't expect an LLC to be as simple as a sole proprietorship. And LLCs don't give you the ability to tap into some of the tax advantages afforded specific fringe benefits that some corporations offer.

FIGURE 2-3:
Page one of IRS
Form 1040
Schedule E,
"Supplemental
Income and
Loss."

SCHEDULE E (Form 1040)	Supplemental Income and Loss	OMB No. 1545-0074
Department of the Treasury Internal Revenue Service (99)	(From rental real estate, royalties, partnerships, S corporations, estates, trusts, REMICs, etc.) ▶ Attach to Form 1040, 1040NR, or Form 1041. ▶ Go to *www.irs.gov/ScheduleE* for instructions and the latest information.	2018 Attachment Sequence No. 13

Name(s) shown on return | Your social security number

Part I Income or Loss From Rental Real Estate and Royalties   Note: If you are in the business of renting personal property, use **Schedule C or C-EZ** (see instructions). If you are an individual, report farm rental income or loss from **Form 4835** on page 2, line 40.

A Did you make any payments in 2018 that would require you to file Form(s) 1099? (see instructions) . . . . . ☐ Yes ☐ No
B If "Yes," did you or will you file required Forms 1099? . . . . ☐ Yes ☐ No

1a Physical address of each property (street, city, state, ZIP code)
A
B
C

1b	Type of Property (from list below)	2 For each rental real estate property listed above, report the number of fair rental and personal use days. Check the **QJV** box only if you meet the requirements to file as a qualified joint venture. See instructions.		Fair Rental Days	Personal Use Days	QJV
A			A			☐
B			B			☐
C			C			☐

Type of Property:
1 Single Family Residence   3 Vacation/Short-Term Rental 5 Land   7 Self-Rental
2 Multi-Family Residence   4 Commercial   6 Royalties   8 Other (describe)

Income:	Properties:		A	B	C
3	Rents received	3			
4	Royalties received	4			
Expenses:					
5	Advertising	5			
6	Auto and travel (see instructions)	6			
7	Cleaning and maintenance	7			
8	Commissions.	8			
9	Insurance	9			
10	Legal and other professional fees	10			
11	Management fees	11			
12	Mortgage interest paid to banks, etc. (see instructions)	12			
13	Other interest.	13			
14	Repairs.	14			
15	Supplies	15			
16	Taxes	16			
17	Utilities	17			
18	Depreciation expense or depletion	18			
19	Other (list) ▶ _____	19			
20	Total expenses. Add lines 5 through 19	20			
21	Subtract line 20 from line 3 (rents) and/or 4 (royalties). If result is a (loss), see instructions to find out if you must file **Form 6198**	21			
22	Deductible rental real estate loss after limitation, if any, on **Form 8582** (see instructions)	22	( )( )( )

23a	Total of all amounts reported on line 3 for all rental properties	23a	
b	Total of all amounts reported on line 4 for all royalty properties	23b	
c	Total of all amounts reported on line 12 for all properties	23c	
d	Total of all amounts reported on line 18 for all properties	23d	
e	Total of all amounts reported on line 20 for all properties	23e	
24	**Income.** Add positive amounts shown on line 21. **Do not** include any losses	24	
25	**Losses.** Add royalty losses from line 21 and rental real estate losses from line 22. Enter total losses here .	25	( )
26	**Total rental real estate and royalty income or (loss).** Combine lines 24 and 25. Enter the result here. If Parts II, III, IV, and line 40 on page 2 do not apply to you, also enter this amount on Schedule 1 (Form 1040), line 17, or Form 1040NR, line 18. Otherwise, include this amount in the total on line 41 on page 2.	26	

For Paperwork Reduction Act Notice, see the separate instructions.   Cat. No. 11344L   Schedule E (Form 1040) 2018

Courtesy of the Internal Revenue Service

LLCs have fewer restrictions regarding shareholders than S corporations. For example, LLCs have no limits on the number of shareholders, and the shareholders can be foreigners, corporations, or partnerships.

Compared with S corporations, the only additional restriction LLCs carry is that sole proprietors and professionals can't always form LLCs (although some states allow this). All states now permit the formation of LLCs, but most state laws require you to have at least two partners for an LLC to be taxed as a partnership and not be a professional firm.

REMEMBER

Single-owner LLCs (which also include married couples in community property states) are treated as sole proprietorships and file Schedule C of Form 1040 for tax purposes, unless the owner elects to file as a corporation on Form 8832, "Entity Classification Election." A domestic entity that has more than one member will default to a partnership. An LLC with multiple owners can either accept its default classification as a partnership, or file Form 8832 to elect to be classified as an association taxable as a corporation. This form is for informational purposes only. Keep in mind that LLCs aren't taxed federally; income is passed through to the company's owners/shareholders. However, numerous states levy a tax on LLCs and require an annual tax filing. Some states like California go even further with fees. California has a fee based on gross receipts, not net income. A California LLC with $500,000 in gross receipts pays $800 tax plus a $2,500 fee for a total of $3,300, even if it reports a net loss for the year after expenses.

Valuing Employee Benefits

Who doesn't like a free lunch?

Well, in this section, I don't actually tell you how to get a free lunch or two, but I do explain how small businesses can offer their employees valuable benefits. These "perks" or "fringe benefits" are usually tax-deductible expenses for the business and often tax-free to the employees. Another plus for the company is that — unlike wages paid to an employee, which cost the business in Social Security, Medicare, and unemployment taxes — benefits can save the company on these taxes.

REMEMBER

A small business owner — or any business owner, for that matter — should never provide a particular employee benefit just because it's tax-deductible. Keep in mind that you have to spend money to qualify for a deduction, and the value of that deduction only recoups part of the outlay the company makes to provide a particular benefit. Providing benefits to your employees can and should be motivated by these factors:

>> **Offering an industry-competitive compensation package:** You compete for employees with other companies in your line of work. If most competitors offer health insurance and a retirement savings plan, you need to know that as you design your benefit package. From a cost standpoint, you need to track

and manage the total cost of the compensation package, which includes benefits provided to employees.

>> **Providing valued benefits:** Another reason to consider particular benefits for your employees is that they'll value them. What benefits your employees value in turn depends on your workforce's makeup. If your employees are primarily older people nearing retirement, they'll value a different mix of benefits, for example, than employees who are younger and single or employees with dependent children.

In this section, I discuss the most common benefits small businesses tend to offer and provide pertinent background for each. I also discuss what tax-deductible benefits are uniquely offered to corporations only.

Retirement plans

Retirement plans are a terrific way for business owners and their employees to tax shelter (defer) a healthy portion of their earnings. Of all the benefits that a small business can offer, a retirement savings plan can be the most valuable in saving employees taxes and helping them accumulate significant savings for their own retirement.

If you don't have employees, regularly contributing to one of these plans is generally a no-brainer. That's because you can set up high-quality retirement plans for little or no cost.

When you have employees, the decision is a bit more complicated but is often a great idea. Self-employed people may contribute to simplified employee pension individual retirement accounts (SEP-IRAs), or SIMPLE plans. Small businesses with a number of employees can also consider 401(k) plans, and those with no employees can consider a solo 401(k) plan.

I discuss all these plans and the impact of the tax rules in detail in Chapter 3.

Health insurance plans

Many employees consider health insurance to be the most valuable benefit a company offers. In reality, it's actually a retirement plan unless you have extensive health problems and use your health insurance a lot, which most people don't.

Almost everyone needs health insurance (except perhaps the super-wealthy, like Bill Gates), but not everyone has it. Before Medicare, the U.S. government-provided insurance program that kicks in at age 65+, most folks obtained their health insurance through their employer. Employer-provided coverage eliminates the headache of each employee having to shop for coverage, and group coverage is usually less costly than coverage that individuals buy on their own.

TIP

Your small business may be eligible for a tax credit by providing health insurance to your employees and their dependents if you pay for at least half that cost. To qualify for the tax credit, which amounts to 35 percent of the health insurance premiums your business pays, your company must have fewer than 25 full-time employees, and their average wages/salaries must be less than $50,000 per year. You claim the credit on IRS Form 8941, "Credit for Small Employer Health Insurance Premiums." (It's available at `www.irs.gov/pub/irs-pdf/f8941.pdf`.) This credit is only permissible for two consecutive tax years after 2013.

The following sections list plan attributes to consider, explain the effect of recent healthcare reform, help you evaluate and buy insurance, and provide pointers on saving money on healthcare.

Looking at plan attributes

Here's what to look for when selecting among the health insurance offerings in the marketplace (important note: the federal legislation known formally as the Patient Protection and Affordable Care Act, discussed in the next section, impacts a number of these issues):

>> **Major medical coverage:** A good health insurance plan covers the big potential expenses: hospitalization, physician, and ancillary charges, such as X-rays and laboratory work.

>> **Choice of healthcare providers:** Plans that allow you to use any healthcare provider you want are becoming less common and more expensive in most areas. Health maintenance organizations (HMOs) and preferred provider organizations (PPOs) are the main plans that restrict your choices. They keep costs down because they negotiate lower rates with selected providers. The main difference is that PPOs still pay the majority of your expenses if you use a provider outside their approved list. If you use a provider outside the approved list with an HMO, you typically aren't covered at all. Although HMO and PPO plans do offer fewer choices when it comes to providers, surveys show that customer satisfaction with these plans is comparatively good.

>> **Deductibles and co-payments:** To reduce your health insurance premiums, choose a plan with the highest deductible and co-payment folks can afford. As with other insurance policies, the more you're willing to share in the payment of your claims, the less you have to pay in premiums. Most policies have annual deductible options (such as $250, $500, $1,000, and so on) as well as co-payment options, which are typically 20 percent or so. When choosing a

co-payment percentage, know that insurance plans generally set a maximum out-of-pocket limit on your annual co-payments (such as $1,000 or $2,000); the insurer covers 100 percent of any medical expenses that go over that cap.

Note: Most HMO plans don't have deductible and co-payment options. Most just charge a set amount — such as $25 — for a physician's office visit.

>> **Guaranteed renewability:** You want a health insurance plan that keeps renewing your coverage without you having to prove continued good health. If you could guarantee good health, you wouldn't need health insurance in the first place.

Making sense of the impact of healthcare reform

In March 2010, President Obama signed into law the Patient Protection and Affordable Care Act and the Health Care and Education Reconciliation Act. Together, these two laws enacted comprehensive healthcare reform in the United States. This mammoth legislation comprised thousands of pages of rules and regulations. This section highlights the most important portions of the legislation that you need to understand.

Now, employer group health plans (with 50 or more full-time employees) are subject to these rules:

>> Plans offering dependent coverage must offer coverage to adult children up to age 26. The coverage isn't taxable to the employee or dependent.

>> Plans must provide preventive care without cost-sharing and must cover certain child preventive care services as recommended by the government. This rule applies only to new group health plans.

>> Employers must offer minimum essential coverage to full-time employees or make nondeductible payments to the government.

>> Plans must remove all annual dollar limits on participants' benefit payments. They may not impose lifetime limits.

>> Plans must limit cost-sharing and deductibles to levels that don't exceed those applicable to a health-savings-account-eligible, high-deductible health plan.

>> Plans must remove all preexisting-condition exclusions on all participants.

>> Plans may not have waiting periods of longer than 90 days.

Higher income taxpayers are now hit with higher tax rates on their investments as well as higher Medicare tax rates to help pay for Obamacare. Taxpayers with total taxable income above $200,000 (for a single return) or $250,000 (for a joint return) from any source are subject to a 3.8 percent tax on the *lesser* of the following:

>> Their net investment income (for example, interest, dividends, and capital gains)

>> The amount, if any, by which their modified adjusted gross income exceeds the dollar thresholds

Taxpayers with earned income above $200,000 (for a single return) or $250,000 (for a joint return) are subject to an additional 0.9 percent Medicare tax (in other words, rising from 1.45 percent to 2.35 percent) on wages in excess of those amounts. Employers aren't required to match the payment of this incremental increase, which is applicable only to the employee.

Buying health insurance

You can buy many health plans through agents, and you can also buy some directly from the insurer. When health insurance is sold both ways, buying through an agent usually doesn't cost more.

Solicit proposals from the larger and older health insurers in your area. Larger plans can negotiate better rates from providers, and older plans are more likely to be here tomorrow. Nationally, Aetna, Anthem, Assurant, Blue Cross, Blue Shield, CIGNA, Kaiser Permanente, and UnitedHealth Group are among the older and bigger health insurers. If your coverage is canceled, you may have to search for coverage that allows an existing medical problem. Other health insurers won't want to insure you. (Find out whether your state department of insurance offers a plan for people unable to get coverage.)

Also check with professional or other associations that you belong to, because plans offered by these groups sometimes provide decent benefits at a competitive price because of the purchasing-power clout that they possess. A competent independent insurance agent who specializes in health insurance can help you find insurers that are willing to offer you coverage.

WARNING

Health insurance agents have a conflict of interest that's common to all financial salespeople working on commission: The higher the premium plan they sell you, the bigger the commission they earn. So an agent may try to steer you into higher-cost plans and avoid suggesting some of the strategies I discuss in the following section for reducing your cost of coverage. (Good agents can help guide you to the best plans that cover preexisting conditions and offer the lowest costs for your medications. Be sure to provide them with this information and compare options carefully.)

Noting other ways to save on healthcare spending

Regarding out-of-pocket medical expenses, you can offer a flexible spending or healthcare reimbursement account. These accounts enable employees to pay for uncovered medical expenses with pretax dollars. The business saves on payroll taxes for the amounts deferred into these accounts. Employees can also use these accounts to pay for vision and dental care.

WARNING

Be forewarned of the major stumbling blocks you face when saving through medical reimbursement accounts:

>> First, you need to elect to save money from your paycheck prior to the beginning of each plan year. The only exception is at the time of a "life change," such as a family member's death, marriage, spouse's job change, divorce, or the birth of a child.

>> You also need to use the money within the year you save it because these accounts contain a "use it or lose it" feature (you have through two and one-half months of the end of the calendar year to spend that year's money).

Health savings accounts (HSAs) are another option, especially for the self-employed and people who work for smaller firms. Employers with fewer than 50 employees can offer HSAs.

To qualify for an HSA, you must have a high-deductible (at least $1,350 for individuals and $2,700 for families) health insurance policy. Then you can put money earmarked for medical expenses into an investment account that offers the tax benefits — deductible contributions and tax-deferred compounding — of a retirement account. And unlike a flexible spending account, you don't have to deplete the HSA by the end of the year: Money can compound tax-deferred inside the HSA for years. Begin to investigate an HSA through insurers offering health plans you're interested in or with the company you currently have coverage through.

Finally, you may be able to save on taxes if you have a substantial amount of healthcare expenditures in a year. You can deduct medical and dental expenses as an itemized deduction on Schedule A of IRS Form 1040 (see Chapter 9) to the extent that they exceed 10 percent of your adjusted gross income for those under age 65 (effective tax year 2019, the threshold is 7.5 percent before). Unless you're a low-income earner, you need to have substantial expenses, usually caused by an accident or major illness, to take advantage of this tax break.

Other benefits

Companies can offer lots of other benefits to their employees. Here are the highlights of some other commonly considered ones:

- >> **Dependent care:** Reimbursed costs for the care of kids under the age of 13 are tax-deductible to the business and a tax-free benefit for employees for up to $5,000 for a married couple filing jointly and $2,500 for others. Note that this is separate from the dependent care tax credit available on your federal tax forms.

- >> **Long-term care insurance:** As with the dependent care benefit, a business can provide long-term care (LTC) insurance, deduct the cost of providing it, and the benefit is tax-free to the employee. Alternatively, individuals can pay for the cost of an LTC policy themselves and deduct the cost as an itemized deduction on Schedule A of their personal income tax return.

- >> **Group term life insurance:** So long as a company has at least ten covered employees, it can deduct the cost of a provided term life policy, and the benefit is tax-free to employees for up to $50,000 of coverage.

- >> **Educational expense reimbursement:** Educational costs that are directly related to an employee's job may be deducted if paid by the business, and the benefit is tax-free to the employee.

- >> **Auto costs:** You can write off the costs of using your car for certain business purposes, and a small business can deduct certain costs as well. Turn to Chapter 8 for the details.

- >> **Meals:** When a company provides food on-site, it can deduct all costs and provide a tax-free benefit to employees, subject to certain criteria being met. For example, if employees are working late or lack sufficient time to get their own food, the business may pay for the cost of a meal. The company can deduct snack costs and have a cafeteria that provides food at cost so long as the employees themselves pay for the actual cost of the food. Meals covered at restaurants by the business are only 50 percent deductible for tax purposes.

- >> **Travel and hotels:** These expenses are deductible for the company when the travel and hotel stays are primarily for business purposes (meal expenses on such trips are 50 percent deductible). That's not to say that you can't enjoy yourself on a trip and do non-work, fun stuff, but the primary purpose of the trip should be business, not pleasure.

- >> **Dues for civic organizations, small business organizations, and trade associations:** If you pay fees to join your local chamber of commerce, other civic clubs, or trade associations relevant to your business, these costs are deductible.

TIP

For more information on benefits and how they work from a tax standpoint, see IRS Publication 15–B, "Employer's Tax Guide to Fringe Benefits."

Benefits that are deductible for corporation owners

A variety of insurance and related benefits are tax-deductible to corporations for all employees. These benefits include

>> Health insurance

>> Disability insurance

>> Term life insurance (up to $50,000 in benefits per employee)

>> Dependent care plans (up to $5,000 per employee may be put away on a tax-deductible basis for childcare and/or care for elderly parents)

>> Flexible spending or cafeteria plans, which allow employees to pick and choose the benefits on which to spend their benefit dollars

For companies that aren't incorporated, the business owners can't deduct the cost of the preceding insurance plans for themselves, but they can deduct these costs for employees. (Self-employed people can deduct 100 percent of their health insurance costs for themselves and their covered family members.)

Chapter **3**

Retirement Accounts and Investments for Small Businesses

S aving and investing through retirement accounts is one of the simplest yet most powerful methods for small business owners and their employees to reduce their current and future income tax burdens and build a retirement nest egg. Unfortunately, many people don't make use of these plans because they fail to establish one or spend too much of what they make.

REMEMBER

To best take advantage of the tax savings that come with retirement savings plans, you should spend less than you earn. Only then can you afford to more fully contribute to these plans (although some plans allow for more of the contributions to come from the business owner if that's something you're interested in).

In this chapter, I detail your retirement account options, how to select a top-notch investment company through which to invest, and how to make wise investment choices for the long term.

Beginning with Retirement Account Basics: Tax Breaks, Penalties, and Saving Guidelines

The single biggest mistake people at all income levels make with retirement accounts is not taking advantage of them. When you're in your 20s and 30s (and for some individuals in their 40s and 50s), spending and living for today and postponing saving for the future seems a whole lot more fun than saving for retirement.

Each decade that you delay contributing approximately doubles the percentage of your earnings that you need to save to meet your goals. For example, if saving 5 percent per year in your early 20s gets you to your retirement goal, waiting to save until your 30s may mean socking away 10 percent per year, waiting until your 40s may mean 20 percent per year, and so on.

So the longer you wait, the more you'll have to save and, therefore, the less that will be left over for spending. As a result, you may not meet your goal, and your golden years may be more restrictive than you hoped.

In this section, I detail the tax breaks you can earn for saving in retirement accounts, address concerns about tapping into your retirement account money if need be without paying a big price, and note how to save a sensible amount.

Instant rewards: Upfront tax breaks

Spend money today and you may get some instant gratification. Put some of that same money into a retirement account, and you may yawn with excitement and then get stressed choosing investments.

Retirement accounts really should be called tax-reduction accounts. If they were, people may be more eager to contribute to them. For many people, avoiding higher taxes is the motivating force that gets them to open the account and start the contributions.

TIP

If you're a moderate-income earner, you probably pay about 25 to 35 percent in federal and state income taxes on your last dollars of income. Thus, with most of the retirement accounts described in this chapter, for every $2,000 you contribute to them, you save yourself about $500 to $700 in taxes in the year that you make the contribution. Contribute five times as much, or $10,000, and whack $2,500 to $3,500 off your tax bill!

Whenever you're working for an employer, always be sure to check with your employer's benefits department because some organizations match a portion of employee contributions. Be sure to partake of this free matching money by contributing to your retirement accounts.

Ongoing tax breaks on your investment earnings

After you place money in a retirement account, any interest, dividends, and appreciation add to the amount in the account without being taxed. You get to defer taxes on all the accumulating gains and profits until you withdraw the money, presumably in retirement. Thus, more money is working for you over a longer period of time.

The percentage tax rate that you pay in retirement need not be less than your tax rate today for you to come out ahead by contributing to retirement accounts. In fact, because you defer paying tax and have more money compounding over more years, you can end up with more money in retirement by saving inside a retirement account, even if your retirement tax rate is higher.

Additional tax credits for lower-income earners

In addition to the upfront tax break you get from contributing to many retirement accounts, lower-income earners may receive a special Saver's Tax Credit worth up to 50 percent on the first $2,000 of retirement account contributions. This tax credit amounts to free money from the government, so you should take advantage!

As you can see in Table 3-1, this retirement account contribution tax credit phases out quickly for higher-income earners, and no such credit is available to single taxpayers with adjusted gross incomes (AGIs) above $32,000, heads of household with AGIs above $48,000, and married couples filing jointly with AGIs above $64,000. (*Note:* This credit isn't available to taxpayers who are claimed as dependents on someone else's tax return or who are under the age of 18 or are full-time students.)

TABLE 3-1 **"Saver's Tax Credit" for the First $2,000 in Retirement Plan Contributions (2019)**

Amount of Credit	Married Couple Filing Jointly	Head of Household	Single/Others
50% of first $2,000 deferred	$0 to $38,000	$0 to $28,875	$0 to $19,250
20% of first $2,000 deferred	$38,000 to $41,500	$28,875 to $31,125	$19,250 to $20,750
10% of first $2,000 deferred	$41,500 to $64,000	$31,125 to $48,000	$20,750 to $32,000

Retirement account penalties for early withdrawals

WARNING

Some folks are concerned about the early withdrawal penalties when contributing to retirement accounts. Specifically, if you withdraw funds from retirement accounts before age 59½, you have to pay not only income taxes on withdrawals but also early withdrawal penalties — 10 percent in federal plus applicable state charges. (Withdrawing from a SIMPLE plan within the first two years incurs a 25 percent penalty, which decreases to 10 percent thereafter; I talk about SIMPLE plans later in this chapter.)

The penalties are in place to discourage people from raiding retirement accounts. Keep in mind that retirement accounts exist for just that reason — saving toward retirement. If you could easily tap these accounts without penalties, the money would be less likely to be there when you need it during retirement.

If you have an emergency, such as catastrophic medical expenses or a disability, you may be able to take early withdrawals from retirement accounts without penalty. (Before considering any withdrawal, take the time to understand the conditions under which you can take a penalty-free withdrawal and what those penalties are.) You may withdraw funds from particular retirement accounts free of penalties (and, in some cases, even free of current income taxes — for example, from a Roth IRA) for educational expenses or a home purchase.

What if you just run out of money because you lose your job or your small business fails? Although you can't bypass the penalties because of such circumstances, if you're earning so little income that you need to tap your retirement account, you'll surely be in a low tax bracket for the year. So even though you pay some penalties to withdraw retirement account money, the lower income taxes that you pay upon withdrawal — as compared to the taxes that you would have incurred when you earned the money originally — should make up for most or all of the penalty.

Know also that if you get in a financial pinch while you're still working, some company retirement plans allow you to borrow against a portion of your cash balance. Just be sure that you can repay such a loan; otherwise, your "loan" becomes a withdrawal and triggers income taxes and penalties.

Another strategy to meet a short-term financial emergency is to withdraw money from your individual retirement account (IRA) and return it within 60 days to avoid paying penalties. I don't generally recommend this maneuver because of the taxes and potential penalties invoked if you don't make the 60-day deadline. (I discuss IRAs in detail later in this chapter.)

TIP

In the event that your only "borrowing" option in an emergency is a credit card with a high interest rate, you should save three to six months' worth of living expenses in an accessible account before funding a retirement account to tide you over in case you lose your income. Money market mutual funds, which are similar to bank savings accounts, are an ideal vehicle to use for this purpose.

If you accumulate enough funds to retire "early," you have a simple way around the pre-age-59½ early withdrawal penalties. Suppose that at age 52 you retire and want to start living off some of the money you've stashed in retirement accounts. No problem. The U.S. tax rules graciously allow you to start withdrawing money from your retirement accounts free of those nasty early withdrawal penalties. To qualify for this favorable treatment, you must commit to withdrawals for at least five continuous years, and the amount of the withdrawals must be at least the minimum required based on your life expectancy per IRS tables.

Guidelines for saving (but not excessively)

TIP

On average, most people need about 70 percent to 80 percent of their pre-retirement income to maintain their standard of living throughout their retirement. For example, if your household earns $60,000 per year before retirement, you'll likely need $42,000 to $48,000 (70 percent to 80 percent of $50,000) per year during retirement to live the way that you're accustomed to living.

Note that 70 percent to 80 percent is just an average. You may need more or less.

>> If you currently save little or none of your annual income, you expect to have a large mortgage payment or growing rent in retirement, or you anticipate traveling or doing other expensive things in retirement, you may need 90 percent or perhaps even 100+ percent of your current income to maintain your standard of living in retirement.

>> On the other hand, if you now save a high percentage of your earnings, you're a high-income earner, you expect to own your home free of debt by retirement, and you anticipate leading a modest lifestyle in retirement, you may be able to make do with, say, 60 percent of your current income.

Over the years, I've seen some clients "over" contribute to retirement accounts. I don't literally mean that these well-intentioned folks broke the contribution limit rules. I'm talking about unusual situations where people have contributed more to their retirement accounts than what makes good financial and tax sense.

For example, it may not make sense for a taxpayer who is temporarily in a low tax bracket (or one who owes no tax at all) to contribute to retirement accounts. Ditto for people who have a large estate already and have piles of money inside retirement accounts that could get walloped by estate and income taxes upon their passing. Few people, of course, have this perhaps enviable "problem."

When in doubt, and if you have reason to believe you should scale back on retirement account contributions, consult with a competent financial/tax advisor who works for an hourly fee and doesn't sell products or manage money. Read Chapter 13 for details on finding such an advisor.

TIP

If you've never thought about what your retirement goals are, looked into what you can expect from Social Security, or calculated how much you should be saving for retirement, now's the time to do it. My book *Personal Finance For Dummies* (John Wiley & Sons, Inc.) goes through all the details and even tells you how to come up with more to invest and do it wisely.

Surveying Your Retirement Account Options

Although setting up a self-employment retirement plan means work for you, you can select and design a plan that meets your needs. You can actually do a better job than many companies do; often, the people establishing a retirement plan don't do enough homework or let some salesperson talk them into high-expense (for the employees, that is) investments. Your trouble will be rewarded; self-employment retirement plans generally enable you to sock away more money on a tax-deductible basis than most employers' plans do.

If you have employees, you're required to make contributions comparable to the company owners' (as a percentage of salary) on their behalf under these plans. Some part-time employees (those who work fewer than 500 to 1,000 hours per year) and newer employees (less than a few years of service) may be excluded. Not all small business owners know about this requirement — or they choose to ignore it, and they set up plans for themselves but fail to cover their employees. The danger is that the IRS and state tax authorities may, in the event of an audit, hit you with big penalties and disqualify your prior contributions if you've neglected to make contributions for eligible employees. Because the IRS audits self-employed people and small businesses at a relatively high rate, messing up in this area is dangerous. So you may want to consult a good tax advisor before setting up a retirement plan for your small business.

Don't avoid setting up a retirement savings plan for your business just because you have employees and you don't want to make contributions on their behalf. In the long run, you can build the contributions you make for your employees into their total compensation package, which includes salary and other benefits like health insurance. Making retirement contributions need not increase your personnel costs.

In this section, I explain how to get the most out of your company's retirement plan, as well as the specific plan options you should consider.

Maximizing your retirement plan's value

To get the most from your contributions as an employer, consider the following:

>> Educate your employees about the value of retirement savings plans. You want them to understand how to save for the future and to value and appreciate your plan. I know some companies, for example, that provided copies of my book *Personal Finance For Dummies* (John Wiley & Sons, Inc.) to employees to do just that.

>> If you have more than 20 or so employees, consider offering a 401(k) or SIMPLE plan, which allows employees to contribute money from their paychecks. (I discuss both of these plans later in this chapter.)

Eligible small employers can claim 50 percent of the costs to set up and administer a retirement plan to a maximum of $500 for the year. The employer's plan must cover no more than 100 employees who make at least $5,000 per year. You claim this credit on IRS Form 8881, "Credit for Small Employer Pension Plan Startup Costs." (Find this form at www.irs.gov/pub/irs-pdf/f8881.pdf.)

Checking out your choices

If you own a small business, you have lots of retirement account choices. The following sections discuss "IRS-approved" retirement accounts, explain how to determine whether you're eligible for them, and cover some nitpicky but important rules.

SEP-IRAs

A simplified employee pension individual retirement account (SEP-IRA) plan requires little paperwork to set up. No annual filing with the IRS is required, and it's less costly to maintain.

Each year, you decide the amount you want to contribute to your SEP-IRA; no minimums exist. Your contributions to a SEP-IRA are deducted from your taxable income, saving you big time on federal and usually state taxes. As with other retirement plans, your money compounds without tax until withdrawal.

SEP-IRAs allow you to sock away 20 percent of your self-employment income (business revenue minus expenses), up to a maximum of $56,000 for tax year 2019. The future contribution limit of SEP-IRA plans will increase in $1,000 increments with increases in the cost of living. You can easily establish one of these plans through major investment firms, including mutual fund companies and brokerage firms.

SIMPLE plans

Employers in small businesses have yet another retirement plan option, known as the SIMPLE-IRA. SIMPLE stands for *savings incentive match plans for employees.* Relative to 401(k) plans (which I discuss later in this chapter), SIMPLE plans enable employers to reduce their costs, thanks to easier reporting requirements and fewer administrative hassles. Employers may escape the nondiscrimination testing requirements — one of the more tedious aspects of maintaining a 401(k) plan — by adhering to the matching and contribution rules of a SIMPLE plan.

The contribution limit for SIMPLE plans is $13,000 for tax year 2019 for younger workers ($16,000 for those age 50 and older). Annual contribution limits increase in increments of $500 with inflation.

Employers must make contributions on behalf of employees. Employers can either match, dollar for dollar, the first 3 percent the employee contributes or contribute 2 percent of pay for everyone whose wages exceed $5,000. Interestingly, if the employer chooses the first option, the employer has an incentive not to educate employees about the value of contributing to the plan because the more employees contribute, the more it costs the employer. And, unlike a

401(k) plan, greater employee contributions don't enable higher-paid employees to contribute more.

Individual 401(k)

Individual 401(k) plans are for sole proprietors or partners with no employees other than the owner, a business partner, or a shareholder of a corporation and their respective spouses (also known as "common law employees").

The contribution limits on these plans is the same as for a SEP-IRA for the employer and for employees; the contribution limit is the same as with traditional 401(k) plans.

401(k) plans for "larger" small companies

In the past, it was prohibitively expensive for small companies to administer a 401(k) plan. This plan is the most common retirement savings plan that larger for-profit companies offer their employees. Over time, increasing numbers of investment companies and administrators have driven down the cost of small company 401(k) plans to the point where these plans can become cost-effective for larger small companies. You can also consider individual or so-called solo 401(k) plans.

The 401(k) name comes from the section of the tax code that establishes and regulates these plans. A 401(k) generally allows you to save up to $19,000 for tax year 2019. Your plan may have lower contribution limits, though, if employees don't save enough in the company's plan. Your contributions to a 401(k) are excluded from your reported income and thus are free from federal and, in some cases, state income taxes.

Older workers — those at least age 50 — are able to put away even more — up to $6,000 more per year than their younger counterparts. The annual contribution limit on 401(k) plans and the additional amounts allowed for older workers rises, in $500 increments, with inflation.

Some employers don't allow their employees to start contributing to their 401(k) plan until they've worked for them for a full year. Others allow you to start contributing right away. Some employers also match a portion of employee contributions.

TIP

If you're interested in exploring a 401(k) plan for your company, contact a mutual fund or discount brokerage organization, such as T. Rowe Price, Vanguard, or Fidelity. Also consider checking out Charles Schwab and ShareBuilder. Increasing numbers of providers are offering 401(k) plans so be careful shopping around; be sure to ask how long each has been in the business and how many customers they service. Understand all fees because they can greatly add up. And, don't be shy about asking for and checking references. In some cases, you may need to work with a separate plan administrator in addition to one of these investment firms.

403(b) plans for nonprofit organizations

Many nonprofit organizations offer 403(b) plans to their employees. Contributions to these plans generally are federal and state tax-deductible. 403(b) plans often are referred to as *tax-sheltered annuities,* the name for insurance company investments that satisfy the requirements for 403(b) plans. For the benefit of 403(b) retirement plan participants, no-load (commission-free) mutual funds also can be used in 403(b) plans.

Nonprofit employees generally are allowed to contribute up to 20 percent or $19,000 of their salaries, whichever is less. Employees age 50 and older may contribute up to $25,000.

Nonprofit organizations have no excuse not to offer 403(b) plans to their employees. These plans have virtually no out-of-pocket setup expenses or ongoing accounting fees. The only requirement is that the organization must deduct the appropriate contribution from employees' paychecks and send the money to the investment company that handles the 403(b) plan.

TIP

Vanguard (800-662-2003; www.vanguard.com), Fidelity (800-343-0860; www.fidelity.com), and T. Rowe Price (800-492-7670; http://corporate.troweprice.com) all offer solid mutual funds and 403(b) plans.

Selecting Top-Notch Investments for Your Retirement Account

A retirement account is simply a shell inside of which you select investments using the money you've contributed. In this section, I discuss the specific vehicles — mutual funds and exchange-traded funds (ETFs) — that I recommend you use. I also give you a short list of some specific fund companies and fund names and discuss how to assemble a portfolio by matching funds to your investing objectives.

Considering fund advantages

Mutual funds are simply pools of money from investors that a mutual fund manager uses to buy a bunch of stocks, bonds, and other assets that meet the fund's investment criteria. The best *exchange-traded funds* (ETFs) are quite similar to mutual funds — specifically, index mutual funds. Each ETF generally tracks a major market index. (Some ETFs, however, track narrowly focused indexes, such as an industry group or a small country.) The most significant difference between a mutual fund and an ETF is that to invest in an ETF, you must buy it through a stock exchange on which the ETF trades, just as individual stocks trade. (I talk about index mutual funds and ETFs later in this chapter.)

Because efficient funds take most of the hassle and cost out of deciding which companies to invest in, they're among the best investment vehicles available today, especially in retirement accounts. Also, funds enable you to have some of the best money managers in the country direct the investment of your money.

REMEMBER

The following list highlights the main reasons for investing in funds rather than individual securities:

>> **Low cost:** When you invest your money in an efficiently managed fund, it should cost you less than trading individual securities on your own. Fund managers can buy and sell securities for a fraction of the cost that you pay. Funds also spread the cost of research over many, many investors. The most efficiently managed mutual funds cost less than 1 percent per year in fees. (Bond funds cost much less — in the neighborhood of 0.5 percent per year or less.) Some of the larger and more established funds can charge annual fees less than 0.2 percent per year; that's less than a $2 annual charge per $1,000 you invest.

>> **Diversification:** Funds generally invest in dozens of securities. Diversification is a big attraction for many investors who choose funds because proper diversification increases the chance that the fund will earn higher returns with less risk. Most funds own stocks or bonds from dozens of companies, thus diversifying against the risk of bad news from any single company or sector. Achieving such diversification on your own is difficult and expensive unless you have a few hundred thousand dollars and a great deal of time to invest.

>> **Professional management:** Fund investment companies hire a portfolio manager and researchers whose full-time jobs are to analyze and purchase suitable investments for the fund. These people screen the universe of investments for those that meet the fund's stated objectives. Fund managers are typically graduates of the top business and finance schools, where they learned portfolio management and securities valuation. Many have additional investing credentials, such as Chartered Financial Analyst (CFA) certification. The best fund managers also typically possess more than ten years' experience analyzing and selecting investments.

For fund managers and researchers, finding the best investments is a full-time job. They do major analysis that you lack the time or expertise to perform. Their activities include assessing company financial statements; interviewing company managers to hear the companies' business strategies and vision; examining competitors' strategies; speaking with companies' customers, suppliers, and industry consultants; attending trade shows; and reading industry periodicals.

>> **Achievable investment minimums:** Many mutual funds have minimums of $1,000 or less. Retirement account investors can often invest with even less. Some funds even offer monthly investment plans so you can start with as little as $50 per month. ETFs have no minimums, although you need to weigh the brokerage costs of buying and selling ETF shares (although some firms waive transaction fees on increasing numbers of ETFs).

>> **Funds to fit varying needs:** You can select funds that match the risk/reward ratio you need to meet your financial goals or that you're comfortable with. If you're relatively young and expect your money to grow over a long period and you can handle some down periods, choose mostly stock-focused funds. If you don't want investments that fluctuate as widely in value, consider investing more in bond funds. (I talk about both types later in this chapter.)

>> **High financial safety:** Fund companies can't fail because the value of fund shares fluctuates as the securities in the fund change value. For every dollar of securities that they hold for their customers, mutual funds have a dollar's worth of securities. The worst that can happen with a fund is that if you want your money, you may get less money than you originally put into the fund because of a market value decline of the fund's holdings.

For added security, a *custodian,* a separate organization independent of the mutual fund company, holds the specific stocks, bonds, and other securities that a mutual fund buys. A custodian ensures that the fund management company can't steal your money.

>> **Accessibility:** Funds are set up for people who value their time and don't like going to a local branch office and standing in long lines. You can fill out a simple form (often online, if you want) and write a check in the comfort of your home (or authorize electronic transfers from your bank or other accounts) to make your initial investment. Then you typically can make subsequent investments by mailing in a check or sending money electronically. Many fund companies also allow you to transfer money electronically back and forth from your bank account. Selling shares of your mutual fund usually is simple, too. Generally, you can do so by calling the fund company's toll-free number or visiting its website.

Maximizing your chances for fund investing success

I recommend using some straightforward, common-sense, easy-to-use criteria to greatly increase your chances of fund investing success. The criteria presented in this section have proved to dramatically increase your fund investing returns, which is great for your retirement. (My website, www.erictyson.com, has details on research and studies that validate these criteria.)

Understanding the role of risk in evaluating performance

A common mistake that many investors make when they select a fund is overemphasizing the importance of past performance. The shorter the time period you analyze, the greater the danger that you'll misuse high past performance as an indicator of a fund's likely future performance.

High past returns for a fund, relative to its peers, are largely possible only if a fund takes more risk or if a fund manager's particular investment style happens to come into favor for a few years. The danger of a fund taking greater risk in the pursuit of market-beating returns is that it doesn't always work the way you hope. The odds are high that you won't be able to pick the next star before it vaults to prominence in the fund universe. You're more likely to jump into a recently high-performing fund and then be along for the ride when it falls back.

Funds make themselves look better by comparing themselves with funds that aren't really comparable. The most common ploy starts with a manager investing in riskier types of securities; then the fund company, in its marketing, compares its performance with that of fund companies that invest in less-risky securities. Always examine the types of securities that a fund invests in and then make sure that the comparison funds or indexes invest in similar securities.

REMEMBER

A fund's historic rate of return or performance is one of several important factors to examine when you select funds. Keep in mind that — as all fund materials must tell you — past performance is no guarantee of future results. In fact, many former high-return funds achieved their results only by taking on high risk or simply by relying on short-term luck. Funds that assume higher risk should produce higher rates of return, but high-risk funds usually decline in price faster during market declines.

Scrutinizing fund management experience

Although the individual fund manager is important, the resources and capabilities of the parent company are equally, if not more, important. Managers come and go, but fund companies usually don't.

Different companies maintain different capabilities and levels of expertise with different types of funds. A fund company gains more or less experience than others not only from the direct management of certain fund types but also through hiring out. Some fund families contract with private money management firms that possess significant experience. In other cases, private money management firms with long histories in private money management offer funds to the general public.

Minimizing fund costs

The charges that you pay to buy or sell a fund and the ongoing fund operating expenses have a major effect on the return that you earn on your fund investments. Given the enormous number of choices for a particular type of fund, there's no reason to pay high costs.

Fund costs are an important factor in the return that you earn because fees are deducted from your investment returns. High fees and charges depress your returns. Here's how to keep your fund fees down:

INVESTIGATE

>> **Minimize operating expenses.** All funds charge fees as long as you keep your money in the fund. The fees pay for the costs of running a fund, such as employees' salaries, marketing, toll-free phone lines, and writing and publishing *prospectuses* (the legal disclosure of the fund's operations and fees). A fund's operating expenses are invisible to you because they're deducted from the fund's share price on a daily basis. Funds with higher operating expenses tend to produce lower rates of return on average. Conversely, funds with lower operating costs can more easily produce higher returns for you than a comparable fund with high costs.

Fund companies quote a fund's operating expenses as a percentage of your investment. The percentage represents an annual fee or charge. You can find this number in the fund expense section of a fund's prospectus, usually in a line that says "Total Fund Operating Expense."

>> **Use no-load funds.** A *sales load* is a commission paid to brokers and financial planners who work on commission. Commissions, or loads, generally are about 5 percent of the amount that you invest. Sales loads are additional and unnecessary costs that are deducted from your investment money.

REMEMBER

Invest in funds that have low total operating expenses and that don't charge sales loads. Both types of fees come out of your pocket and reduce your rate of return. Plenty of excellent funds are available at reasonable annual operating-expense ratios (less than 1 percent for stock funds and less than 0.5 percent for bond funds). See my recommendations of specific funds later in this chapter.

Understanding and using index funds

In some funds, the portfolio manager and a team of analysts scour the market for the best securities. An index fund manager, however, simply invests to match the makeup — and, thus, the performance — of an index such as the Standard & Poor's 500 index of 500 large U.S. company stocks. Index funds, which are a type of mutual fund, operate with far lower operating expenses because research isn't needed to identify companies in which to invest.

With actively managed stock funds, a fund manager can make costly mistakes, such as not being invested when the market goes up, being too aggressive when the market plummets, or just being in the wrong stocks. An actively managed fund can easily underperform the overall market index that it's competing against. On the other hand, index funds deliver relatively solid returns by keeping expenses low, staying invested, and not changing investments. Over ten years or more, index funds typically outperform about three quarters of actively managed funds, which can't overcome the handicap of high operating expenses that pull down their rates of return.

Vanguard (www.vanguard.com) is the largest and most successful provider of index funds because it maintains the lowest annual operating fees in the business. Vanguard has all types of bond and stock (both U.S. and international) index funds. There are some other index providers with low fees and demonstrated success - iShares, Schwab, and SPDR have some worthwhile funds. See my recommended fund sections later in this chapter.

Considering exchange-traded funds

Index mutual funds, which track particular market indexes and the best of which feature low costs, have been around for decades. Exchange-traded funds (ETFs) represent a twist on index funds. ETFs trade as stocks do and offer some potential advantages over traditional mutual funds, but they also have some potential drawbacks.

As with index funds, the promise of ETFs is low management fees. I say *promise* because the vast majority of ETFs actually have expense ratios far higher than those of the best index funds.

If you can't meet the minimum investment amounts for index funds (typically, several thousand dollars), you face no minimums when buying an ETF, but you must factor in the brokerage costs of buying and selling ETF shares through your favorite brokerage firm. Suppose that you pay a $10 transaction fee through an online broker to buy $1,000 worth of an ETF. That $10 may not sound like much, but it represents 1 percent of your investment and wipes out the supposed cost advantage of investing in an ETF. Because of the brokerage costs, ETFs aren't good vehicles for investors who seek to make regular monthly investments.

Here are some drawbacks of ETFs:

>> **The perils of market timing:** Being able to trade in and out of an ETF during the trading day presents challenges. In my experience working with individual investors, most people find it both nerve-racking and futile to try to time their moves in and out of stocks with the inevitable fluctuations that take place during the trading day. In theory, traders want to believe that they can buy at relatively low prices and sell at relatively high prices, but that's far easier said than done.

>> **Brokerage commission every time you trade:** With no-load index funds, you generally don't pay fees to buy and sell. With ETFs, however, because you're actually placing a trade on a stock exchange, you typically pay a brokerage commission every time you trade. (**Note:** Some brokers offer certain ETFs without brokerage charges in the hope of getting your account and making money on other investments.)

>> **Fluctuating prices:** Because ETFs fluctuate in price based on supply and demand, when you place a trade during the trading day, you face the complication of trying to determine whether the current price on an ETF is above or below the actual value. With an index fund, you know that the price at which your trade was executed equals the exact market value of the securities it holds.

>> **Poorly diversified investments:** Many ETFs invest in narrow segments, such as one specific industry or country. Such funds undermine the diversification value of fund investing and tend to have relatively high fees.

>> **Excessive risks and costs with leverage:** ETF issuers have come out with increasingly risky and costly ETFs. One particular class of ETFs that I especially dislike are leveraged ETFs. These ETFs claim to magnify the move of a particular index, such as the Standard & Poor's 500 stock index, by double or triple. So a double-leveraged S&P 500 ETF is supposed to increase by 2 percent for every 1 percent increase in the S&P 500 index. My investigations of whether the leveraged ETFs actually deliver on their objectives show that they don't even come close. Leveraged ETFs aren't investments; they're gambling instruments for day traders. Don't ever use these, especially in a retirement account, and never offer them to employees if you don't want to get sued!

Using asset allocation in your retirement fund portfolio

When you invest money for the longer term, such as for retirement, you can choose among the various types of funds that I discuss later in this chapter. Most people get a big headache when they try to decide how to spread their money among the choices. This section helps you begin cutting through the clutter for longer-term investing.

Asset allocation simply means that you decide what percentage of your investments you place, or allocate, in bonds versus stocks and in international stocks versus U.S. stocks. (Asset allocation can include other assets, such as real estate and small business.)

In your 20s and 30s, time is on your side, and you should use that time to your advantage. You may have many decades before you need to draw on some portion of your retirement account assets. If your investments drop over a year or even over several years, the value of your investments has plenty of time to recover before you spend the money during retirement.

TIP

Your current age and the number of years until you retire are the biggest factors in your allocation decision. The younger you are and the more years you have before retirement, the more comfortable you should be with volatile, growth-oriented investments, such as stock funds.

Table 3-2 provides my guidelines for allocating fund money that you've earmarked for long-term purposes, such as retirement. It's a simple but powerful formula that uses your age and the level of risk you're willing to take with your investments.

TABLE 3-2

Longer-Term Fund Asset Allocation

Your Investment Attitude	Bond Allocation (%)	Stock Allocation (%)
Play it safe	= Age	= 100 – Age
Middle of the road	= Age – 10	= 110 – Age
Aggressive	= Age – 20	= 120 – Age

Suppose that you're an aggressive type who prefers taking a fair amount of risk to make your money grow faster. Using Table 3-2, if you're 35 years old, consider putting 15 percent (35 – 20) into bond funds and 85 percent (120 – 35) into stock funds.

TIP

Now divvy up your stock investment money between U.S. and international funds. Here are the portions of your stock allocation that I recommend investing in overseas stocks:

>> 20 percent for a play-it-safe attitude

>> 35 percent for a middle-of-the-road attitude

>> 50 percent for an aggressive attitude

If, in Table 3-2, the 35-year-old aggressive type invests 85 percent in stocks, she then can invest about 50 percent of the stock fund investments (which works out to be around 42 percent of the total) in international stock funds. So the 35-year-old aggressive investor's portfolio asset allocation would look like 15 percent bonds, 42.5 percent U.S. stocks, and 42.5 percent international stocks.

How do you go about implementing such a recommendation? Which specific funds do you choose? As I explain in the next section, stock funds differ on several levels. You can choose among growth-oriented stocks and funds and those that focus on value stocks, as well as funds that focus on small-, medium-, or large-company stocks. You also need to decide what portion you want to invest in index funds versus actively managed funds that try to beat the market.

TIP

Deciding how much you should use index versus actively managed funds is a matter of personal taste. If you're satisfied knowing that you'll get the market rate of return and that you can't underperform the market (after accounting for your costs), index your entire portfolio. On the other hand, if you enjoy the challenge of trying to pick the better managers and want the potential to earn better-than-market returns, don't use index funds at all. Or, invest in a happy medium of both, as I do.

Selecting the best stock funds

Stock funds differ from one another on several dimensions. The following characteristics are what you need to pay most attention to:

>> **Company location:** Stocks and the companies that issue them are classified based on the location of their headquarters. Funds that specialize in U.S. stocks are, not surprisingly, called U.S. stock funds; the rest are called international or overseas funds.

>> **Company size:** Another dimension on which a stock fund's stock selection differs is based on the size of the company in which the fund invests: small, medium, or large. The total market value — *capitalization,* or cap for short —

of a company's outstanding stock defines the categories that define the stocks that the fund invests in. (**Note:** The following definitions can change over time.)

- Small-cap stocks are usually defined as stocks of companies that possess total market capitalization of less than $2 billion.

- Medium-cap stocks have market values of $2 billion to $10 billion.

- Large-cap stocks are those of companies with market values greater than $10 billion.

» **Growth stocks versus value stocks:** Stock fund managers and their funds are categorized by whether they invest in growth or value stocks.

- *Growth stocks* have high prices in relation to the company's assets, profits, and potential profits. Growth companies typically experience rapidly expanding revenue and profits. These companies tend to reinvest most of their earnings in the company to fuel future expansion; thus, these stocks pay no or low dividends.

- *Value stocks* are priced cheaply in relation to the company's assets, profits, and potential profits. Value stocks tend to pay higher dividends than growth stocks and historically have produced higher total returns.

Putting together two or three of these major classifications, you can start to comprehend those lengthy names that are given to stock funds. You can have funds that focus on large-company value stocks or small-company growth stocks. You can add U.S., international (non U.S.), and worldwide (global) funds to further subdivide these categories into more fund types. So you can have international stock funds that focus on small-company stocks.

TIP

You can purchase several stock funds, each focusing on a different type of stock, to diversify into various types of stocks. Two potential advantages result from doing so:

» Not all your money rides in one stock fund and with one fund manager.

» Each of the different fund managers can look at and track particular stock investment possibilities.

The following sections describe the best stock funds in different geographic categories. *Note:* With stock funds, you have the option of investing in ETFs as well as traditional mutual funds.

U.S. stock funds

Of all the types of funds offered, U.S. stock funds are the largest category. The only way to know for sure where a fund currently invests (or where the fund may invest in the future) is to ask. You can call the mutual fund company that you're interested in to start your information search or visit its website. You can also read the fund's annual report. (The prospectus generally doesn't tell you what the fund currently invests in or has invested in.)

ERIC'S
PICKS

Here's my short list of recommended U.S. stock funds:

>> Dodge & Cox Stock (800-621-3979; www.dodgeandcox.com)

>> Fidelity Low-Priced Stock (800-544-8544; www.fidelity.com)

>> Harbor Capital Appreciation (800-422-1050; www.harborfunds.com)

>> Vanguard Dividend Appreciation Index Fund, Total Stock Market Index, Primecap, Selected Value and Strategic Value (800-662-7447; www.vanguard.com)

International stock funds

Be sure to invest in stock funds that invest overseas for diversification and growth potential. You usually can tell that you're looking at a fund that focuses its investments overseas if its name contains the word *international*, which typically means that the fund's stock holdings are foreign only. If the fund name includes the word *global* or *worldwide*, the fund holds both foreign and U.S. stocks.

TIP

Shun foreign funds that invest in just one country. As with investing in a sector fund that specializes in a particular industry, this lack of diversification defeats a major benefit of investing in funds. Funds that focus on specific regions, such as Southeast Asia, are better but generally still problematic because of poor diversification and higher expenses than those of other, more-diversified international funds.

If you want to invest in more geographically limiting international funds, take a look at T. Rowe Price's and Vanguard's offerings, which invest in broader regions, such Europe, Asia, and the volatile but higher-growth-potential emerging markets.

In addition to the risks normally inherent with stock fund investing, changes in the value of foreign currencies relative to the U.S. dollar cause price changes in international stocks. A decline in the value of the U.S. dollar helps the value of foreign stock funds. Conversely, a rising dollar versus other currencies can reduce the value of foreign stocks. Some foreign stock funds hedge against currency changes. Although this hedging helps reduce volatility, it does cost money.

ERIC'S PICKS

Here are my picks for diversified international funds:

>> Dodge & Cox International (800-621-3979; www.dodgeandcox.com)

>> Harbor International (800-422-1050; www.harborfunds.com)

>> Litman Gregory Masters International (800-960-0188; www.mastersfunds.com)

>> T. Rowe Price Spectrum Growth — actually a global fund that invests in some foreign stocks (800-638-5660; www.troweprice.com)

>> Oakmark International and Global — holds some U.S. stocks (800-625-6275; www.oakmark.com)

>> Vanguard Global Equity (invests in the United States too), International Growth, and Total International Stock Index (800-662-7447; www.vanguard.com)

Investing in the best exchange-traded funds

Like the vast majority of investors, you don't need to complicate your life by investing in ETFs. Use them only if you're an advanced investor who understands index funds and you've found a superior ETF for a given index fund that you're interested in.

The most significant difference between a mutual fund and an ETF is that to invest in an ETF, you must buy it through a stock exchange on which the ETFs trade. Unlike a mutual fund, you can trade ETFs during the trading day rather than simply at the market closing price.

TIP

Use the buy-and-hold mentality that I advocate in my investing books. Don't hop in and out of ETFs because you'll inevitably pay more in taxes, earn lower returns, and incur higher brokerage fees. Also, you should buy only the ETFs that track the broader market indexes and that have the lowest expense ratios. Avoid those that track narrow industry groups or single small countries.

INVESTIGATE

Check whether the ETF you're considering is selling at a premium or discount to its net asset value (which is the value of all the securities an ETF holds). You can find this information on the ETF provider's website after the market's close each business day.

The best ETFs, like the best index funds, have low expense ratios. My top picks among the leading providers of ETFs include the following:

>> **iShares:** BlackRock is a leading provider of these cost effective ETFs based upon indexes from Russell, Morningstar, S&P and Dow Jones. (www.ishares.com; 800-474-2737).

>> **State Street Global Advisor SPDRs:** This group utilizes indexes from Dow Jones, MSCI, Russell, and S&P. (www.ssgafunds.com; 866-787-2257).

>> **Vanguard:** Historically, Vanguard has been the low-cost leader with index funds, and now it has low cost ETFs as well. (www.vanguard.com; 800-662-7447)

>> **WisdomTree:** Developed by Wharton business professor Jeremy Siegel, these ETFs have higher fees but offer a broad family of index choices for investors seeking stocks that pay higher dividends. (www.wisdomtree.com; 866-909-9473)

Balancing your act: Funds that combine stocks and bonds

Some funds — generally known as *balanced funds* — invest in both bonds and stocks. These funds are usually less risky and less volatile than funds that invest exclusively in stocks. In an economic downturn, bonds usually hold value better than stocks do.

Balanced funds make it easier for investors who are skittish about investing in stocks to hold stocks because they reduce the volatility that normally comes with pure stock funds. Because of their extensive diversification, balanced funds are also excellent choices for an investor who doesn't have much money to start with.

Here's my short list of great balanced funds:

>> Dodge & Cox Balanced (800-621-3979; www.dodgeandcox.com)

>> Fidelity Freedom Funds and Fidelity Puritan (800-343-3548; www.fidelity.com)

>> T. Rowe Price Balanced (800-638-5660; www.troweprice.com)

>> Vanguard LifeStrategy Funds, Star, Wellesley Income, and Wellington (800-662-7447; www.vanguard.com)

Finding the best bond funds

Although there are thousands of bond fund choices, not many remain after you eliminate high-cost funds, low-performance funds, and funds managed by fund companies and fund managers with minimal experience investing in bonds (all key points that I address in the earlier section "Maximizing your chances for fund investing success").

Among the key considerations when choosing bond funds are:

» **Bond credit quality:** The lower the issuer's credit rating, the riskier the bond. As with the risk associated with longer maturities, a fund that holds lower-quality bonds should provide higher returns for the increased risk you take. A higher yield compensates you for taking greater risk. Funds holding higher-quality bonds provide lower returns but more security.

» **Fees and costs:** After you settle on the type of bonds that you want, consider a bond fund's costs, including its sales commissions and annual operating fees. Stick with no-load funds with lower annual operating expenses.

» **Taxability:** Pay attention to the taxability of the dividends that bonds pay. When you invest in bonds inside retirement accounts, you want taxable bonds. (Outside retirement accounts, the choice between taxable and tax-free bonds depends on your tax bracket.)

» **Type of bond issuer:** Bonds can be issued by corporations, government entities, and foreign entities (corporate and governments). While some bond funds hold an eclectic mix, many focus on specific types of bonds (corporate bonds, for example).

» **Years to maturity:** Bond fund objectives and names usually fit one of three maturity categories: short-, intermediate-, and long-term. You can generally earn a higher yield from investing in a bond fund that holds longer-term bonds, but such bond prices are more sensitive to changes in interest rates. (*Duration,* which quantifies a bond fund's sensitivity to changes in interest rates, is another term you may come across. A fund with a duration of six years means that if interest rates rise by 1 percent, the fund should decline by 6 percent.)

The following sections warn you about yield chasing and provide recommendations for short-, intermediate-, and long-term bond funds. *Note:* With bond funds, you have the option of investing in ETFs as well as traditional mutual funds.

The dangers of yield-chasing

When selecting bond funds to invest in, investors are often led astray as to how much they can expect to make. The first mistake is looking at recent performance and assuming that they'll get that return in the future.

Investing in bond funds based on recent performance is particularly tempting after a period where interest rates have declined because declines in interest rates pump up bond prices and, therefore, bond funds' total returns. Keep in mind that an equal but opposite force waits to counteract high bond returns as bond prices fall when interest rates rise.

To make performance numbers meaningful and useful, you must compare bond funds that are comparable, such as intermediate-term funds that invest exclusively in high-grade corporate bonds.

INVESTIGATE

Bond funds calculate their yield after subtracting their operating expenses. When you contact a fund company seeking a fund's current yield, make sure that you understand what time period the yield covers. Fund companies are supposed to give you the Securities and Exchange Commission (SEC) yield, which is a standard yield calculation that allows for fairer comparisons among bond funds. The SEC yield, which reflects the bond fund's yield to maturity, is the best yield to use when you compare funds because it captures the effective rate of interest that an investor can receive in the future.

WARNING

If you select bond funds based on advertised yield, you're quite likely to purchase the wrong bond funds. Bond fund companies can play games to fatten a fund's yield. Higher yields make it easier for salespeople and funds to hawk their bond funds. Know that yield-enhancing shenanigans can leave you poorer. Here's what you need to watch out for:

>> **Longer-maturity bonds:** Bond funds usually can increase their yield just by increasing their maturity a bit. So if one short-term bond fund invests in bonds that mature in an average of two years, and another fund has an average maturity of seven years, comparing the two is comparing apples and oranges.

>> **Lower-credit-quality bonds:** When comparing one bond fund with another, you may discover that one pays a higher yield. You may find out later, however, that the higher-yielding fund invests a sizable chunk of its money in junk (non-investment-grade) bonds, whereas the other fund fully invests only in high-quality bonds.

>> **Return of principal as dividends:** Some funds return a portion of your principal in the form of dividends. This move artificially pumps up a fund's yield but depresses its total return. When comparing bond funds, make sure that you compare their total return over time in addition to seeing whether they have comparable portfolios of bonds.

>> **Temporary waivers of expenses:** Some bond funds, particularly newer ones, waive a portion or even all of their operating expenses to inflate the fund's yield temporarily.

Recommended short-term bond funds

Short-term bond funds are the least sensitive to interest rate fluctuations in the bond fund universe. The stability of short-term bond funds makes them appropriate investments for money on which you seek a better rate of return than a money market fund can produce for you.

TIP

With short-term bond funds, however, you also have to tolerate the risk of losing a percentage or two in principal value if interest rates rise. Short-term bonds work well with money that you plan to withdraw from your retirement account in the near future.

ERIC'S
PICKS

My favorite is the Vanguard Short-Term Investment-Grade fund (800-662-7447; www.vanguard.com).

Recommended intermediate-term bond funds

Intermediate-term bond funds hold bonds that typically mature in a decade or so. They're more volatile than shorter-term bonds but can also be more rewarding. The longer you own an intermediate-term bond fund, the more likely you are to earn a higher return on it than on a short-term fund unless interest rates continue to rise over many years.

TIP

As an absolute minimum, don't purchase an intermediate-term fund unless you expect to hold it for at least three to five years. Therefore, you need to make sure that the money you put in an immediate-term fund is money that you don't expect to use in the near future.

ERIC'S
PICKS

Taxable intermediate-term bond funds to consider include the following:

>> Dodge & Cox Income (800-621-3979; www.dodgeandcox.com)

>> DoubleLine Total Return (877-354-6311; www.doubleline.com)

>> Vanguard Total Bond Market Index (800-662-7447; www.vanguard.com)

Recommended long-term bond funds

Long-term bond funds are the most aggressive and volatile bond funds. If interest rates on long-term bonds increase substantially, you can easily see the principal value of your investment decline 10 percent or more.

Long-term bond funds are generally used for retirement investing by investors who

>> Don't expect to tap their investment money for a decade or more.

>> Want to maximize current dividend income and are willing to tolerate volatility.

TIP

Don't use long-term bond funds to invest money that you plan to use within the next five years because a bond market drop can leave your portfolio short of your monetary goal.

ERIC'S
PICKS

I have just one favorite taxable bond fund that holds longer-term bonds: the Vanguard Long-Term Investment-Grade fund (800-662-7447; www.vanguard.com).

Developing Realistic Investment Return Expectations

In my experience as a former financial advisor and as a writer interacting with many folks, I still find it noteworthy how many people have unrealistic and inaccurate return expectations for particular investments. Where do these wrong expectations come from? There are numerous sources, most of which have a vested interest in convincing you that you can earn really high returns if you simply buy what they're selling. Examples include newsletter writers, financial advisors, websites, blogs, and various other financial publishing outlets.

In this section, I discuss the actual returns you can reasonably expect from common investments used toward retirement. I also illustrate the power of compounding those returns over the years and decades ahead and show you why you don't need huge returns to accomplish your personal and financial goals for retirement.

Estimating your investments' likely future returns

WARNING

When examining expected investment returns, you have to be careful because you're largely using historic returns as a guide. Using history to predict the future, especially the near future, is dangerous. History may repeat itself, but not always in exactly the same fashion and not necessarily when you expect it to.

Use historical returns only as a guide, not as a guarantee. Keep that in mind as I discuss the returns on various investments such as bonds and stocks in the following sections. For comparative purposes, I also discuss historic returns from real estate investing.

Bond returns

When investing in a bond (at least when it's originally issued), you're effectively lending your money to the issuer of that bond (borrower), which is generally the federal government or a corporation, for a specific period of time. Companies can and do go bankrupt, in which case you may lose some or all of your investment. Government debt can go into default as well. Typically, you get paid in the form of a higher yield for taking on more risk when you buy bonds that have a lower credit rating.

Jeremy Siegel, a professor of finance at the Wharton School, has amassed data showing the performance of investments such as bonds and stocks over more than two centuries! His research has found that bond investors generally earn about 4 to 5 percent per year on average.

WARNING

Returns, of course, fluctuate from year to year and are influenced by inflation (increases in the cost of living). Generally speaking, increases in the rate of inflation, especially when those increases aren't expected, erode bond returns.

Consider a government bond that was issued at an interest rate of 4 percent when inflation was running at just 2 percent. Thus, an investor in that bond was able to enjoy a 2 percent return after inflation, or what's known as the *real return* — real meaning after inflation is subtracted. Now, if inflation jumps to, say, 6 percent per year, why would folks want to buy your crummy 4 percent bond? They wouldn't unless the price drops enough to raise the effective yield higher.

Longer-term bonds generally yield more than shorter-term bonds because they're considered to be riskier because of the longer period until they pay back their principal. What are the risks of holding a bond for more years? There's more time for the credit quality of the bond to deteriorate (and for the bond to default), and there's also more time for inflation to come back and erode the bond's purchasing power.

Stock returns

The returns from stocks that investors have enjoyed, and continue to enjoy, have been remarkably constant from one generation to the next. Since 1802, the U.S. stock market has returned an annual average of about 6 to 7 percent per year above the rate of inflation. That's a remarkable track record, but don't forget that it's an annual average return.

Stocks have significant downdrafts and can easily drop 20 percent, 30 percent, or more in relatively short periods of time. Stocks can also rise dramatically in value over short periods. The keys to making money in stocks are to be diversified, to invest consistently, and to own stocks over the long run.

Stocks exist worldwide, of course, not just in the United States. When investing in stocks, go global for diversification purposes. International (non-U.S.) stocks don't always move in tandem with U.S. stocks. As a result, overseas stocks help diversify your portfolio. In addition to enabling U.S. investors to diversify, investing overseas has proved to be profitable over the years.

WARNING

Now, some folks make stock investing riskier than need be by doing some foolish things:

>> **Chasing after specific stocks or sectors that have recently been hot:** Yes, what a rich genius you'd be if you had invested in Apple, McDonald's, Google, and so on when those stocks went public. With the benefit of hindsight, it's easy to spot the "best" stock investments (companies or sectors) over specific periods. It's quite another thing to put your money on the line now and hope and expect that you have the ability to pick the best-performing stocks of the future.

>> **Excessive trading and market timing:** Another type of wishful thinking occurs when folks like to believe that they can jump into and out of the market at the right times to join in moves higher and sidestep declines.

Real estate returns

Real estate is a solid long-term investment. Real estate, as an investment, has produced returns comparable to those of investing in the stock market. Both stocks and real estate have down periods but have historically produced attractive long-term returns.

Real estate does well in the long run because of growth in the economy, in jobs, and in population. Real estate prices in and near major metropolises and suburbs generally appreciate the most because people and businesses tend to cluster in those areas.

Compounding your returns

In the preceding section, I discuss the historic investment returns on common investments. During the past century, stocks and investment real estate returned around 9 percent per year and bonds around 5 percent.

Compounding seemingly modest investment returns can help you accumulate a substantial sum of money to help you accomplish your personal and financial goals for retirement.

The stock market can be risky, which logically raises the question of whether investing in stocks is worth the anxiety and potential losses. Why bother for a few extra percent per year? Here's a good answer to that sensible question: Over many years, a few extra percent per year increases your nest egg dramatically. The more years you have to invest, the greater the difference a few percent makes in your returns (see Table 3-3).

TABLE 3-3

How Compounding Grows Your Investment Dollars

For Every $1,000 Invested at This Return	In 25 Years, You'll Have	In 40 Years, You'll Have
1%	$1,282	$1,489
2%	$1,641	$2,208
3%	$2,094	$3,262
4%	$2,666	$4,801
5%	$3,386	$7,040
6%	$4,292	$10,286
7%	$5,427	$14,974
8%	$6,848	$21,725
9%	$8,623	$31,409

Here's a practical example to show you what a major difference earning a few extra percent can make in accomplishing your financial goals. Consider a 30-year-old investor who's saving toward retirement on his $40,000 annual salary. Suppose that his goal is to retire by age 67 with about $30,000 per year to live on (in today's dollars), which is 75 percent of his working salary.

If he begins saving at age 30, he needs to save about $460 per month if you assume that he earns about 5 percent per year average return on his investments. That's a big chunk to save each year — amounting to about 14 percent of his gross (pretax) salary.

But what if this investor can earn just a few percent more per year on average from his investments — 8 percent instead of just 5 percent? In that case, he could accomplish the same retirement goal by saving just half as much: $230 per month!

Chapter **4**

Real Estate and Your Small Business

E ven if you operate your business in the virtual world of the Internet, you need a place from which to run your company. Many new businesses are started out of folks' homes, but others require or benefit from space in an office building, retail center, or somewhere else.

What expenses you may or may not deduct on your small business tax return are a function of where you operate your company and also what business entity you choose (for example, a sole proprietorship, C corporation, LLC, and so on; see Chapter 2 for details on entities). And, of course, where you work can affect many important business issues, including the ease with which customers can find and patronize your business, the receptivity of employees to come work for you, the length of your commute, and so on.

In this chapter, I discuss the realities — both good and bad — of working from home and help you decide whether to work at home or seek outside space if those are options for your company. I also cover leases and possible purchases of real estate that you can use for your business.

Deciding Whether to Work out of Your Home

No matter what type of business you have in mind, you need space to work from, whether it's a spare room in your home, shared office space, a retail store, or a small factory. With some businesses, such as a restaurant, the options for where you can sensibly and legally operate your company are limited. With many other businesses, especially in the early days, months, and years, you may be able to operate the company out of your home.

In this section, I walk you through the important issues to consider regarding where you should operate your business. In particular, I help you determine whether working out of your home makes sense. *Note:* I use the term "home" generically to mean where you live, whether you rent or own and regardless of the type of property — single family home, apartment, condo, and so forth.

Researching local ordinances and issues

Government officials like to regulate things and make rules. As a small business owner, it's your responsibility to find out what rules may apply to your company and where you're seeking to operate it.

(Now, I'm not suggesting that people don't need rules and regulations. After all, would you like to buy a home and then find out next year that your neighbor is opening up a commercial chicken farm on his property or a junkyard that recycles and sells scrap metal?)

INVESTIGATE

Check with the governing authorities of your town or city to find out what local regulations exist for home-based businesses. Here are some examples of good questions to ask:

>> How many employees can you have working at your home?

>> Can customers come to your home and, if so, what limits apply to how many people and/or vehicles are allowed?

>> Must you file any paperwork or get any permits to operate a business out of your home?

>> Will you owe any local tax because of your business operations and equipment?

How can you find answers to these types of questions? Pick up the phone or visit your local government offices, small business association, chamber of commerce, or another, similar local organization. Of course, you can also surf the Internet sites of such organizations.

TIP

In addition to researching what specific rules may apply to your business, do some basic research and use some good, old-fashioned common sense:

>> What are the needs of your business and customers? If you don't require fancy office space to impress others or to meet with clients, working from home may make more sense.

>> If you operate a retail company that requires lots of customers to come to you, using outside space is probably the best (and legally correct) choice.

Controlling costs

The biggest potential appeal of running your business out of your home is to save money, or more specifically, to minimize your expenses. If you have space in your home that you can use, you've essentially found yourself a rent-free business office.

As I strongly advocate in my book *Small Business For Dummies* (John Wiley & Sons, Inc.), *bootstrapping* — keeping your expenses and overhead low so that you can largely self-finance your business — can make great financial and business sense. Having a home-based office can certainly be part of your bootstrapping strategy.

Another part of the low-cost appeal of a home-based office is the tax write-offs you may be eligible for by running a business out of your home. If you own your home and qualify for the home office deduction, you can take depreciation on your property as a business expense as well as operating expenses attributable to the portion of your home you use for business purposes. Renters can deduct their relevant expenses including a portion of the rent, utilities, Internet access, and so on. Chapter 9 covers the details for claiming the home office deduction on your income tax return.

WARNING

Some seminar operators and other promoters talk up running a business out of your home just for the supposedly great tax deductions. They pitch that you can write off all sorts of homeownership and personal expenses. It sounds too good to be true because it is! Regardless of where you elect to operate your company, the reality is that you may only deduct expenses directly related to operating your business. Also, keep in mind that if you secure space outside of your home for your company, you may take the costs for that space as legitimate business expenses. Chapter 8 details the expenses you may take for office and other expenses.

Separating your work life from your personal life

One of the biggest challenges of running your small business out of your home is separating your work life from your personal life. Of course, some folks who work outside their home have trouble "getting away" from work when they're at home, especially with all the increasingly invasive and addictive technologies in people's lives.

REMEMBER

But working at home presents unique challenges in compartmentalizing work and home lives:

>> **Discipline:** At home, do you have the discipline to work the number of hours that you need to or will the kitchen goodies tempt you to make half a dozen snack trips? Can you refrain from turning on the TV every hour for late-breaking news or constantly surfing the Internet for stock quotes, personal research, and entertainment? The sometimes amorphous challenge of figuring out how to grow the business may cause you to focus your energies elsewhere.

>> **Shutting down:** At the other "extreme" are folks who have workaholic tendencies and find it difficult to literally stop working. The close proximity of your office and associated working stuff can make it too easy to go back to work even after you've tried to leave it for the day.

>> **Privacy:** When you work out of your home, others who come into your home — employees, service providers, and so on — will know much more about your personal life. This isn't all bad or even a negative at all depending on how you feel about it and what's going on in your life. But it's definitely something to consider before you commit to running a business out of your home.

>> **Family matters:** Last but not least, your home life should factor into where you decide to work. One advantage to working at home when you're a parent is that you can be a more involved parent. If nothing else, you can spend the one to two hours per day with your kids that many people spend commuting! Just make sure you try to set aside work hours during which time your office is off-limits.

Ask other family members how they feel about your working at home. Be specific about what you plan to do, where, when, and how. Will clients come over? What time of day and where in the home will you meet with them? You may not think that your home office is an imposition, but your spouse may. Home business problems come between many couples. If you're single and living alone, home life is less of an issue.

Doing a cost comparison

While there are plenty of qualitative issues to weigh regarding working at home versus getting outside space, you should also crunch some numbers. Specifically, you should compare the costs, after factoring in taxes, of the alternatives. Those options include working out of your home, leasing a space somewhere, or buying an office or retail building, topics that I cover later in this chapter.

The Tax Cuts and Jobs Act that took effect in 2018 impacts the tax deductibility of some of the items real estate owners can claim on their tax returns. Of particular importance are the limitations on so-called SALT — state and local taxes. For your owner-occupied home, if you're able to itemize your tax deductions on Schedule A, you'll be limited to a $10,000 annual deduction for all state and local taxes and property taxes. For mortgages taken out after December 14, 2017, you may deduct interest on the first $750,000 of mortgage debt. With real estate used for business, you won't face these SALT limitations.

REMEMBER

When pricing out working from home (if that's an option), be careful not to fall into the trap of assuming that using space in your home is "free." Such space isn't really free, especially if you're considering buying or renting a larger home to have more space in part for your business.

Leasing Space for Your Business

If you want and/or need some sort of commercial, office, or retail space for your business, unfortunately you have to master an often ugly contract known as a lease. In this section, I define the term *lease* and explain why, especially in the early years of a business, leasing is often superior to buying a business property. I also talk about different types of space you can lease and discuss how to negotiate a lease.

Leaning toward leasing

Unless you can run your business from your home, you may be in the market for office or retail space. Finding good space and buying or leasing it both take tons of time if you do it right.

A *lease* is a contractual obligation between a lessor (landlord) and a lessee (tenant) to transfer the right to exclusive possession and use of certain real property for a defined time period for an agreed consideration (money). A verbal lease can be enforceable, but it's much better for all parties involved to have a written lease that defines the rights and responsibilities of the landlord and the tenant.

TIP

In the early years of your business, buying, owning, and managing an office or a retail building generally doesn't make sense. The down payment consumes important capital, and you may end up spending lots of time and money on a real estate transaction for a location that may not interest you in the long term. Buying this type of real estate rarely makes sense unless you plan to stay put for five or more years (I talk about buying business property in detail later in this chapter). Leasing a space for your business is far more practical.

Leasing burdens of retail businesses

Renting office space is simpler than renting retail space because a building owner worries less about your business and its financial health. Your company generally needs more credibility to rent a retail building because your retail business affects the nature of the strip mall or shopping center where you lease. Owners of such properties don't want to move in a fledgling small business that quickly ends up failing or a business that's run in an unprofessional, slipshod fashion.

TIP

If you and your business don't have a track record with renting space, getting references is useful. These references can be folks you've interacted with over the years in the course of your work and can speak to your integrity, ethics, competence, and financial acumen. If you seek well-located retail space, you usually end up competing with national chain stores, so you better have a top-notch credit rating and track record. Consider subletting — circulate flyers to businesses that may have some extra space in the area you want to locate your company. Spending time in those business locations may help you identify businesses with excess space and a lack of customers. Also prepare financial statements that show your personal and business creditworthiness.

Negotiating a lease

Brokers list most spaces for lease. Working with a broker can be useful, but the same conflicts exist as with residential real estate brokers. Brokers are salespeople who get paid on commission, which doesn't make them bad people but does create conflicts of interest that may be at odds with what's in your best interests. That's why you need to do your homework before hiring a broker to be sure you're hiring someone who has expertise and ethics and is a good listener.

You may also consider examining spaces for lease without a broker and deal with the landlord directly. Such landlords may give you a better deal because they don't have to pay a brokerage commission. It's imperative if you go direct that you learn enough about leases and what to for and look out for. (Check out my book *Real Estate Investing For Dummies*, published by John Wiley & Sons, Inc., for more information.)

The biggest headaches with leasing space are understanding and negotiating the lease contract. Odds are that the lessor presents you with a standard, preprinted lease contract that she says is fair and is the same lease that everyone else signs. Don't sign it! This contract is the lessor's first offer. Have an expert review it and help you modify it. Find yourself an attorney who regularly deals with similar real estate lease contracts.

Office leases are usually simpler than retail leases. About the most complicated issue you face with office leases is that they can be full service, which includes janitorial services. Retail leases, however, are usually triple-net, which means that you as the tenant pay for maintenance (for example, resurfacing the parking lot, snow plowing, cleaning, and gardening), utilities, and property taxes. You're correct to worry about these open-ended charges in a triple-net retail lease because you can't control many of these expenses. And, if the property is sold, property taxes can jump.

Here are provisions to keep in mind when dealing with a triple-net lease:

» Compare your site's costs to other sites to evaluate the deal that the lessor offers you.

» Your lease contract should include a cap for the triple-net costs at a specified limit per square foot.

» Try to make sure that the lease contract doesn't make you responsible for removal costs for any toxic waste that may be discovered during your occupation of the space. Also exclude increased property taxes that the sale of the property may cause.

» If feasible, get your landlord to pay for remodeling. It's cheaper for the landlord to do it and entails fewer hassles for you.

» With retail leases, get an option for renewal. This renewal option is critical in retail, where location is important. The option should specify the cost — for example, something like 5 percent below market, as determined by arbitration.

» Get an option that the lease can be transferred to a new owner if you sell the business. This protects you from getting booted out simply because ownership of the property changes hands.

If you really think you want to purchase (not lease) because you can see yourself staying in the same place for at least five years, see the next section.

Buying Business Property

If you've been in a business for at least several years, things are going well, and you have the financial wherewithal, you may consider buying a property for your business. As with buying a home instead of renting, owning puts you squarely in control of the property and your use of the property — recognizing of course that local zoning ordinances restrict what you may and may not do with your property.

In this section, I assist you with assessing whether your money situation will enable you to successfully and safely buy business property, do a simple rent-versus-buy analysis to see whether buying makes sense in your local market, and walk you through how to evaluate property for sale.

Taking stock of your financial situation

If you can't pay, you can't play. Or, I should say, you want to be sure you can really afford a property purchase before you ever consider buying instead of leasing a business property.

REMEMBER

As a small business owner, your priority is the financial health and success of your business. It makes no sense whatsoever to jeopardize your business's health and possible survival by taking on excessive debt to buy a property. That said, buying a business property will never be a risk-free proposition, just like any other significant decision affecting your small business.

INVESTIGATE

Here are critical issues to resolve regarding your financial situation before you contemplate looking for business property to buy:

» **Do you have sufficient capital (cash)?** Capital is a big barrier to most small business owners buying property for their business. The down payment and closing costs on a business property can easily take 30 percent or more of the sales price of a property. For example, if you're considering a business property that costs $200,000, between the down payment and closing costs, you could easily need at least $60,000 in cold hard cash just to do the deal.

» **Do you understand what improvements you need to make to a property and the cost of those improvements?** It's unlikely you'll be able to jump right into a property you buy without making some modifications and changes to it to suit your business.

» **Are you regularly producing financial statements for your business?** In recent years and recent quarters, do you have an income statement or cash flow analysis? How about a recent balance sheet? If not (or even worse, if you don't know what these are), don't consider buying business property. Get yourself a copy of the latest edition of my book *Small Business For Dummies* (John Wiley & Sons, Inc.) which I co-authored with small business veteran and guru Jim Schell.

>> **Have you examined your personal finances and developed a personal financial plan?** Do you know how much you should be saving toward your important goals such as retirement? Do you have proper personal insurance protection in place? Have you completed proper wills and other needed estate planning documents?

Doing a rent-versus-buy analysis

A rent-versus-buy analysis is the single most powerful piece of analysis you can do to assess whether buying or leasing makes more financial sense in your local area. You can lease (rent) property or you can buy property. If you can afford to buy a business property, it would be foolish to commit to buying (or renting) if you haven't compared the two options financially.

A rent-versus-buy analysis is based on the prices for business property for sale and the cost for you to lease a similar or comparable property. Specifically, after identifying some business properties that would meet your requirements and that you can afford, you first need to calculate what it would cost you on a monthly basis, after factoring in tax benefits, to buy and own those properties.

Then, you need to determine what it would cost you on a monthly basis to lease those same or similar properties. For each property, what you're trying to do is an apples-to-apples comparison of the monthly, after-tax cost of owning that property and the monthly cost of renting that same property.

After you have that information, how can it help you? You use it the same way to make a purchase decision for competing products or services. For example, if your analysis shows that leasing is far less costly than buying/owning, that may tip the scales of your decision toward leasing.

Evaluating leases as a real estate investor

If you're interested in possibly buying a particular business property, it's essential that you understand the lease terms that currently exist on the property. Why? For starters, the current lessee may have the right to continue leasing if the property is sold. Second, if the property is large enough for your business plus others, you may end up using the property yourself as well as leasing to others.

TIP

From an investment standpoint, owning a nice property with attractive and well-maintained buildings may give you a sense of pride of ownership, but you're really investing in the leases. Successful real estate investors know that an excellent opportunity is to find properties with leases that offer upside potential in the form of higher income and/or stability of tenancy.

Regardless of the type of property you're considering as an investment, make sure that the seller provides all the leases. And don't accept just the first page or a summary of the salient points of the lease — insist on the full and complete lease document, along with any addendums or written modifications with the seller's written certification that the document is accurate and valid. (Verbal modifications to the written lease aren't generally enforceable.) Have your real estate legal advisor review the leases as well.

In the sections that follow, I discuss how to understand and evaluate leases.

Lease transferability and analysis

REMEMBER

Existing leases almost always run with the property upon transfer of ownership and thus are enforceable. The new owner of the property can't simply renegotiate or void the current leases he doesn't like. Because you'll be legally obligated for all terms and conditions of current leases if you buy a property, be sure that you thoroughly understand all aspects of the property's current leases.

You may find that you're presented with the opportunity to purchase properties with leases that are detriments to the property and actually bring down its current and future value. For example, the leases may be so far above the current market conditions that an investor should discount the likelihood that the leases will be in place and enforceable in the future.

Other common problems with leases include:

>> Preprinted boilerplate forms (as opposed to a customized lease tailored to the specific tenant-landlord agreement) that may or may not comply with current laws or issues relevant for the specific tenant.

>> The charges for late payments, returned checks, or other administrative fees may not be clearly defined or may be unenforceable.

>> The rules and regulations may not be comprehensive or enforceable.

>> There's no rent escalation clause or it isn't clearly defined.

This isn't to suggest that you pass on purchasing any properties with leases with the preceding problems. Just be aware and factor the effect, if any, into your decision making to determine whether you want to buy the property, or just simply note that you need to change the onerous terms upon renewal.

A seller should be honest and disclose all material facts about the property she's selling, but most states don't have the same written disclosure requirements that are mandated for residential transactions. So even though your broker or sales agent and other members of your due diligence investigation team may be assisting you with inspecting the property and reviewing the books provided during the transaction, keep in mind that you need to be the one who cares the most about your best interests.

Note the expiration dates of the leases because any lease that's about to expire should be evaluated based on current market conditions. Future leases may not be at the same rent level, plus you must consider the concessions or tenant improvements that will be necessary to get the lease renewed:

>> Residential lease renewals may require a monetary concession or possibly a perk for the tenants, such as cleaning their carpets or installing microwaves or ceiling fans. You may end up with such a lease to review if you buy a mixed-use property.

>> Commercial lease renewals can require significant tenant improvements or rent concessions.

Factor these costs into your analysis because renewing a tenant, even with the associated costs, is typically much more cost effective than the turnover of a tenant.

Making sense of commercial leases

Commercial (business) leases, which can include office and retail space, are much more complicated than residential ones. Thus, the commercial real estate investor must have a thorough understanding of the contractual obligations and duties of the lessor (landlord) and lessee (tenant).

The analysis of commercial leases is typically called lease abstraction. A *lease abstract* is a written summary of all the significant terms and conditions contained in the lease and is much more than a rent roll. Although a good rent roll covers the lease basics — rent, square footage, length of lease, and renewal date or options — a good abstract covers other key tenant issues such as signage, rights of expansion and contraction, and even restrictions or limitations on leasing to other tenants that offer similar products and services. Have written lease abstracts prepared for any commercial property you're considering to ensure that you understand all the terms.

When obtaining financing for commercial properties, lenders typically require a certified or signed rent roll, along with a written lease abstract for each tenant. However, because the income of the property is critical to the owner's ability to make the mortgage payments, most lenders don't simply rely on the buyer's numbers but independently derive their own income projections based on information they require the purchaser to obtain from the tenants. This information includes:

>> **Lease estoppel:** A lease estoppel certificate is a legal document completed by the tenant that outlines the basic terms of his lease agreement and certifies that the lease is valid without any breaches by either the tenant or the landlord at the time it's executed. These estoppel certificates are also beneficial for the property's purchaser. You should seriously consider requiring estoppels from all tenants when you purchase a commercial building, regardless of the lender's requirements. Tenants may, for example, dispute the amount of the security deposit or claim that they were entitled to unwritten promises by the previous owner (for example, new carpet or the waiving of late charges).

>> **Financial statements:** The rent provided in the lease is a concern, but it's the amount you actually collect that determines the profitability of your real estate investment. Because of this, many leases require the commercial tenant to periodically provide (or present upon request) a recent financial statement.

>> **Recent sales info:** Most retail leases have provisions for percentage rents in which the tenant pays a base rent plus additional rent based on a percentage of sales. The percentage rent is often on a sliding scale, whereby the percentage paid by the tenant increases as sales increase. Be sure that you receive and review recent sales information and ensure that tenants are current on their percentage rent payments.

TIP

A proven way to make money in real estate is to find commercial property for sale with leases where the person in charge of the property isn't collecting the proper rent due under the lease's terms. For example, you may find that the rent roll from the seller of a property you're considering for purchase hasn't implemented rent increases when due. Even more common is the failure of landlords and their property managers to correctly calculate and collect the common area maintenance charges or ancillary fees and reimbursements due from the tenant. Of course, you may also find that the landlords are actually overcharging the tenants, and thus, you'd never want to purchase a property relying on phantom income that you wouldn't have the legal right to collect. For more insights regarding investing in business real estate, see the latest edition of *Real Estate Investing For Dummies* (John Wiley & Sons, Inc.), which I co-authored with Robert Griswold.

Chapter **5**

Estate Planning

Among the dreariest of tax and financial topics is the issue of what happens to your assets when you pass away. Depending on how your finances are structured and when you die, you (actually, your estate) may get socked with estate taxes.

Unfortunately, you can't predict when the grim reaper will pay a visit. That doesn't mean, however, that you need to participate in complicated and costly estate planning. To the contrary, especially when your assets are modest, a few simple moves may be all you need.

In this chapter, I discuss how the estate tax system works (especially at the federal level), the particular issues that may affect your small business, and the strategies you may consider to reduce the possibility of future estate taxes hitting your assets.

REMEMBER

Estate planning takes time and money, which are precious commodities for most people. Whether spending your time and money on estate planning is worthwhile depends on your personal and financial circumstances, both now and in the near future.

Determining Your Estate's Tax Concerns

As a small business owner, you have two potential major areas of concern regarding planning your estate:

>> **Minimizing estate taxes:** The more you owe, the more your assets will be depleted. Even worse, your heirs may be forced to sell your business to pay the estate taxes you owe. The good news is that, given the currently high limits of assets that can be passed along to heirs, few people and families are subject to estate taxes at the federal level. (*Note:* Some states have much lower state estate and inheritance tax limits.)

>> **Preserving your business:** In the event of your untimely passing, you'll probably want to ensure that your business can continue to operate as smoothly as possible.

The following sections help you sort out your estate's exact tax concerns by explaining the federal estate tax exemption, how to figure out your taxable estate, various estate tax rates, and special estate tax treatment for small businesses. (I describe strategies for minimizing estate taxes and preserving your business later in this chapter.)

WARNING

With all the warnings about the enormous estate taxes that you may owe upon your death, you may think that owing estate taxes is a common problem. It isn't, but that hasn't stopped some insurance agents, attorneys, and estate-planning "specialists" from using scare tactics to attract prospective clients, often by luring them to free estate-planning seminars. The later section "Getting advice and help" explains how to find the best advisors.

Understanding the federal estate tax exemption

Thanks to the recent passage of the Tax Cuts and Jobs Act, in tax year 2019, an individual who dies can pass $11.4 million to beneficiaries without paying federal estate taxes. A married couple can pass up to $22.8 million to beneficiaries without paying federal estate taxes (these amounts will increase in future years along with inflation). Because most people still are trying to accumulate enough money to retire or take a trip around the world someday, most folks typically don't have to pay federal estate taxes because they don't have this much money around when they die.

Note: I must mention here that estate tax laws are set by Congress, and the rules evolve over time. That said, the current laws should stick for a number of years.

Figuring out your taxable estate

To calculate the value of your estate upon your death, the IRS totals up your assets and subtracts your liabilities:

>> Assets include your personal property, home and other real estate, savings and investments (such as bank accounts, stocks, bonds, and mutual funds held inside and outside of retirement accounts), and small business(es) and life insurance death benefits (unless properly placed in a trust, as described later in this chapter).

>> Liabilities include any outstanding loans (such as a mortgage), bills owed at the time of your death, legal and other expenses to handle your estate, and funeral expenses.

The IRS also deducts any charitable contributions or bequests that you dictate in your will from your assets before calculating your taxable estate.

Examining estate tax rates

Under current federal estate tax law, if your estate totals more than $11.4 million at your death ($22.8 million for a married couple), you may owe federal estate taxes. In addition to raising the amounts that can be passed on free of federal estate taxes, recent tax law changes lowered for the tax rate that applies to estates large enough to be subject to estate taxes. The federal estate tax rate for 2019 is a hefty 40 percent.

Be aware that states also can levy additional estate taxes (levied on the estate) and inheritance taxes (charged to the recipient). That said, more states are scrapping these taxes or significantly raising the threshold limits. A few states have their own estate tax exemptions that differ from the federal amount, and even fewer have an inheritance tax (see Table 5-1). One state — Maryland — has an estate and inheritance tax.

Surveying special estate tax treatment afforded small businesses

Here's another caveat to the list of states in Table 5-1 that whack estates or inheritors when someone passes away and leaves assets. Some states include special additional exemptions for small business owners. For example, consider the exemptions granted by Pennsylvania. Farmland is exempt from the state's inheritance tax, so long as the land is inherited by family members and continues to be used for agriculture for seven years. Also, family-owned businesses that have less than 50 employees and assets under $5 million are exempt from the Pennsylvania inheritance tax. To qualify, the business must have been in existence for five or more years, be inherited by family members, and remain in business for at least seven more years.

TABLE 5-1   **States with an Estate or Inheritance Tax**

State	Exemption	Maximum Tax Rate	Tax Levied
Connecticut	$2.6 million	12%	Estate
District of Columbia	$11.2 million	16%	Estate
Hawaii	$11.2 million	16%	Estate
Illinois	$4 million	16%	Estate
Indiana	$100	20%	Inheritance
Iowa(1)	none	15%	Inheritance
Kentucky(2)	$500	16%	Inheritance
Maine	$11.2 million	12%	Estate
Maryland(3)	$4 million $1000	16% 10%	Estate Inheritance
Massachusetts	$1 million	16%	Estate
Minnesota	$2 million	16%	Estate
Nebraska(4)	$10,000	18%	Inheritance
New Jersey(5)	none	16%	Inheritance
New York	$5.25 million	16%	Estate
Oregon	$1 million	16%	Estate
Pennsylvania(6)	none	15%	Inheritance
Rhode Island	$910,725	16%	Inheritance
Vermont	$2,75 million	16%	Estate
Washington	$2.13 million	19%	Estate

(1) Iowa has an inheritance tax that applies to family members and other lineal ancestors and most charities and nonprofit organizations.
(2) Kentucky's inheritance tax doesn't apply to closest family members.
(3) Maryland's inheritance tax doesn't apply to close relatives and charities.
(4) Nebraska's inheritance tax doesn't apply to surviving spouses.
(5) New Jersey's inheritance tax doesn't apply to close family members.
(6) Pennsylvania's inheritance tax doesn't apply to surviving spouses, charities, and government entities.

Recognizing the burden that could be placed on the heirs of an estate that has a small business as a substantial part of the estate, the IRS cuts some slack in paying an estate tax bill in such situations. These special installment payment provisions apply when the small business is at least 35 percent of the estate's total value. Federal estate tax owed in such a case may be spread out over 14 years at a relatively low interest rate.

Reducing Expected Estate Taxes with a Few Strategies

Thanks to all the changes in tax laws and the army of attorneys and tax advisors working to find new ways around paying estate taxes, a dizzying array of strategies exists to reduce estate taxes — including taking up residence in a foreign country! In the following sections, I start with the simpler stuff and work toward the more complex; I also provide pointers on finding advice and help from professionals.

WARNING

You have your work cut out for you as you try to educate yourself about estate planning. Many attorneys and non-attorneys sell estate-planning services, and many insurance agents hawk life insurance. All are pleased to sell you their services. Most people don't need to do complicated and costly estate planning with high-cost attorneys. Here, I also give you the straight scoop on what, if anything, you need to be concerned with now and at other junctures in your life, and I tell you the conflicts of interest that these "experts" have in rendering advice.

Giving away your assets

TIP

Current tax law allows you to give up to $15,000 per individual each year to as many people — such as your children, grandchildren, or best friends — as you desire without any gift tax consequences or tax forms required. If you're married, your spouse can do the same. The benefit of giving is that it removes the money from your estate, and if you have a large estate, you can save the 40 percent in federal estate taxes, plus whatever your state levies in estate and inheritance taxes. By directing some of your money to people and organizations now while you're still alive, you can experience the satisfaction of seeing the good that your money can do. Even better is the fact that all future appreciation and income on the gifted money also is removed from your estate because the money now belongs to the gift recipient. (The current annual tax-free gifting limit of $15,000 per recipient will increase in future years with inflation.)

WHERE THERE'S A WILL THERE'S AN EASIER WAY

Wills are legal documents that detail your instructions for what you want done with your personal property and assets upon your death. Wills don't save you on taxes or on *probate* (the legal process for administering and implementing the directions in a will), but they're an estate-planning basic that most people should have but don't. Most of the world doesn't bother with wills because contemplating one's demise and drafting a will aren't enjoyable and laws and customs divvy up a person's estate among the spouse and children or other close relatives.

The main benefit of a will is that it ensures that your wishes for the distribution of your assets are fulfilled. If you die without a will — known in legalese as *intestate* — your state decides how to distribute your money and other property, including your small business, according to state law. Therefore, your friends, more-distant relatives, and favorite charities will probably receive nothing. For a fee, the state appoints an administrator to supervise the distribution of your assets.

If you have little in the way of personal assets and don't really care who gets your possessions and other assets (state law usually specifies the closest blood relatives), you can neglect creating a will. You can save yourself the time and sadness that inevitably accompany this gloomy exercise.

If you have minor (dependent) children, a will is necessary to name a guardian for them. In the event that you and your spouse both die without a will, the state (courts and social service agencies) decides who raises your children. Therefore, even if you can't decide at this time who would raise your children, you at least need to appoint a trusted guardian who can decide for you.

Living wills, medical powers of attorney, and durable powers of attorney are useful additions to a standard will. Here's what each of these is:

- **Living will:** This tells your doctor what, if any, life-support measures you would accept.

- **Medical power of attorney:** This grants authority to someone you trust to make decisions with a physician regarding your medical options when you aren't able.

- **Durable power of attorney:** This gives someone else the authority to act for you in other legal transactions if you're away or incapacitated, including signing your tax returns.

These additional documents are usually prepared when a will is drawn up.

You can use gifting to remove a substantial portion of your assets from your estate over time. Suppose that you have three children. You and your spouse each can give each of your children $15,000 per year for a total gift of $90,000. If your kids are married, you can make additional $15,000 gifts to their spouses for another $90,000 per year.

Note: Yet another tax — the federal *generation-skipping transfer tax* — can be assessed on a gift (some states levy this tax as well). This tax applies if the gift giver is a grandparent making a gift to a grandchild (and the grandparent's son or daughter is still alive) or if the gift is made to an unrelated individual who is more than 37½ years younger. Seek the advice of a qualified tax advisor if this tax may apply to you (check out the later section "Getting advice and help" for guidance in finding such an advisor).

The following sections go into more detail on the assets you can give away and what happens when you give gifts greater than $15,000.

Knowing what you should/can give

As a business owner, you can give away ownership interests in your company. Usually, you do this by incorporating the business — forming a family limited partnership or limited liability company (LLC) to make it easier to pass along a portion of the ownership and continue the operations (I discuss these business entities in Chapter 2). You can give away stock annually worth up to $15,000 to each recipient you designate. Don't worry about giving up control when you give away stock in this fashion; you can designate the shares that you give away as nonvoting shares. (*Note:* You must value the stock as you give it away, so you need to enlist tax and other experts to help you with this process.)

TIP

You, of course, have other options in terms of what money or assets you give to others. Start with cash or assets (mutual funds, stocks, and so on) that haven't appreciated since you purchased them. If you want to transfer an asset that has lost value, consider selling it first; then you can claim the tax loss on your tax return and transfer the cash.

TIP

Rather than giving away assets that have appreciated greatly in value, consider holding on to them. If you hold such assets until your death, your heirs receive what's called a *stepped-up basis.* That is, the IRS assumes that the effective price your heirs "paid" for an asset is the value on your date of death, which wipes out the capital gains tax that otherwise is owed when selling an asset that has appreciated in value. (Donating appreciated assets to your favorite charity can make sense because you get the tax deduction for the appreciated value and avoid realizing the taxable capital gain.)

Making gifts greater than $15,000 per year

You can make gifts of greater than $15,000 per year to an individual; however, you have to prepare and file IRS Form 709, "United States Gift (and Generation-Skipping Transfer) Tax Return." (Find this form at www.irs.gov/pub/irs-pdf/f709.pdf.) Chances are good that you won't have to pay any tax on the transfer, but when giving gifts that large, the IRS does want to have a record as it reduces your lifetime exclusion amount (which is currently $11.4 million).

You don't need to file Form 709 in the following situations:

>> You're allowed to make gifts larger than $15,000 per year to pay for another person's tuition or medical expenses without filing Form 709. If you decide you want to pay your beloved niece's tuition to her costly college (how nice of you), just make sure that you write the check directly to the school. Likewise, in the case of paying someone else's medical expenses, send your check directly to the medical care provider or institution.

>> If you make a large gift of cash or property to charity and you otherwise aren't required to file Form 709, you don't need to report this gift, even if its value exceeds $15,000, provided that you gave up all interest in the property you transferred. Don't forget to include your gift on Schedule A of your Form 1040 (see Chapter 9) — even though the property you're giving may not be part of this year's income, you're still entitled to an income tax deduction.

>> Gifts to political organizations aren't really gifts at all. If you're so inclined and make large payments to political organizations, you don't trigger a requirement to file Form 709, even if your gift is greater than $15,000.

A more complicated way to give money to your heirs without giving them absolute control over the money is to set up a Crummey trust (named after the first man to gain approval to use this type of trust). Although the beneficiary has a short window of time (a month or two) to withdraw money that's contributed to the trust, you can verbally make clear to the beneficiary that, in your opinion, leaving the money in the trust is in his or her best interest. You also can specify in the trust document itself that the trust money be used for particular purposes, such as tuition. Some of the other trusts I discuss in the later section "Setting up trusts" may meet your needs if you want more control over the money you intend to pass to your heirs.

Leaving all your assets to your spouse

Tax laws wouldn't be tax laws without exceptions and loopholes. Here's one: If you're married at the time of your death, any and all assets that you leave to your spouse are exempt from estate taxes normally due upon your death. In fact, you may leave an unlimited amount of money to your spouse, hence the name *unlimited marital deduction.* Assets that count are those willed to your spouse or for which he or she is named as beneficiary (such as retirement accounts).

TIP

Even in the typical cases where the deceased spouse's estate isn't subject to federal estate tax because it's less than $11.4 million as of 2019, the surviving spouse must file IRS Form 706, "United States Estate (and Generation-Skipping Transfer) Tax Return." This must be done to make use of the deceased spouse's unused federal estate tax exemption; otherwise, it will be wasted and lost. (Find this form at www.irs.gov/pub/irs-pdf/f706.pdf.)

WARNING

Although leaving all your assets to your spouse is a tempting estate-planning strategy for married couples, this strategy can have problems:

>> You and your spouse could die simultaneously.

>> The unlimited marital deduction isn't allowed if your spouse isn't a U.S. citizen.

>> Some states don't allow the unlimited marital deduction, so be sure to find out about the situation in your state.

Buying cash-value life insurance

Two major types of life insurance exist.

>> Most people who need life insurance — and who have someone dependent on their income — should buy *term life insurance,* which is pure life insurance: You pay an annual premium for which you receive a predetermined amount of life insurance protection. If the insured person passes away, the beneficiaries collect; otherwise, the premium is gone. In this way, term life insurance is similar to auto or homeowner's insurance.

>> The other kind of life insurance, called *cash-value life insurance,* is probably one of the most oversold financial products in the history of Western civilization. With cash-value policies (whole, universal, variable, and so on), your premiums pay for life insurance, and some of your dollars also are credited to an account that grows in value over time, assuming that you keep paying your premiums.

On the surface, a cash-value life policy sounds potentially attractive. However, better ways to reduce your estate taxes exist. The following sections give details on agent conflicts of interest and the rare circumstances when buying life insurance is the best solution to help with estate taxes.

Agent conflicts of interest

WARNING

Some insurance salespeople aggressively push cash-value policies because of the high commissions (50 percent to 100 percent of the first year's premium paid by you) that insurance companies pay their agents. These policies are expensive ways to purchase life insurance. Because of their high cost (about eight times the cost of the same amount of term life insurance), you're more likely to buy less life insurance coverage than you need, which, unfortunately, is the sad result of the insurance industry pushing this stuff. The vast majority of life insurance buyers need more protection than they can afford to buy in cash-value coverage.

Agents know which buttons to push to get you interested in buying the wrong kind of life insurance. Insurance agents show you all sorts of projections implying that after the first 10 or 20 years of paying your premiums, you won't need to pay more premiums to keep the life insurance in force. The only reason you may be able to stop paying premiums is that you've poured too much extra money into the policy in the early years of payment.

Insurance agents also argue that your cash value grows tax-deferred. But if you want tax-deferred retirement savings, you first need to take advantage of retirement savings plans such as 401(k)s, 403(b)s, SEP-IRAs, and so on. These plans give you an immediate tax deduction for your current contributions in addition to growth without taxation until withdrawal. Money paid into a cash-value life policy gives you no upfront tax breaks. When you've exhausted the tax-deductible plans, then variable annuities or a nondeductible IRA can provide tax-deferred compounding of your investment dollars (see Chapter 3 for details on retirement accounts and investments).

REMEMBER

Life insurance tends to be a mediocre investment anyway. The insurance company quotes you an interest rate for the first year only. After that, the rate is at the company's discretion. If you don't like the future interest rates, you can be penalized for quitting the policy. Would you invest your money in a bank account that quoted an interest rate for the first year only and then penalized you for moving your money in the next seven to ten years?

WARNING

Insurance companies aren't stupid. In fact, they're quite smart. If you purchase a cash-value life insurance policy that provides a death benefit of, say, $1 million, you have to pay substantial insurance premiums, although far less than $1 million. Is that a good deal for you? No, because the insurance company invests your premium dollars and earns a return the same way as you otherwise would have, had you invested the money instead of using it to buy the life insurance.

Through the years, between the premiums you pay on your life insurance policy and the returns the insurance company earns investing your premiums, the insurance company is able to come up with more than $1 million on average on policies like yours. Otherwise, how could it afford to pay out a death benefit of $1 million on policies like yours?

Rare instances when life insurance can help with estate taxes

When bought and placed in an irrevocable life insurance trust, life insurance, it's true, receives special treatment with regard to estate taxes. Specifically, the death benefit or proceeds paid on the policy upon your death can pass to your designated heirs free of estate taxes. (Some states, however, don't allow this.)

People who sell cash-value insurance — that is, insurance salespeople and other life insurance brokers masquerading as estate-planning specialists and financial planners — too often advocate cash-value life insurance as the best, and only, way to reduce estate taxes. But the other methods I discuss in this chapter are superior in most cases.

TIP

Using life insurance as an estate-planning tool is beneficial if your estate includes assets that you don't want to subject to a forced sale to pay estate taxes after you die. For example, small business owners whose businesses are worth millions may want to consider cash-value life insurance under special circumstances. If your estate lacks the other necessary assets to pay expected estate taxes and you don't want your beneficiaries to be forced to sell the business, you can buy life insurance to pay expected estate taxes.

For advice on whether life insurance is an appropriate estate-planning strategy for you, don't expect to get objective information from anyone who sells life insurance. See the later section "Getting advice and help" for guidance.

Setting up trusts

If estate planning hasn't already given you a headache, understanding the different types of trusts could. A *trust* is a legal device used to pass to someone else the management responsibility and, ultimately, the ownership of some of your assets. I discuss some trusts, such as Crummey and life insurance trusts, earlier in this chapter; in this section, I talk about other trusts you may hear about when planning your estate.

Living trusts

When you use a revocable living trust, you control the assets placed into the trust and can revoke the trust whenever you desire. The advantage of a living trust is that upon your death, assets can pass directly to your beneficiaries without going through *probate,* the legal process for administering and implementing the directions in a will.

Living trusts keep your assets out of probate but, in and of themselves, do nothing to help you deal with estate taxes. Living trusts can contain bypass trusts and other estate tax–saving provisions.

Property and assets that are owned by *joint tenants with a right of survivorship* (owned by two or more individuals, with the deceased owner's share passing upon death to the surviving owner) or inside retirement accounts — such as IRAs or 401(k)s — and have designated beneficiaries generally pass to heirs without going through probate. Many states also allow a special type of revocable trust for bank accounts called a *Totten trust,* sometimes also referred to as a *payable-on-death* or POD account, which also insulates the bank accounts from probate. Such trusts are established for the benefit of another person, and the money in the trust is paid to that beneficiary upon the account holder's death.

Probate can be a lengthy, expensive hassle for your heirs. Attorney probate fees may approach 5 percent to 7 percent of the estate's value. In addition, the details of your assets become public record because of probate. Properly drafted and funded, living trusts can save on probate fees and maintain your financial privacy. They're also useful in naming someone to administer your affairs in the event you become incapacitated.

TIP

You can't escape the undertaker or the lawyers. Setting up a trust and transferring property in and out costs money and time. Thus, living trusts are likely to be of greatest value to people who are age 60 and older, are single, and own assets worth more than $100,000 that must pass through probate (including real estate, nonretirement accounts, and businesses). Small estates are often less expensive to probate in some states than the cost and hassle of setting up a living trust. The key is to maintain an independent administration, which is when the probate court trusts the executor to make most of the decisions without the court's supervision.

Charitable trusts

If you're feeling philanthropic, charitable trusts may be for you. With a *charitable remainder trust,* you or your designated beneficiary receives income from assets that you donate to a charity.

TIP

At the time you fund a charitable remainder trust, you're also entitled to a current charitable deduction on IRS Form 1040 Schedule A, calculated by a complicated formula that includes reference to life expectancies and the gift's present value. Although not inexpensive to set up or to administer, a charitable remainder trust makes especially good sense in cases where a person holds an asset that he or she wants to donate that has greatly appreciated in value. By not selling the asset before the donation, a hefty tax on the profit is avoided.

In a *charitable lead trust,* the roles of the charity and beneficiaries are reversed. The charity receives the income from the assets for a set number of years or until you pass away, at which point the assets pass to your beneficiary. You get a current income tax deduction for the value of the expected payments to the charity.

Getting advice and help

The number of people who happily will charge you a fee for or sell you some legal advice or insurance far exceeds the number actually qualified to render objective estate-planning advice. Attorneys, accountants, financial planners, estate-planning specialists, investment companies, insurance agents, and even some nonprofit agencies stand ready to help you figure out how to dispense your wealth.

WARNING

Most of these people and organizations have conflicts of interest and lack the knowledge necessary to do sound estate planning for you. Attorneys are biased toward drafting legal documents and devices that are more complicated than may be needed. Insurance agents and financial planners who work on commission try to sell cash-value life insurance. Investment firms and banks encourage you to establish a trust account that requires them to manage the assets in the future. Although the cost of free estate-planning seminars is tempting, you get what you pay for — or worse.

TIP

Start the process of planning your estate by first looking at the big picture. Talk to your family members about your financial situation. Many people never take this basic but critical step. Your heirs likely have no idea what you're considering or what you're worried about. Conversely, how can you develop a solid action plan without understanding your heirs' needs and concerns? Be careful not to use money to control or manipulate other family members.

For professional advice, you need someone who can look objectively at the big picture. Attorneys and tax advisors who specialize in estate planning are a good starting point. Ask the people you're thinking of hiring whether they sell life insurance or manage money. If they do, they can't possibly be objective and likely aren't sufficiently educated about estate planning, given their focus.

TIP

For preparation of wills and living trusts, check out the high-quality software programs on the market. Legal software may save you from the often difficult task of finding a competent and affordable attorney. Preparing documents with software also can save you money.

Using legal software is generally preferable to using fill-in-the-blank documents. Software has the built-in virtues of directing and limiting your choices and keeping you from making common mistakes. Quality software also incorporates the knowledge and insights of the legal eagles who developed the software. As for the legality of documents that you create with software, keep in mind that you and your witnesses properly signing the document (for example, a will) makes it legal and valid. An attorney preparing a document isn't what makes it legal. If your situation isn't unusual, legal software may work well for you.

For will and living trust preparation, check out WillMaker Plus by Nolo Press. In addition to enabling you to prepare wills (in every state except Louisiana), WillMaker Plus can help you create a living will, medical power of attorney, and living trust. Living trusts are fairly standard legal documents that serve to keep property out of probate in the event of your death (keep in mind that they don't address the issue of estate taxes). The software package advises you to seek professional guidance for your situation, if necessary.

If you want to do more reading on estate planning, pick up a copy of *Plan Your Estate* by attorney Denis Clifford (Nolo Press). When you have a large estate that may be subject to estate taxes, consulting an attorney or tax advisor who specializes in estate planning may be worth your time and money. Get smarter first and figure out the lingo before you seek and pay for advice.

2
Ongoing Tax Jobs

IN THIS PART . . .

Track your business revenues and costs, and understand record-keeping issues (like when to stash and when to trash).

Peruse your Form 1040 filing options: Form 1040EZ (a breeze!), Form 1040A (known as the short form), and Form 1040 (known as the long form).

Make sense of Schedule C and C-EZ. The following are among the qualifications for Schedule C-EZ: Your deductible expenses can't exceed $5,000, you can't have an inventory of items for sale, you must operate only one business as a sole proprietor, and you must use the cash method of accounting.

Report the business use of your home; to do so, you need to fill out IRS Form 8829. Watch out, though; be aware of the downsides of home office deductions.

Complete self-employment and other small business–related tax forms, such as IRS Form 1040-ES ("Estimated Tax for Individuals") and IRS Form 8889 ("Health Savings Accounts").

Chapter **6**

Keeping Track of Your Small Business Revenues and Costs

Running your own business means hard work and long hours.

One of the ways that you keep score is to track your business revenue and expenses; the difference between the two is the profit or loss for your company. I strongly recommend that you utilize a system for accounting for your business inflows and outflows to stay on top of what's going on in your business and to ease the pains of completing the never-ending stream of tax forms required by state and federal government tax authorities quarterly and annually.

In this chapter, I explain the basics of developing a business accounting process for your small business. I also discuss how to fulfill the myriad filing requirements of the tax authorities by keeping proper records.

Establishing an Accounting System for Your Business

If you're thinking about starting a business or you're already in the thick of one, make sure you keep a proper accounting of your income and expenses. If you don't, you'll have a lot more stress and headaches when it comes time to complete and submit the necessary tax forms for your business.

Besides helping you over the annual tax-filing hurdle and fulfilling quarterly requirements, accurate records allow you to track your company's financial health and performance during the year. How are your profits running compared with last year? Can you afford to hire new employees? Analyzing your monthly or quarterly business financial statements (profit and loss statement, balance sheet, and so on) can help you answer these and other important questions.

WARNING

Here's another reason to keep good records: The IRS may audit you, and if that happens, you'll be asked to substantiate particular items on your return. Small business owners who file IRS Form 1040 Schedule C, "Profit or Loss From Business," with their tax returns are audited at a much higher rate than other taxpayers (see Chapter 8 for more about this form). Although that dubious honor may seem like an unfair burden to business owners, the IRS targets small businesses because more than a few small business owners break the tax rules, and many areas exist where small business owners can mess up.

REMEMBER

If your small business is audited, well-prepared and organized financial records will help. Being organized in and of itself helps establish you in the auditor's eyes as a responsible business person.

The following sections cover the key tax-organizing things that small business owners need to keep in mind and get right.

Separating business from personal finances

One of the IRS's biggest concerns is that, as a small business owner, you'll try to minimize your company's profits (and therefore taxes) by hiding business income and inflating business expenses. Uncle Sam thus looks suspiciously at business owners who use personal checking and personal credit card accounts for company transactions. You may be tempted to use your personal accounts this way because opening separate accounts is a hassle — not because you're dishonest.

TIP

Take the time to open separate accounts (such as bank accounts and credit card accounts) for your business and your personal use. Doing so not only makes the tax authorities happy but also makes your accounting easier. And don't make the mistake of thinking that paying for an expense through your business account proves to the IRS that it was a legitimate business expense. If the IRS finds that the expense was truly for personal purposes, it will likely dig deeper into your company's financial records to see what other shenanigans are going on.

Documenting expenses and income in the event of an audit

It doesn't matter whether you use file folders, software, apps, or a good old-fashioned shoe box to collate receipts and other important financial information. What does matter is that you keep complete and accurate records of both expenses and income.

>> **Expenses:** You'll probably lose or misplace some of those little pieces of paper that you need to document your expenses. Thus, one advantage of charging expenses on a credit card or paying by check is that these transactions leave a trail, which makes it easier to total your expenses come tax time and prove your expenses if you're audited.

WARNING

Just be careful when you use a credit card because you may buy more things than you can really afford. Then you're stuck with a lot of debt to pay off. I generally recommend only charging on a credit card what you can pay off in full by the time your statement payment due date rolls around.

On the other hand (as many small business owners know), finding lenders when you need money is difficult. Borrowing on a low-interest-rate credit card can be an easy and quick way for you to borrow money without groveling to bankers for a loan. (See the latest edition of my book *Personal Finance For Dummies*, published by John Wiley & Sons, Inc., for details.)

>> **Income:** Likewise, leave a trail with your revenue. Depositing all your receipts in one account helps you when tax time comes or if you're ever audited. Be sure to use a dedicated account for your business; don't be tempted to deposit business income into a personal account. (See the next section for details.)

The later section "Keeping Good Tax Records for Your Small Business" provides full details on the process of stashing the right items.

Keeping current on income, employment/payroll and sales taxes

When you're self-employed, you're responsible for the accurate and timely filing of all your income taxes. Without an employer and a payroll department to handle the paperwork for withholding taxes on a regular schedule, you need to make estimated tax payments on a quarterly basis.

If you have employees, you need to withhold taxes from each paycheck they receive, and you must make timely payments to the IRS and the appropriate state and local authorities. In addition to federal and state income taxes, you must withhold and send in Social Security and any other state or locally mandated employment (payroll) taxes, sales taxes and you need to issue W-2s annually for each employee and 1099-MISCs for each independent contractor paid $600 or more. Got a headache yet? (See Chapter 1 for more on these taxes.)

For paying taxes on your own self-employment income, you can obtain Form 1040-ES, "Estimated Tax for Individuals." This form comes complete with an estimated tax worksheet and four payment coupons to send in with your quarterly tax payments. It's amazing how user-friendly government people can be when they want your money! The form itself has some quirks and challenges, but you'll be happy to know that I explain how to deal with it in Chapter 10.

To discover all the amazing rules and regulations of withholding and submitting taxes from employees' paychecks, ask the IRS for Form 941, "Employer's Quarterly Federal Tax Return." Once a year, you also need to complete Form 940, "Employer's Annual Federal Unemployment (FUTA) Tax Return," for unemployment insurance payments to the feds.

TIP

If your business has a part-time or seasonal employee and the additional burden of filing Form 941 quarterly, the IRS has made the paperwork a tad easier. You may be able to file Form 944, "Employer's Annual Federal Tax Return," if your tax withholding on behalf of employees doesn't exceed $1,000 for the year (which translates to about $4,000 in wages). If you qualify, you need to file only once each year. To see whether you qualify, call the IRS at 800-829-0115 or visit its website at www.irs.gov. If you do qualify, the IRS will send you something in writing.

Also check to see whether your state has its own annual or quarterly unemployment insurance reporting requirements. Look for your state's department of labor or use the links on the U.S. Department of Labor website at www.dol.gov/whd/contacts/state_of.htm. And, unless you're lucky enough to live in one of those rare states with no state income taxes, don't forget to get your state's estimated income tax package.

TIP

Falling behind in paying taxes ruins some small businesses. When you hire employees, for example, you're particularly vulnerable to tax land mines. If you aren't going to keep current on taxes for yourself and your employees, hire a payroll company or tax advisor who can help you jump through the necessary tax hoops. (For info on finding a good tax advisor, see Chapter 13.) Payroll companies and tax advisors are there for a reason, so use them selectively. They take care of all the tax filings for you, and if they mess up, they pay the penalties. Check with a tax advisor you trust for the names of reputable payroll companies in your area. Generally, using a payroll service for form preparation and tax deposits is money well spent. The cost is much less than the potential penalties (and time) if you prepare yourself.

Reducing your taxes by legally shifting income and expenses

Many small business owners elect to keep their business accounting on what's called a *cash basis.* This choice doesn't imply that all business customers literally pay in cash for goods and services or that the company owners pay for all expenses with cash. Cash-basis accounting simply means that, for tax purposes, you recognize and report income in the year you received it and expenses in the year you paid them.

By operating on a cash basis, you can exert more control over the amount of profit (revenue minus expenses) that your business reports for tax purposes from year to year. If your income fluctuates from year to year, you can lower your tax burden by doing some legal shifting of income and expenses.

Suppose that you recently started a business. Assume that you have little, but growing, revenue and somewhat high startup expenses. Looking ahead to the next tax year, you can already tell that you'll be making more money and will likely be in a much higher tax bracket. Thus you can likely reduce your tax bill by paying more of your expenses in the next year. Of course, you don't want to upset any of your company's suppliers. However, you can pay some of your bills after the start of the next tax year (January 1) rather than in late December of the preceding year (presuming that your business's tax year is on a regular January 1 through December 31 calendar-year basis). *Note:* Credit card expenses are recognized as of the date you charge them, not when you pay the bill.

Likewise, you can exert some control over when your customers pay you. If you expect to make less money next year, don't invoice customers in December of this year. Wait until January so that you receive more of your income next year.

WARNING

Be careful with this revenue-shifting game. You don't want to run short of cash and miss a payroll! Similarly, if a customer mails you a check in December, IRS laws don't allow you to hold the check until January and count the revenue then. For tax purposes, you're supposed to recognize the payment as revenue when you receive it.

Note: One final point about who can and who can't do this revenue and expense two-step. Sole proprietorships, partnerships (including limited liability companies, also known as LLCs), S corporations, and personal-service corporations generally can shift revenue and expenses. On the other hand, C corporations and partnerships that have C corporations as partners may not use the cash-accounting method if they have annual receipts of more than $5 million per year. Chapter 2 has details on all these business entities.

Keeping Good Tax Records for Your Small Business

Tax records pose a problem for many people because the IRS doesn't require any particular form of record-keeping. In fact, the IRS recommends, in general terms, that you keep records only to file a "complete and accurate" return. This section explores what records you should keep, where you should maintain them, and for how long.

Ensuring a complete and accurate tax return

In case you don't feel like flipping through countless pages of government instructions on what constitutes a "complete and accurate" return, here are some common tax situations at a glance and the types of records normally required:

>> **Business expenses:** As I mention in the earlier section "Separating business from personal finances," the IRS is especially watchful in this area, so be sure to keep detailed proof of any expenses that you claim. This proof can consist of many items, such as receipts of income, expense account documentation and statements, and so on. Keep in mind that the IRS doesn't always accept canceled checks as the only method of substantiation, so make sure that you hang on to the bill or receipt for every expense you incur.

>> **Car expenses:** If, for the business use of your car, you choose to deduct the actual expenses rather than the standard mileage rate (which is 54.5 cents per mile for tax year 2018), you need to show the cost of the car and when you started using it for business. You also must record your business miles, your total miles, and your expenses, such as insurance, gas, and maintenance. You need a combination of a log and written receipts, of course! Stationery and office supply stores carry inexpensive logbooks that you can buy for your vehicle usage and expense tracking. You can also obtain smartphone apps to serve the same purpose.

>> **Home expenses:** If you own your home, you need to keep records of your mortgage and real estate tax payments, the purchase price and purchase expenses, and the cost of all the improvements and additions you make over time (save your receipts). Although you may not be selling your house this year, when you do, you'll be thankful you have all your receipts in a neat little file. If you rent a portion of your house or run a business from it, you also need your utility bills, general repair bills, and housecleaning and lawn-mowing costs to calculate your net rental income or your home office expense. (See Chapter 9 for information on the home office deduction.)

Setting up a record-keeping system

TIP

The tax year is a long time for keeping track of records that you need (and where you put them) when the filing season arrives. So here are some easy things you can do to make your tax-preparation burden a little lighter:

>> **Use an accordion file.** You can buy one with slots already labeled by month, by category, or by letters of the alphabet, or you can make your own filing system with the extra labels. All this can be yours for less than $15.

>> **Set up a manila file folder system.** Decide on the organizational method that best fits your needs, and get into the habit of saving all bills, receipts, and records that you think you may use someday for tax purposes or for things that affect your overall financial planning. This basic advice is good for any taxpayer, whether you file a simple tax return or a complicated one with far more supplemental schedules. Note that this plan, which should set you back about $5, is only minimal, but it's much better than the shoe-box approach to record-keeping. (A scanning program for documents may also be of interest here.)

>> **Track tax information on your computer and/or through smartphone apps.** A number of financial software packages and smartphone apps enable you to keep track of your spending for tax purposes. Just don't expect to reap the benefits without a fair amount of upfront and continuing work. You need

to figure out how to use the software, and you must enter a great deal of data for the software to be useful to you. Don't forget, though, that you still need your receipts to back up your claims; in an audit, the IRS may not accept your computer records without verifying them against your receipts.

If you're interested in software, consider a business-oriented program, such as QuickBooks, for your small-business accounting. Check out their smart-phone apps as well. For really simple businesses, consider Quicken. You can merge data into QuickBooks at a later date if you desire. Whichever software you choose, keep in mind that the package tabulates only what you enter or download into it. So if you use the software to write your monthly checks but neglect to enter data for things you pay for with cash, for example, you won't have the whole picture.

Deciding when to stash and when to trash

REMEMBER

One of the most frequently asked questions is how long a taxpayer needs to keep tax records. The answer is easy — a minimum of three years. That's because the statute of limitations for tax audits and assessments is three years. If the IRS doesn't adjust or audit your 2018 tax return by April 15, 2022 (the three years start running on April 15, 2019), it missed its chance.

On April 15, 2022, feel free to celebrate another auditless year with a "Shredding the 2018 Tax Return" party. (If you filed after April 15 because you obtained an extension, you must wait until three years after the extension due date rather than the April 15 tax date. The same is true when you file late — the three-year period doesn't start until you actually file your return.)

TIP

However, I must add one point to the general three-year rule: Save all records for the assets that you continue to own. These records can include stocks and bonds, automobiles, your home (along with its improvements), and expensive personal property, such as jewelry, video cameras, or computers. Keep these records in a safe-deposit box in case you suffer a (deductible casualty) loss, such as a fire. You don't want these records going up in smoke!

Some taxpayers take the practical step of videotaping their home and its contents, but if you do, make sure that you keep that record outside your home. You can save money on safe-deposit box fees by leaving your video with relatives who may enjoy watching it because they don't see you often enough. (Of course, your relatives may also suffer a fire or an earthquake.)

WARNING

In situations where the IRS suspects that income wasn't reported, IRS agents can go back as far as six years. And if possible tax fraud is involved, forget all time limitations!

Watching out for state differences

Although the IRS requires that you keep your records for only three years, your state may have a longer statute of limitations with regard to state income tax audits. If you're curious what your state's rules are, check with your state's income tax collecting authority. Also, some of your tax-related records may be important to keep for other reasons. For example, suppose that you throw out your receipts after three years. Then the fellow who built your garage four years ago sues you, asserting that you didn't fully pay the bill. You may be out of luck in court if you don't have the canceled check showing that you paid.

The moral: Hang on to records that may be important (such as home improvement receipts) for longer than three years — especially if a dispute is possible. Check with a legal advisor whenever you have a concern because statutes of limitations vary from state to state.

Replacing lost business records

If your business records have been lost or destroyed, you can often obtain duplicate bills from major vendors. You shouldn't have a great deal of trouble getting copies of the original telephone, utility, rent, credit card, oil company, and other bills. Reconstructing a typical month of automobile use can help you make a reasonable determination of the business use of your car. If that month's use approximates an average month's business use of an auto, the IRS usually accepts such reconstructed records as adequate substantiation.

If you deposited all your business income in a checking or savings account, you can reconstruct that income from duplicate bank statements. Although banks usually don't charge for copies of bank statements, they do charge for copies of canceled checks if you can't obtain them online. These charges can be quite expensive, so do some legwork before ordering copies of all your checks. For example, obtain a copy of your lease and a statement from your landlord saying that all rent was paid on time before you request duplicate copies of rent checks.

By ordering copies of past returns with Form 4506, "Request for Copy of Transcript of Tax Form," you can have a point of reference for determining whether you accounted for typical business expenses. Past returns reveal not only gross profit percentages or margins of profit but also the amounts of recurring expenses. (You can find this form at www.irs.gov/pub/irs-pdf/f4506.pdf.)

» Making sense of income lines and strategies to reduce your taxable income

» Understanding the impact of the new tax bill in 2018 and beyond

» Using deductions and credits to your best advantage

Chapter **7**

Form 1040 Filing Options

Face it: Completing tax forms ranks right up there with visiting the department of motor vehicles or the dentist among activities you'd least like to spend your free time on. But taxes gobble lots of your money. So it pays to know how to legally minimize your tax bill and make the best use of the various tax forms and schedules. Legally reducing your taxes and keeping and saving more of your money can actually be, dare I say, fun!

In this chapter, I cover the common Form 1040s at your disposal and go into detail about how to complete the lines on common income reporting, deductions, and tax credits.

The New and Improved Form 1040

Prior to the 2017 tax reform bill's passage, you had a few choices of tax forms — three, to be exact. In order, from mind-challenging (read: simplest in IRS jargon) to mind-numbing (read: complex), they are Form 1040EZ, Form 1040A, and Form 1040. (Find all these forms at www.irs.gov.)

Effective for Tax Year 2018, Forms 1040A and Form 1040EZ have been eliminated and everyone will instead use the "new and improved" (simpler) Form 1040.

The vast majority of tax filers, especially those previously who were able to use Forms 1040A or 1040EZ will find they only need to file Form 1040 and no schedules and will have far fewer lines and calculations to complete.

There are actually more Schedules now for the Form 1040 because in addition to the prior Schedules that are known by their letters — Schedules A, B, C, D, and so on, there are now six numbered schedules (1 through 6) that each contain a number of lines that used to be part of the main pages of the Form 1040 (refer to Table 7-1; see the instructions for the Schedules for more information.). Many Form 1040 filers will pleasantly find that they only need to complete Form 1040 without any of those Schedules.

TABLE 7-1: **A General Guide to What Schedule(s) You'll Need to File**

If you. . .	Then use . . .
Have additional income, such as business income, capital gains, unemployment compensation, prize or award money, or gambling winnings. Have any deductions to claim, such as student loan interest deduction, self-employment tax, educator expenses.	Schedule 1
Owe AMT (alternative minimum tax) or need to make an excess advance premium tax credit repayment.	Schedule 2
Can claim a nonrefundable credit other than the child tax credit or the credit for other dependents, such as the foreign tax credit, education credits, or general business credit.	Schedule 3
Owe other taxes, such as self-employment tax, household employment taxes, or additional tax on IRAs or other qualified retirement plans and tax-favored accounts.	Schedule 4
Can claim a refundable credit other than the earned income credit, American opportunity credit, or additional child tax credit. Have other payments, such as an amount paid with a request for an extension to file or excess Social Security tax withheld.	Schedule 5
Have a foreign address or a third-party designee other than your paid preparer.	Schedule 6

Before the 2017 tax reform, Form 1040 was widely known as the one that everybody loved to hate. The *Wall Street Journal* believed that tax professionals invented the prior form — the newspaper's editors even refer to the tax laws as the "Accountants and Lawyers Full Employment Act." I think that complicated tax laws should be called the "IRS Guaranteed Lifetime Employment Act."

One factor that may have forced you in the past to have to complete the complicated Form 1040 with various schedules was that you itemized your deductions on Schedule A, "Itemized Deductions." Thanks to the Tax Cuts and Jobs Act bill that took affect in 2018, the standard deduction amounts were greatly increased (approximately doubled) so fewer taxpayers will be able to or need to itemize. Such taxpayers will enjoy a simpler Form 1040.

Tackling the Income Lines

Income is, in brief, money or something else of value that you receive regardless of whether you work for it. Most people know that wages earned from toiling away at jobs are income. But income also includes receipts of alimony, certain interest, dividends, profits on your investments, and even your lottery winnings or prizes won on a game show or the latest reality TV program.

CAN YOU ITEMIZE YOUR DEDUCTIONS?

Deductions are just that: You subtract them from your income before you calculate the tax you owe. (Deductions are good things!) To make everything more complicated, the IRS gives you two methods for determining your total deductions: itemized and standardized deductions. The good news is that you get to pick the method that leads to the best solution for you — whichever way offers greater deductions. If you can itemize, you should, because it saves you tax dollars. The bad news is that if you choose to itemize your deductions, you must complete additional schedules.

The first method — taking the standard deduction — requires no thinking or calculations. If you have a relatively uncomplicated financial life, taking the standard deduction is generally the better option (for example, it provides you with a greater deduction than if you itemized). Symptoms of a simple tax life are not earning a high income, renting your house or apartment instead of owning, and lacking unusually large expenses, such as medical bills or losses from theft or catastrophe. Single folks qualify for a $12,000 standard deduction, heads of household receive an $18,000 standard deduction, and married couples filing jointly get a $24,000 standard deduction in tax year 2018. If you're age 65 or older, or blind, your standard deduction is increased by a modest additional amount.

Some deductions are available even if you don't itemize your deductions. The bad news: You have to complete Form 1040's Schedule A to be able to claim all of them.

The other method of determining your total allowable deductions is to itemize them on your tax return. This method is definitely more of a hassle, but if you can tally up more than the standard deduction amounts, itemizing saves you money. If you have large unreimbursed medical expenses, have a mortgage on your home, give a lot to charity, or pay a lot in state and local taxes, you probably want to add these amounts up, just in case. Use Schedule A of IRS Form 1040 to total your itemized deductions.

In this section, I explain the common types of income reported on your personal income tax return, with special attention paid to issues relating to small business owners. *Note:* This isn't meant to be comprehensive for those topics covered — seek out a tax advisor (with the help of Chapter 13) or a more detailed tax preparation book. Also, the line numbers referenced are per the 2018 version of Form 1040 — the actual line numbers may change slightly in future years. You can get the most recent version at www.irs.gov/pub/irs-pdf/f1040.pdf. See Page 2 of Form 1040 in Figure 7-1.

FIGURE 7-1:
Page 2 of
Form 1040.

Courtesy of the Internal Revenue Service

Line 1: Wages, salaries, tips, etc.

If you work for an employer (because you haven't started your small business yet), you'll receive a Form W-2, "Wage and Tax Statement," which your employer is required to mail to you no later than January 31 (unless that's a weekend day, in which case the deadline is the next business day after the weekend) of the year your tax return is due. This form helps you find out what you earned during the year and how much your employer withheld from your wages for taxes.

REMEMBER

You may notice that there are multiple copies of the W-2. That's because if you use regular mail to file your tax return, one copy goes with your federal return and another copy goes with your state return. You keep one copy and any other copies your employer gave you with your neat and organized tax records. If you file electronically, keep all the copies in your files with a copy of your completed tax return. In case you're wondering, your employer has already sent the information on the W-2 to the Social Security Administration. If you look at the lower-left corner of your W-2s, you see what to do with each copy.

If you're self-employed and you don't receive a W-2, you get to skip this line, but you'll end up doing much more work completing Schedule C so you can also fill in line 12 of the Form 1040 Schedule 1. (Chapter 8 has details on filling out Schedule C; I discuss line 12 later in this chapter.) For farmers, it's Schedule F; see the later section "Line 18: Farm income (or loss)" for details.

Line 2a: Tax-exempt interest

In the distant past, because municipal bond interest wasn't taxable, you didn't receive a 1099 showing the tax-exempt interest you received. Now box 8 of Form 1099-INT lists the municipal bond interest paid to you, and box 9 gives you the portion of the box 8 number that comes from so-called *private activity bonds*, or municipal bonds that are actually funding joint public-private projects, such as privately owned utilities or football stadiums.

Even though you may not have to pay tax on tax-exempt interest, these numbers are important in figuring out how much of your Social Security benefits may be subject to tax and in allocating itemized deductions between taxable and tax-exempt income. Interest from private activity bonds is listed because it's taxable under the dreaded alternative minimum tax (described later in this chapter).

TIP

Surprisingly, some people who invest money in tax-exempt bonds actually shouldn't. These people often aren't in a high enough income tax bracket to benefit. You'd be better off moving at least some of your money into taxable bonds or stocks (where longer-term capital gains are taxed at lower rates than ordinary income). See the latest edition of my book *Investing For Dummies* (Wiley) for more information on investing strategies.

Line 2b: Taxable interest

Add up all your interest income from boxes 1 and 3 of all your Form 1099-INTs and boxes 1, 2, and 6 of any Form 1099-OIDs you may have (for any so-called *zero coupon bonds* you may own). If the total is $1,500 or less, enter that amount on this line. If this amount is more than $1,500, you must complete Schedule B (or Schedule 1, if you file Form 1040A). No biggie! Schedule B and Schedule 1 are both easy to complete and are essentially identical, with the exception of a couple of questions regarding foreign accounts at the bottom of Schedule B. When you get the total, come back and fill it in.

Except for interest from municipal bonds, all the interest you earn is taxable. If you need examples, the IRS publications have pages of them. But don't report the interest you earn inside your IRA or other retirement accounts; that interest is taxed (possibly) only when you withdraw the funds (a Roth IRA allows for tax-free investment returns, even at withdrawal).

If you keep lots of your money in bank accounts, you may be missing out on free opportunities to earn higher interest rates. Check out money market funds, a higher-yielding alternative to bank accounts. For longer-term investment ideas and the basics of retirement accounts, see Chapter 3.

Lines 3a and 3b: Ordinary dividends and qualified dividends

Just as long-term capital gains are taxed at lower rates, so too are corporate dividends paid out from stock holdings.

Box 1a of your Form 1099-DIV includes the amount of all the ordinary dividends (not capital gains), whether qualified for the lower rate or not. If you have more than one 1099-DIV, add together all the amounts in box 1a and plop the total on line 3a of your Form 1040. If you're using Schedule B (because your total dividend income is greater than $1,500), carry the number from line 6 of those schedules over to line 3a of your Form 1040.

Form 1099-DIV includes all kinds of dividends and distributions from all sorts of companies, credit unions, real estate investment entities, and so forth. Some of these may qualify for the special *qualified dividends* tax rates; others don't. Box 1b of Form 1099-DIV shows you the amount of qualified dividends.

Although you aren't required to file 1040 Schedule B or 1040A Schedule 1 when your dividend income is less than $1,500, if you have more than a couple of Form 1099-DIVs arriving in your mailbox, you may want to anyway. One of the most common reasons for the IRS to contact you is because what you report on your return doesn't match the information it has gathered about you from other sources. The more detail you can give on your return, the easier it is to find the discrepancies when they occur. These schedules are probably the easiest IRS forms ever devised, and you'll have absolutely no problems completing them.

Lines 4a and 4b: Total pensions and annuities

Here's where you report your retirement benefits paid out from your taxable pension, profit-sharing, 401(k), SEP, or Keogh plans. How these plans are taxed depends on whether you receive the funds in the form of an annuity (paid over your lifetime) or in a lump sum.

The amounts you fill in on lines 4a and 4b are reported on a Form 1099-R that you receive from your employer or your plan's custodian. If the amount that you receive is fully taxable, complete only line 4b and leave line 4a blank.

If you didn't pay or contribute to your pension or annuity using money you already paid tax on — or if your employer didn't withhold part of the cost from your pay while you worked — then the amount that you receive each year is fully taxable. The amount that you contributed, for which you received a deduction — such as tax-deductible contributions to a 401(k), SEP, IRA, or Keogh — isn't considered part of your cost.

If you paid part of the cost (that is, if you made nondeductible contributions or contributions that were then added to your taxable income on your W-2), you aren't taxed on the part that you contributed because it represents a tax-free return of your investment. The rest of the amount that you receive is taxable.

Lines 5a and 5b: Social Security benefits

Politicians don't want to do away with Social Security; they just want to pay fewer benefits and to tax more of it. As a result, they've made retirement (and the taxes associated with it) more complicated.

REMEMBER

Don't forget that if you're married and file a joint return, you and your spouse must combine your incomes and your benefits when figuring whether any of your combined benefits are taxable. Even if your spouse didn't receive any benefits, you must add your spouse's income to yours when figuring whether any of your benefits are taxable.

Every person who receives Social Security benefits receives a Form SSA-1099, even if the benefit is combined with another person's in a single check. If you receive benefits on more than one Social Security record, you may receive more than one Form SSA-1099. Your gross benefits are shown in box 3 of Form SSA-1099, and your repayments are shown in box 4. The amount in box 5 shows your net benefits for the tax year (box 3 − box 4). This is the amount you use to figure whether any of your benefits are taxable. If you misplace Form SSA-1099, you can order a duplicate at the Social Security website (www.ssa.gov/1099) or by phone at 800-772-1213.

To determine the taxable portion of your Social Security income, add one half of your Social Security income to all your other income, including tax-exempt interest. You must also include the following: interest from qualified U.S. savings bonds, employer-provided adoption benefits, foreign earned income or housing, and income earned by bona fide residents of American Samoa or Puerto Rico.

IRS Publication 17 gives you the worksheets you need to figure out what part, if any, of your Social Security benefits you need to include on line 20b of your Form 1040. To get this publication, call 800-829-3676 or visit www.irs.gov.

Line 7: Adjusted gross income

The next step is subtracting the amount in line 36 (which are your total adjustments) from line 6 (total income). The result is your adjusted gross income (AGI).

This number is used to determine a host of deductions and tax credits. So, elsewhere in this chapter as well as in other chapters, I refer to this line.

Line 8: Standard deduction or itemized deductions (from Schedule A)

This section refers to what can be a critical choice, so don't make a quick decision between the two choices the IRS offers for deductions. Either choice is good in the sense that the result reduces your taxable income — the income that you owe tax on. However — and note, this is a big however — you may be cheating yourself if you automatically jump into the easier of the two choices and take the standard deduction.

The standard deduction is tempting to take because, without any complicated figuring, you simply take the deduction that corresponds to your filing status and that amount was greatly increased in 2018 thanks to the recently passed Congressional tax bill. If you're filing as a single, you can take a standard deduction of $12,000; married couples filing jointly can take $24,000.

Itemizing your deductions on Schedule A (refer to Chapter 9) requires more work than just claiming the standard deduction, but if the total of your itemized deductions adds up to more than your standard deduction, don't waste them.

If you're in doubt about whether itemizing saves you money or what expenses you may actually itemize, examine the line items on Schedule A. Even if itemizing can't save you money for this year's return, educating yourself about deductions that are available is a good idea for the future. The major expenses that you may itemize include

>> Some homeownership expenses, which includes mortgage interest, property taxes, and in some cases, private mortgage insurance (for mortgages

originated after December 15, 2017, interest on up to $750,000 of mortgage debt may be deducted, down from the prior $1,000,000 for mortgages originated before that date)

>> State income or sales taxes (state and local taxes now including property taxes are limited to a $10,000 annual deduction limit)

>> Medical and dental expenses that exceed 10 percent of your AGI beginning in 2019, up from 7.5 percent

>> Gifts to charity

>> Casualty and theft losses, in a federally declared disaster area, that exceed 10 percent of your AGI

You may have noticed that this list has gotten shorter and stingier. That's correct. However, some higher earners may benefit from getting rid of the overall phase out of a portion of itemized deductions for high income earners.

Schedule 1: Additional Income and Adjustments to Income

With the simplified Form 1040, most of the lines that used to be on the bottom two-thirds of the front (first) page of the form have been moved over to Schedule 1 (see Figure 7-2). This section discusses the most important of these lines that you may deal with as a small business owner.

Line 12: Business income (or loss)

If you're self-employed, you must complete Schedule C to report your business income and expenses. If you just receive an occasional fee and don't have any business expenses, you can report that fee on line 21 (Schedule 1) as other income. And keep in mind that if you're a statutory employee (a life insurance salesperson, agent, commission driver, or traveling salesperson, for example), report the wages shown in box 1 of your W-2 form on Schedule C along with your expenses. How do you know whether you're a statutory employee? Simple: Box 13 of your W-2 will be checked.

TIP

As a general rule, you're better off reporting your self-employment income on Schedule C, if you're eligible. You can deduct business-related expenses against your income on Schedule C, and that can lower your income and the tax that you have to pay.

FIGURE 7-2:
Schedule 1 of
Form 1040.

SCHEDULE 1
(Form 1040)

Additional Income and Adjustments to Income

OMB No. 1545-0074

20**18**

Department of the Treasury
Internal Revenue Service

▶ Attach to Form 1040.
▶ Go to *www.irs.gov/Form1040* for instructions and the latest information.

Attachment
Sequence No. **01**

Name(s) shown on Form 1040

Your social security number

Additional Income	1–9b	Reserved	**1–9b**
	10	Taxable refunds, credits, or offsets of state and local income taxes	**10**
	11	Alimony received	**11**
	12	Business income or (loss). Attach Schedule C or C-EZ	**12**
	13	Capital gain or (loss). Attach Schedule D if required. If not required, check here ▶ ☐	**13**
	14	Other gains or (losses). Attach Form 4797	**14**
	15a	Reserved	**15b**
	16a	Reserved	**16b**
	17	Rental real estate, royalties, partnerships, S corporations, trusts, etc. Attach Schedule E	**17**
	18	Farm income or (loss). Attach Schedule F	**18**
	19	Unemployment compensation	**19**
	20a	Reserved	**20b**
	21	Other income. List type and amount ▶ _____	**21**
	22	Combine the amounts in the far right column. If you don't have any adjustments to income, enter here and include on Form 1040, line 6. Otherwise, go to line 23 . .	**22**

Adjustments to Income	23	Educator expenses	**23**	
	24	Certain business expenses of reservists, performing artists, and fee-basis government officials. Attach Form 2106 . .	**24**	
	25	Health savings account deduction. Attach Form 8889 .	**25**	
	26	Moving expenses for members of the Armed Forces. Attach Form 3903	**26**	
	27	Deductible part of self-employment tax. Attach Schedule SE	**27**	
	28	Self-employed SEP, SIMPLE, and qualified plans . .	**28**	
	29	Self-employed health insurance deduction	**29**	
	30	Penalty on early withdrawal of savings	**30**	
	31a	Alimony paid **b** Recipient's SSN ▶	**31a**	
	32	IRA deduction	**32**	
	33	Student loan interest deduction	**33**	
	34	Reserved	**34**	
	35	Reserved	**35**	
	36	Add lines 23 through 35	**36**	

For Paperwork Reduction Act Notice, see your tax return instructions.   Cat. No. 71479F   Schedule 1 (Form 1040) 2018

Courtesy of the Internal Revenue Service

The amount that you enter on line 12 (of Schedule 1) is the result of the figuring and jumbling you do on Schedule C or C-EZ, which is a shorter version. See Chapter 8 for more information on those schedules.

Line 13: Capital gain (or loss)

You have a capital gain (or loss) when you sell stocks, bonds, or investment property for a profit (or loss). Losses on investments such as stocks, bonds, and mutual funds made outside of retirement accounts are generally deductible.

You report capital gains and losses on Schedule D, putting the net result on line 13. If all you have are capital gain distributions from a mutual fund, you can skip Schedule D and enter your capital gain distribution(s) on line 13. If you fall into this category, don't forget to check that little box to the left of the amount you entered on line 13.

Line 14: Other gains (or losses)

You guessed it, grab another form — Form 4797, "Sales of Business Property." (Check it out at www.irs.gov/pub/irs-pdf/f4797.pdf.) Fill out that form and enter the final figure on line 14. Use Form 4797 when you sell property that you've used in your business or that you've been depreciating (such as a two-family house that you've been renting out).

Line 17: Rental real estate, royalties, partnerships, S corporations, trusts, etc.

This line is an important one for all you self-starters who are landlords, business owners, authors, taxpayers collecting royalties, and those people lucky enough to have someone set up a trust fund for them. Schedule E, "Supplemental Income and Loss," is the necessary form to wrestle with for this line (see Chapter 2).

Don't let the term *supplemental income* throw you. That's just IRS-speak for the income you receive from rental property or royalties, or through partnerships, S corporations (corporations that don't pay tax; the owners report the corporation's income or loss on their personal tax returns), trusts, and estates. To report your rental or royalty income, you use Schedule E, which is laid out in the form of a profit or loss statement (income and expenses). From your income, you subtract your expenses. The remainder is your net income, the income that you have to pay taxes on. If you have a loss, the rules get a little sticky as to whether you can deduct it; consult a qualified tax advisor for help.

Line 18: Farm income (or loss)

Schedule F, "Profit or Loss from Farming," is the form that you use to report income and expenses from selling crops or livestock. (See this form at www.irs.gov/pub/irs-pdf/f1040sf.pdf.) All types of farms and farming income are included here, including farms that produce livestock, dairy, poultry, fish, aquaculture products, bee products, and fruit, as well as truck farms (because produce isn't the only thing farmers raise and harvest). Even though Schedule F is titled "Profit or Loss from Farming," you use this form to tell the IRS what you took in from operating a plantation, ranch, nursery, orchard, or oyster bed.

Schedule F isn't as bad as it looks. In fact, it's set up in exactly the same way as Schedule C, "Profit or Loss from Business" (see Chapter 8). Although a business is a business (and farming is certainly a business), the IRS clearly thought that enough tax items were peculiar to farming that it deserved its own schedule.

TIP

Before you even attempt to prepare your Schedule F, obtain a copy of IRS Publication 225 ("Farmer's Tax Guide") either by calling 800-829-3676 or from the Internet at www.irs.gov.

Line 19: Unemployment compensation

Losing your job is bad enough. And then you receive another nasty surprise — the news that the unemployment compensation you receive is taxable. The government should send you a Form 1099-G to summarize these taxable benefits that you receive. You enter the total compensation on line 19.

You can elect to have tax withheld at the rate of 10 percent on your unemployment, so you won't be caught short next April 15. This is one offer most people are likely to refuse.

Line 21: Other income

Line 21 of Form 1040 is a catchall for reporting income that doesn't fit the income categories listed on page one of Form 1040. Hey, even if you find some money, the IRS treats it as income! Just report all this miscellaneous income here. Don't forget to write a description of these earnings on the dotted line next to the amount.

Here are some examples of stuff that goes on line 21:

>> **Bartering:** *Bartering* is the trading of your services for goods or other services. You usually must declare the fair market value of goods you receive. If you participate in a barter exchange, you may get a Form 1099-B — and the IRS gets a copy, too.

>> **Canceled debt:** A *canceled debt,* or a debt paid for you by another person, is generally income to you and must be reported. If you're eligible for one of the many student loan forgiveness programs that seek to encourage recent college grads to go into less in-demand occupations, the loan amounts forgiven are taxable income for you to report! Another example is a discount offered by a financial institution for the prepaying of your mortgage is income from the cancellation of the debt. However, you have no income from the cancellation of a debt if the cancellation is a gift. For example, suppose you borrow $10,000 from a relative who tells you that you don't have to repay it. It's a gift!

If you received a sweetheart deal on a loan, make sure that you read the IRS rules on below-market interest rates for loans. There is some relief for beleaguered homeowners who've lost their homes to foreclosure. When the bank forecloses on your home (as opposed to investment real estate), provided your mortgage was a nonrecourse loan, you realize no ordinary income. A *nonrecourse loan* is one where the lender can repossess the property held as collateral for that loan (that is to say, your home) but can't come after you personally for additional money. If a debt is canceled as the result of bankruptcy or because you're insolvent, the cancellation of the debt negates your having to pay tax on the income. And you don't have to report it as income if your student loan is canceled because you agreed to certain conditions to obtain the loan and then performed the required services.

>> **Fees:** Maybe you're a corporate director or a notary public, and you made some extra cash. If these payments are $600 or more from a single source, you'll receive Form 1099-MISC from the person or company that paid you. If you receive a fee or commission from an activity you're not regularly engaged in for business, you report it instead on line 21. Fees are considered self-employment income, which means that you may owe Social Security tax on them. You compute the Social Security tax you owe on Schedule SE ("Self-Employment Tax"; see Chapter 10 for info). You then report the amount of Social Security tax you owe on line 57 of Form 1040, Schedule 4, "Other Taxes," and you get a deduction for half of the tax on line 27 (discussed later in this chapter).

>> **Life insurance:** The death benefit paid to the beneficiary of a life insurance contract is exempt from tax. It's also possible to receive the death benefit prior to death *(viatical settlements)* as advance, or accelerated, payments, provided that the insured is terminally ill and has been certified by a physician as being expected to die within 24 months of that certification. If the payments are made to someone who has been certified as chronically ill, that person may exclude from her income the larger of $250 per day or the actual long-term care expenses incurred.

>> **Prizes and awards:** If you get lucky and hit the lottery or win a prize in a contest, the winnings are taxable. Sorry! However, some employee achievement awards may be nontaxable. These include noncash awards, such as a watch, golf clubs, or a TV, given in recognition for length of service or safety achievement. The tax-free limit is $400 if given from a nonqualified employer plan and $1,600 from a qualified plan.

Adjustments to Income

After totaling all your income with the help of the preceding section, you may think that all you have to do is figure your tax on that amount. But wait! All you've done so far is figure out your total income. Your taxable income will be much, much less.

In the "Adjusted Gross Income" (line 7) of your Form 1040 tax return, you add your adjustments to income on lines 23 through 35 (from Schedule 1) and subtract them from your total income on line 6. The result of this subtraction is called your *adjusted gross income* (AGI). Your AGI is an important number because it's used as the benchmark for calculating many allowable deductions, such as medical and miscellaneous itemized deductions, and the taxable amount of your Social Security income.

REMEMBER

You don't have to itemize your deductions on Schedule A to claim adjustments to income in this section. Everyone gets to make these adjustments. (I talk about Schedule A in Chapter 9.)

The following sections present the line-by-line rundown of the more important adjustments you may be able to make to your total income. The headings refer to line numbers where you plug your data into your Form 1040, Schedule 1.

Line 23: Educator expenses

Teachers who spend their own money for items they supply for the classroom are entitled to deduct these expenses from their income. You can deduct up to $250 of these expenses on line 23. You can then deduct any remaining expenses on Schedule A as a miscellaneous itemized deduction. Expenses that qualify include books, supplies, computer software and equipment, and supplemental material used in the classroom. If you're married filing jointly and both of you are educators, you may deduct up to $500.

To claim this deduction, you must be an educator, or more precisely, a teacher, instructor, counselor, principal, or aide in a public or private elementary or secondary school who works a minimum of 900 hours during the school year. Educators who exclude U.S. savings bond interest from income that was used to pay college tuition or payments from a 529 plan, or made withdrawals from a Coverdell Education Savings Account, can claim this deduction only if the amount they paid for classroom supplies exceeds the amount that is tax-free under these other education tax breaks.

Line 24: Certain business expenses of reservists, performing artists, and fee-basis government officials

If you believe you fall into the category of an armed forces reservist, a performing artist, or a fee-basis government official, read up! You may be able to deduct certain business expenses from your total income on this line Before you can, though, you need to know whether your job and your expenses qualify.

> >> Armed forces reservists may deduct travel expenses if they travel more than 100 miles away from home in connection with their service.

> >> Performing artists may deduct all their employee business expenses on line 24, provided that they meet several requirements.

> >> Government officials paid on a fee basis may deduct all their employee business expenses on line 24 if they're employed by state or local government and are paid in whole or in part on a fee basis ($5,000 to prepare a particular report, for example).

If you do qualify, you need to fill out Form 2106 or Form 2106-EZ before you fill in an amount on line 24. (I talk about these forms in more detail in Chapter 9.)

Line 25: Health savings account deduction

Health savings accounts (HSAs) may allow you to pay for unreimbursed medical expenses on a tax-free basis. You may establish an HSA if you're covered by a qualified high-deductible health plan with annual deductibles of at least $1,350 for individuals and $2,700 for families for tax year 2018. You may not open or fund one of these accounts if you have other general health insurance (separate dental, accident-only, vision, workers' comp, disability, or long-term care policies don't count against you here). You also can't be claimed as a dependent on someone else's return.

An HSA works similarly to an individual retirement account (IRA). In this case, your HSA is invested and allowed to grow income tax–free until you need to access the money to pay for qualified medical expenses (medical insurance premiums are excluded). Payouts for qualified medical expenses are tax-free. Unlike flexible spending accounts that may be offered by your employer, there's no "use it or lose it" feature here. Your money continues to grow from year to year until you need to use it. You may contribute a maximum of $3,450 for individuals and $6,900 for families for tax year 2018. If you're age 55 or older, you may make an additional contribution of $1,000 (if married and both spouses are 55 or older, each can contribute an extra $1,000). After you enroll in Medicare at age 65, contributions are no longer allowed, although you may continue to take distributions.

If you funded an HSA during the tax year, you need to complete Form 8889, "Health Savings Accounts (HSAs)," to figure out the amount to include on line 25. Check out Chapter 2 for an introduction to HSAs; flip to Chapter 10 for more information about Form 8889.

MOVING EXPENSES NO LONGER DEDUCTIBLE

Before 2018, if you incurred moving expenses because you had to relocate for job reasons, you could deduct those moving expenses for which your employer didn't reimburse you. Self-employed individuals could also deduct their moving expenses.

The Tax Cuts and Jobs Act eliminated the moving expense deduction effective with tax year 2018. It was one of those smaller tax breaks that had to go in order to pay for the across-the-board tax breaks and other perks that took effect beginning in 2018.

Line 27: Deductible part of self-employment tax

One of the great drawbacks of being self-employed is that you get hit not only with income tax on your earnings but also with self-employment tax. This wonderful invention combines the 7.65 percent ordinary wage earners pay for combined Social Security and Medicare contributions with the employer's matching 7.65 percent. So because self-employed people are both the employer and the employee, they get stuck with both halves of this tax, or a whopping 15.3 percent of all earnings from self-employment up to $128,400, and 2.9 percent on all earnings above that.

If you're subject to this additional tax, line 27 provides some tax relief. You're generally allowed to deduct one half of your self-employment tax from your total income.

Line 28: Self-employed SEP, SIMPLE, and qualified plans

SEP-IRA or SIMPLE retirement accounts allow you to make substantial pretax contributions toward your retirement savings.

A SEP is a combination IRA/profit-sharing plan and is available only for self-employed individuals and their employees (but not corporations). With a SEP (simplified employee pension), you're allowed to stash up to 20 percent of your net income from self-employment but not to exceed a $55,000 contribution (for tax year 2018). You can set up your plan and make this contribution for the most recent tax year up until the day, including extensions, that you file your income tax return. Your contributions to the plan are not only deductible but also exempt from tax until you start receiving benefits.

Note that if you have employees and want to contribute to a SEP plan for yourself, you can't ignore your employees. Check out Chapter 3 for more details on all your small business retirement plan options, including SIMPLE plans.

Line 29: Self-employed health insurance deduction

If you're self-employed, you may deduct 100 percent of your health and dental insurance premiums from your income, with one caveat: You may not deduct more than your net profit from your business. A general partner (but not a limited partner), an independent contractor, or a shareholder in an S corporation may also claim this deduction. The deduction is allowed for premiums paid for you, your spouse, and your dependents.

Subject to age-specific limits, your long-term care premiums also qualify for this deduction. These are the limits for tax year 2018:

>> Age 40 and below: $420

>> Age 41–50: $780

>> Age 51–60: $1,560

>> Age 61–70: $4,160

>> Age 71 and over: $5,200

TIP

For more information, see IRS Publication 535, "Business Expenses." To get this publication, call 800-829-3676 or visit www.irs.gov.

Line 32: IRA deduction

Saving for your eventual retirement is a good thing, which is why the tax laws are structured to give you all sorts of benefits if you do save for retirement. The IRA is one way that you may sock away some money for your golden years.

Line 32 is concerned only with the deduction you can take for a contribution to a traditional IRA. Even though you don't get a deduction for the nondeductible IRA or Roth IRA, for some people, these accounts can be useful retirement planning tools. You can find out more about all retirement plans, including the amounts that you may contribute, in Chapter 3.

TIP

Nondeductible regular IRA contributions are reported to the IRS on Form 8606, even if you don't have to file a tax return for the year. If you're filing a Form 1040, you attach Form 8606 to your 1040. The penalty for not filing your Form 8606 is $50, and if your IRA contributions are more than the permissible amount, you must correct the overpayment; otherwise, you may be subject to a penalty.

Line 33: Student loan interest deduction

Although most types of personal interest are no longer deductible, you may deduct up to $2,500 of interest on a loan used to pay higher education and certain vocational school expenses (ask the vocational school whether it qualifies for this deduction if you have to borrow to pay the tab). You can claim this deduction as long as it takes to pay off the loan and as long as you're paying interest on it.

WARNING

Students usually take out these loans because they can obtain lower interest rates, but their parents aren't able to claim the deduction, even if they make all the payments. That's because the parents didn't borrow the money. If the student is liable for the loan, the student can't claim the interest deduction if he can be claimed as a dependent on someone else's return. But in an interesting twist, if a nondependent student takes the loan but the parents make the payments, the student may be allowed to take the interest deduction on his return.

For single filers, the deduction doesn't start to get eliminated until income hits $65,000 and doesn't completely disappear until $80,000. For joint filers, the phaseout of the deduction starts at the $135,000 income level, with the deduction getting wiped out at $165,000.

TIP

The beauty of the student loan interest deduction is that you don't have to itemize your deductions to claim it. You can claim both the standard deduction and the student loan deduction. This deduction should be of great benefit to recent graduates and folks wanting to further their education.

To take this deduction, you must meet the following requirements:

>> You're not filing as married filing separately, and no one else can claim you as a dependent.

>> You must incur the loan to pay the higher education expenses of you, your spouse, or anyone you claimed as a dependent when you took out the loan.

>> You must pay the expenses within a reasonable amount of time after the loan is taken out. I want I could tell you what's "reasonable," but you know how it is: The IRS knows what's reasonable when it sees it. One way the IRS views as reasonable is when you use the loan proceeds within 60 days before the start or end of an academic semester to pay your allowable higher education expenses.

- >> You must be the person primarily responsible for the loan.

- >> The student must carry at least half the normal workload of a full-time student or be attributable to a period during which she met this requirement.

- >> You must take out the loan to pay higher education expenses for tuition, fees, room and board, books, supplies, and other necessary expenses, such as transportation.

- >> Loans from related family members don't qualify for the deduction.

- >> Revolving lines of credit don't qualify unless you agree that the line will be used only to pay for education expenses.

TIP

With these rules, high-income taxpayers may be able to do better with home equity loans, although interest on loans secured by your home whose proceeds are used to pay non-home related expenses isn't deductible under the alternative minimum tax. You may want to check with a tax advisor before you head down this road.

Line 34: Tuition and fees

For 2018, Congress has extended the tuition and fees deduction, which allows you to deduct up to $4,000 of qualified tuition and fees paid to an eligible educational institution of higher education for yourself, your spouse, or your dependent. You may not claim this credit if you're already claiming an American Opportunity or Lifetime Learning Credit for the same student (see the later section "Line 50: Education credits"), and you may not file as married filing separately. Tuition paid for part-time students qualifies; however, income limits apply. The deduction is eliminated for single taxpayers who earn more than $80,000 and for married-filing-jointly taxpayers who earn more than $160,000.

Sport, hobby, and noncredit courses don't qualify for the deduction, unless the course is required as part of a degree program or you take it to improve job skills. If someone else can claim you as a dependent on his return, you can't claim the deduction. As a result, if your income prohibits you from claiming the deduction, your child on whose behalf the expense was incurred can't claim the deduction either.

TIP

This higher education deduction, which you can claim even if you don't itemize your deductions, enables taxpayers to deduct education expenses without having to substantiate that those expenses are job-related. You can claim education expenses above $4,000 as a miscellaneous itemized deduction if they're employment-related.

Nonrefundable Credits: Lines 48 to 55

Now it's time for your credits — and each one has a nice form for you to fill out. The credits are on lines 48 to 53 of Form 1040's Schedule 3 (refer to Figure 7-3).

REMEMBER

Tax credits reduce your tax bill dollar for dollar. Deductions reduce only your taxable income. A $1,000 tax deduction reduces the tax for someone in the 30 percent tax bracket by only $300. A $1,000 tax credit reduces that same person's taxes by $1,000.

SCHEDULE 3 (Form 1040)	**Nonrefundable Credits**	OMB No. 1545-0074
Department of the Treasury Internal Revenue Service	▶ Attach to Form 1040. ▶ Go to *www.irs.gov/Form1040* for instructions and the latest information.	20**18** Attachment Sequence No. **03**
Name(s) shown on Form 1040		Your social security number

Nonrefundable Credits			
	48	Foreign tax credit. Attach Form 1116 if required	48
	49	Credit for child and dependent care expenses. Attach Form 2441	49
	50	Education credits from Form 8863, line 19	50
	51	Retirement savings contributions credit. Attach Form 8880	51
	52	Reserved	52
	53	Residential energy credit. Attach Form 5695	53
	54	Other credits from Form a ☐ 3800 b ☐ 8801 c ☐	54
	55	Add the amounts in the far right column. Enter here and include on Form 1040, line 12	55

For Paperwork Reduction Act Notice, see your tax return instructions.   Cat. No. 71480G   Schedule 3 (Form 1040) 2018

FIGURE 7-3: Schedule 3 of Form 1040.

Courtesy of the Internal Revenue Service

Line 48: Foreign tax credit

If you paid tax to a foreign country on income earned in that country, you're allowed to take a credit for it if you also paid U.S. income tax on that same income. Use Form 1116, "Foreign Tax Credit (Individual, Estate, or Trust)," to figure this credit. (This form is at www.irs.gov/pub/irs-pdf/f1116.pdf.) If you don't itemize your deductions, you have to claim the foreign tax that you paid as a credit if you want to use it to reduce your tax.

You don't have to be a multinational corporation to pay foreign taxes. With more and more people investing in international mutual funds, the foreign tax credit is being used more than ever before to reduce investors' U.S. tax bills for their share of the foreign taxes paid by the funds that they own.

Unfortunately, the computation of this credit is a nightmare. If you hate number-crunching, a computer tax software program can help, or see a tax advisor. Attach Form 1116 to your return and bid it good riddance! You can either claim the foreign tax that you paid as a credit here on line 48 or as an itemized deduction on Schedule A (see Chapter 9).

TIP

As a general rule, taking the credit produces a larger savings. You can also use the foreign tax credit for foreign taxes paid on income earned overseas that exceeds the $104,100 exclusion and the housing allowance. You can ignore the fiendish Form 1116 if the foreign tax you paid is $300 or less ($600 for joint filers). Simply enter the foreign tax you paid on line 48 if your foreign tax is less than these amounts. This simplified method of claiming the credit is available if the only type of foreign income you had was from dividends, interest, rent, royalties, annuities, or the sale of an asset.

Line 49: Credit for child and dependent care expenses

If you hire someone to take care of your children so that you can work for income (doing housework and errands don't cut it), you're entitled to the credit that you figure on Form 2441, "Child and Dependent Care Expenses." This credit may save you several hundred dollars. To be eligible, your child must be younger than 13 or a dependent of any age who is physically or mentally handicapped. (See this form at www.irs.gov/pub/irs-pdf/f2441.pdf.)

The maximum credit for one child or other qualifying individual in 2018 is $1,050 (based on a maximum $3,000 of qualifying expenses) and $2,100 (based on a maximum $6,000 of qualifying expenses) for two or more children or other qualifying individuals. Employers who provide child care for their employees are allowed a tax credit for a percentage of their expenses.

The cost of your baby sitter, day care, or after-school care counts toward this credit (but not after-school activities, such as dance, music, and sports); options like summer day camps (overnight camps don't make the grade) do, too. Note that if you weren't sending your child to that camp in the summer, you'd need to hire a sitter or day care instead.

Line 50: Education credits

On this line you claim the American opportunity credit and the lifetime learning credit. Keep in mind that credits reduce your tax, dollar for dollar. You claim both credits on Form 8863, "Education Credits (American Opportunity and Lifetime Learning Credits)." Here are snapshots of how these credits work:

» The American opportunity credit provides a credit of $2,500 per student per year for up to four years of college. The credit is equal to 100 percent of the first $2,000 of tuition expenses (but not room, board, or books) and 25 percent of the next $2,000 of tuition paid. A student must carry at least one-half the normal course load. The credit can be claimed for you, your spouse, and your dependents. But if you earn too much, you aren't eligible. For married taxpayers (filing jointly only), the credit starts to phase out at $160,000 of income and is gone at $180,000. For single taxpayers, the phaseout starts at $80,000 and is done at $90,000.

>> The lifetime learning credit is a 20 percent credit on up to $10,000 of tuition expenses (but not room, board, or books). This credit doesn't have a limit on the number of years you may claim it. This credit phases out for single taxpayers with $56,000 of income and is gone completely at $66,000. For married taxpayers filing jointly, the income phase-out range is $112,000 to $132,000. Any course to acquire or improve job skills qualifies, but not courses involving sports or hobbies.

TIP

You can claim the American opportunity credit for one child and the lifetime credit for another, but you can't claim both credits for the same student. Families with more than one child can use both credits in concert, but doing so requires careful planning. You need to make sure tuition payments are made in the correct tax year for the correct student.

Line 51: Retirement savings contributions credit

The retirement savings contribution credit encourages joint filers with adjusted gross incomes of less than $63,000 (single filers below $31,500) to save for retirement by enabling them to claim a tax credit tax for a percentage of up to the first $2,000 that they contribute to Roth or traditional IRAs, 401(k)s, or elective deferrals to their employer's retirement plan.

To claim the credit, you need to fill out yet another form, Form 8880, "Credit for Qualified Retirement Savings Contributions". (See this form at www.irs.gov/pub/irs-pdf/f8880.pdf. For an introduction to retirement accounts, check out Chapter 3.)

Chapter **8**

Schedules C and C-EZ

unning your own business really can be the American dream. In fact, the only thing better than working for yourself is knowing how to keep more of what you earn. It's like giving yourself an immediate pay raise at tax time.

If you're self-employed, you report your income and business expenses on Schedule C (or C-EZ) of Form 1040. You determine your profit, on which you pay tax, by subtracting your expenses from your income. (Farmers use Schedule F instead, but many of the same principles apply; see Chapter 7 for an introduction to this form.)

In this chapter, I discuss Schedules C and C-EZ, which most small business owners use when filing their taxes. I explain the most common lines of these forms and how to legally reduce your taxes.

Schedule C-EZ

Schedule C-EZ, "Net Profit from Business (Sole Proprietorship)," is a form that's relatively EZ to complete. (Don't believe me? See it for yourself at www.irs.gov/pub/irs-pdf/f1040sce.pdf.) The only catches are that your deductible expenses can't exceed $5,000, you can't have an inventory of items for sale, you must operate only one business as a sole proprietor, and you must use the cash method of accounting (explained later in this chapter). You also can't use Schedule C-EZ if you have a net loss from your business, you're claiming expenses for the business use of your home (see Chapter 9), you had employees, or you're required to file Form 4562, "Depreciation and Amortization."

If you qualify to use Schedule C-EZ, have a go at it. After you fill in the easy background information in Part I, figure your net profit in Part II (I explain how to calculate gross income and expenses later in this chapter):

>> **Line 1:** Fill in the gross income from your business (the amount of money you brought in before you started paying for any of your expenses).

>> **Line 2:** Fill in your business expenses.

>> **Line 3:** Subtract line 2 from line 1; this amount is your net profit. Note that if you have a negative number here, you need to use Schedule C to report a loss.

That's it! Carry the profit over to Form 1040, Schedule 1, line 12. Unless you're a statutory employee (independent contractor) or you and your spouse are only reporting rental real estate income not subject to self-employment tax, also carry the profit to line 2 of Schedule SE to calculate your self-employment tax (I discuss Schedule SE in Chapter 10).

If you deduct automobile expenses on line 2, you have to fill out Part III and answer a few more questions so the IRS is sure that your expenses are legitimate.

Schedule C

Schedule C isn't so EZ, but it isn't as bad as it looks for many small business owners. In this section, I walk you through this schedule line by line. You can follow along with my guidelines by checking out Figure 8-1; you can also download the most recent version at www.irs.gov/pub/irs-pdf/f1040sc.pdf.

Basic information

Lines A through E are pretty easy background stuff: principal business or profession, business code, business name, employer ID number, and business address.

You can pick your business code from the list located in the Schedule C section of your Form 1040 instruction booklet. You can now obtain an employer identification number (EIN) instantly by applying online at www.irs.gov: Click "Filing," then click "Self-Employed & Small Businesses," and then select "EIN." You can also call 800-829-4933 or go the paper route by sending a completed Form SS-4, "Application for Employer Identification Number," to the IRS. (When filing online, be sure to write the number down as soon as it appears on-screen and before attempting to print the confirmation letter.)

SCHEDULE C
(Form 1040)
Department of the Treasury
Internal Revenue Service (99)

Profit or Loss From Business
(Sole Proprietorship)
▶ Go to *www.irs.gov/ScheduleC* for instructions and the latest information.
▶ Attach to Form 1040, 1040NR, or 1041; partnerships generally must file Form 1065.

OMB No. 1545-0074
2018
Attachment
Sequence No. **09**

Name of proprietor

Social security number (SSN)

A Principal business or profession, including product or service (see instructions)

B Enter code from instructions
▶

C Business name. If no separate business name, leave blank.

D Employer ID number (EIN) (see instr.)

E Business address (including suite or room no.) ▶
City, town or post office, state, and ZIP code

F Accounting method: **(1)** ☐ Cash **(2)** ☐ Accrual **(3)** ☐ Other (specify) ▶

G Did you "materially participate" in the operation of this business during 2018? If "No," see instructions for limit on losses · ☐ Yes ☐ No

H If you started or acquired this business during 2018, check here · · · · · · · · · · ▶ ☐

I Did you make any payments in 2018 that would require you to file Form(s) 1099? (see instructions) · · · · · ☐ Yes ☐ No

J If "Yes," did you or will you file required Forms 1099? · · · · · · · · · · · · · · · · · · ☐ Yes ☐ No

Part I Income

1	Gross receipts or sales. See instructions for line 1 and check the box if this income was reported to you on Form W-2 and the "Statutory employee" box on that form was checked · · · · · · · · ▶ ☐	1	
2	Returns and allowances ·	2	
3	Subtract line 2 from line 1 ·	3	
4	Cost of goods sold (from line 42) ·	4	
5	**Gross profit.** Subtract line 4 from line 3 · · · · · · · · · · · · · · · · · ·	5	
6	Other income, including federal and state gasoline or fuel tax credit or refund (see instructions) · · · ·	6	
7	**Gross income.** Add lines 5 and 6 · · · · · · · · · · · · · · · · · · · ▶	7	

Part II Expenses. Enter expenses for business use of your home **only** on line 30.

8	Advertising · · · · ·	8		18	Office expense (see instructions)	18
9	Car and truck expenses (see instructions) · · · ·	9		19	Pension and profit-sharing plans ·	19
				20	Rent or lease (see instructions):	
10	Commissions and fees ·	10		a	Vehicles, machinery, and equipment	20a
11	Contract labor (see instructions)	11		b	Other business property · · ·	20b
12	Depletion · · · · ·	12		21	Repairs and maintenance · · ·	21
13	Depreciation and section 179 expense deduction (not included in Part III) (see instructions) · · · · ·	13		22	Supplies (not included in Part III) ·	22
				23	Taxes and licenses · · · · ·	23
				24	Travel and meals:	
14	Employee benefit programs (other than on line 19) · ·	14		a	Travel · · · · · · · · ·	24a
15	Insurance (other than health)	15		b	Deductible meals (see instructions) · · · · ·	24b
16	Interest (see instructions):			25	Utilities · · · · · · · ·	25
a	Mortgage (paid to banks, etc.)	16a		26	Wages (less employment credits) ·	26
b	Other · · · · · · ·	16b		27a	Other expenses (from line 48) · ·	27a
17	Legal and professional services	17		b	**Reserved for future use** · · ·	27b

28	**Total expenses** before expenses for business use of home. Add lines 8 through 27a · · · · · ▶	28	
29	Tentative profit or (loss). Subtract line 28 from line 7 · · · · · · · · · · · · · · · ·	29	
30	Expenses for business use of your home. Do not report these expenses elsewhere. Attach Form 8829 unless using the simplified method (see instructions). **Simplified method filers only:** enter the total square footage of: (a) your home: _____ and (b) the part of your home used for business: _____ . Use the Simplified Method Worksheet in the instructions to figure the amount to enter on line 30 · · · · · · · ·	30	
31	**Net profit or (loss).** Subtract line 30 from line 29. • If a profit, enter on both **Schedule 1 (Form 1040), line 12** (or Form 1040NR, line 13) and on **Schedule SE, line 2.** (If you checked the box on line 1, see instructions). Estates and trusts, enter on **Form 1041, line 3.** • If a loss, you **must** go to line 32.	31	

32 If you have a loss, check the box that describes your investment in this activity (see instructions).
• If you checked 32a, enter the loss on both **Schedule 1 (Form 1040), line 12** (or Form 1040NR, line 13) and on **Schedule SE, line 2.** (If you checked the box on line 1, see the line 31 instructions). Estates and trusts, enter on **Form 1041, line 3.**
• If you checked 32b, you **must** attach Form 6198. Your loss may be limited.

32a ☐ All investment is at risk.
32b ☐ Some investment is not at risk.

For Paperwork Reduction Act Notice, see the separate instructions. Cat. No. 11334P Schedule C (Form 1040) 2018

FIGURE 8-1:
Schedule C.

Part III **Cost of Goods Sold** (see instructions)

33   Method(s) used to
value closing inventory: **a** ☐ Cost   **b** ☐ Lower of cost or market   **c** ☐ Other (attach explanation)

34   Was there any change in determining quantities, costs, or valuations between opening and closing inventory?
If "Yes," attach explanation . . . . ☐ **Yes**   ☐ **No**

35   Inventory at beginning of year. If different from last year's closing inventory, attach explanation . . . | **35** |

36   Purchases less cost of items withdrawn for personal use . . . . | **36** |

37   Cost of labor. Do not include any amounts paid to yourself . . . . | **37** |

38   Materials and supplies . . . . | **38** |

39   Other costs . . . . | **39** |

40   Add lines 35 through 39 . . . . | **40** |

41   Inventory at end of year . . . . | **41** |

42   **Cost of goods sold.** Subtract line 41 from line 40. Enter the result here and on line 4 . . . . . . | **42** |

Part IV **Information on Your Vehicle.** Complete this part **only** if you are claiming car or truck expenses on line 9 and are not required to file Form 4562 for this business. See the instructions for line 13 to find out if you must file Form 4562.

43   When did you place your vehicle in service for business purposes? (month, day, year)   ▶   _____ / _____ / _____

44   Of the total number of miles you drove your vehicle during 2018, enter the number of miles you used your vehicle for:

   a   Business _____   **b** Commuting (see instructions) _____   **c** Other _____

45   Was your vehicle available for personal use during off-duty hours? . . . . ☐ **Yes**   ☐ **No**

46   Do you (or your spouse) have another vehicle available for personal use?. . . . . ☐ **Yes**   ☐ **No**

47a   Do you have evidence to support your deduction? . . . . ☐ **Yes**   ☐ **No**

   b   If "Yes," is the evidence written? . . . . ☐ **Yes**   ☐ **No**

Part V **Other Expenses.** List below business expenses not included on lines 8–26 or line 30.

-- | |

-- | |

-- | |

-- | |

-- | |

-- | |

-- | |

-- | |

-- | |

48   **Total other expenses.** Enter here and on line 27a . . . . | **48** |

FIGURE 8-1:
continued

Courtesy of the Internal Revenue Service

Two topics in the basic information section may give you pause: the accounting method your company uses and material participation in your business. The following sections provide some guidelines.

Accounting methods

Line F of the basic information section asks for the accounting method you use. The two main methods to report income are cash and accrual.

With the cash method, you report income when you actually receive it, and you deduct expenses when you actually pay them. This rule has an exception: If you charge an expense on a credit card, you deduct this expense in the year charged, even if you pay the charge in a later year.

Does your business take in $10 million or less? If so, then you can use the cash method of accounting, but only if a bunch of restrictions don't apply. If you're in a purely service business, then you don't have to worry about these restrictions. You can use the cash method.

If you're in the wholesale or retail trade, manufacturing, information services, or mining, then you can't use the cash method. However, this rule does have its exceptions: Even if you're in one of these businesses that disqualifies you from using the cash method, you still can use it if providing a service is the main thing you do. For example, suppose you're a publisher (information services) whose main activity is the sale of advertising space. You can use the cash method even though information services isn't one of the businesses normally allowed to use the cash method. The reason? The sale of advertising space is considered a service. Similarly, businesses that manufacture or modify a product to a customer's specifications and design may use the cash method even though manufacturing isn't an eligible business.

TIP

A small business whose average annual income (over the current year and two previous years) is $1 million or less can use the cash method regardless of its line of business. However, it can deduct the purchase of merchandise for resale only when it's sold and not when it's purchased, so read on. Even though some people are permitted to use the cash method, if they use materials and supplies that aren't incidental to the services they perform, they face a hitch: They have to use or pay for those materials and supplies before they can deduct the cost. Roofing contractors are an example. Even though they may use the cash method, they aren't allowed to deduct the cost of the materials they purchase until the later of either when they use the materials on a customer's job or when they pay for them. Say a contractor paid $5,000 for shingles in December, 2018 but didn't install them until January, 2019. Sorry, it's a 2019 tax deduction, not a 2018 deduction. (The amount the contractor charges the customer is reported in the year the contractor receives it because the contractor is using the cash method.)

With the accrual method, you record revenue and expenses when the work or transaction is actually completed rather than when money changes hands. Say you must use the accrual method because you operate a clothing store. You report income from a sale in the year that you make it, even when you bill the customer or collect the money for the sale in a later year. You deduct expenses in the year that you incur them, even if you don't pay those expenses until a later year.

TIP

A hybrid method of accounting also exists. Even if you have to use the accrual method to report income and deduct merchandise sold, you nevertheless can use the cash method for the rest of your expenses, rent, telephone bill, wages, and so on. Doing so can make your bookkeeping less complicated.

REMEMBER

If you have the choice, the cash method of accounting gives you more control over how much profit your business reports year to year. For example, if next year looks like a slower year for you, perhaps because you plan to take a sabbatical, you may elect to push income that you could realize this year into next year instead, when you may be in a lower tax bracket because you'll have less income. You legally can do this by not invoicing for work you've performed late in the current year until January. Instead of billing that work and being paid for it in December, for example, you can send those bills in January. Likewise, you can pay more of your expenses in December instead of waiting until January. Keep in mind that if you sell merchandise, you have to comply with the accrual method rules, unless your average income is $1 million or less. However, you can't deduct your merchandise purchases until you sell those goods. If you provide a service, you can use the cash method.

This general rule may not apply to everyone. For example, if you operate a business that receives large cash advances (deposits) from customers before you undertake the work, you're better off using the accrual method. That way you don't have to report the cash advances until you actually do the work.

Material participation

WARNING

Line G asks about material participation. "Did you 'materially participate' in the operation of this business?" is a trick question designed to limit losses that someone can deduct as a silent partner. If you put up the dough but someone other than your spouse operated a business that lost money, then you can't deduct the loss. The reason? You didn't materially participate in the operation of the business, and (as a result) you're considered to be operating a tax shelter.

Seven criteria determine material participation. The instructions for Schedule C of your 1040 instruction booklet has them all. The basic criteria include whether you meet either the 500- or 100-hour rules regarding material participation, whether you were the only one who did the work, and whether you participated on a regular, continuous, and substantial basis. Pass any one of the seven and you're okay.

Part I: Income

Time to tally. This section wants you to find some gross things: gross sales, gross profits, and gross income.

Line 1: Gross receipts or sales

If you operate a service business, enter the income from fees that you actually collected (because you're reporting income under the cash method described in the earlier section "Accounting methods"). If clients have given you Form 1099-MISC to report their payments to you to the IRS, add up the amounts in box 7. Note that even if you didn't receive a Form 1099-MISC, you're still obligated to report all the income you received.

If you're required to use the accrual method, enter the total of all the sales that you billed to your customers on this line.

Line 2: Returns and allowances

If you had to return any fees, enter that amount here. If any customers returned merchandise, that amount also goes on this line, along with any discounts that those customers took. You then subtract line 2 from line 1 and put the total on line 3.

Line 4: Cost of goods sold

The IRS must think that you're an accountant; otherwise, it would simply tell you to subtract the amount you paid for merchandise that you sold from your sales to arrive at this figure. Businesses that don't sell products don't have to put an amount on this line.

But because you're not an accountant, you have to compute the cost of the merchandise that you sold in Part III (on page 2 of Schedule C). Part III is a ten-line schedule where you enter your beginning inventory, the merchandise that you purchased, the salary that you paid to your production workers (if you manufacture the product that you sell), and the cost of production supplies. You total all these expenses on line 40. From this total, you subtract your ending inventory to arrive, on line 42, at the cost of the goods that you sold. This amount goes back to this line, 4.

Note that you may only deduct the cost of merchandise you sold during the year, not the cost of all the merchandise that you purchased. That's why you have to subtract your ending inventory, which is the stuff that you didn't sell. You get to deduct what's on hand when it's sold. You enter the amount of your ending inventory on line 41 and carry it over to your next year's return. So don't forget to enter the amount from line 41, which becomes your inventory at the beginning of the year, on line 35 of your next year's Schedule C.

The following example explains what this inventory business is all about. Say you own a retail furniture store. In 2017, you purchased two identical chairs, one for $1,200 and the other for $1,000. You sold only one chair. Which one did you sell? The inventory method that you select determines that.

>> Under the *FIFO method* — first in, first out — the first chair purchased is deemed the first one sold. If that's the $1,200 chair, then enter the cost of the $1,000 chair on line 41, because that's the one considered on hand at the end of the year.

>> Under the *LIFO method* — last in, first out — the chair purchased last is deemed to be sold first. Under this method, the $1,000 chair is considered to be sold first, so enter $1,200 on line 41, because that's the cost of the chair that's considered the unsold one.

TIP

Which method is better? In a period of rising costs, it's the LIFO method. FIFO is better when costs are declining.

Line 33 also requires you to select the method that you used to value your inventory. Three methods are available — cost (box a), lower of cost or market (box b), and other (box c). Skip box c because it's too complicated. Most people check box a because it's the easiest. Although using the lower of cost or market method can increase deductions if your inventory declines in value (you get to deduct the amount of the decline), it requires you to revalue your inventory every year.

WARNING

After you select a valuation method, you can change it only with permission from the IRS.

After all that calculation to get the amount for line 4, subtract it from line 3 and enter the total on line 5. This amount is your *gross profit.*

Line 6: Other income

For line 6, just do what the schedule orders you to do — see page C-3 of the 1040 booklet if you have any questions about other income. Some of the more common — and more obscure — examples of other income include the following:

>> Federal and state gasoline or fuel tax credit

>> Fee for allowing a company to paint an advertisement on the side of your building

>> Interest on accounts receivable

>> Scrap sales

If you enter anything on line 6, add it to the amount on line 5 and then put the total on line 7. If you don't enter anything for line 6, just repeat line 5's amount on line 7. The amount on line 7 is your *gross income.*

Part II: Expenses

Take a breath and get ready for all those wonderful expense-tabulating lines that are split into two columns — so they'd all fit on one page!

Line 8: Advertising

On this line, enter the cost of any advertising that your business does to promote itself, including radio, newspaper, Internet, and print ads and promotional brochures and mailers. Don't forget the little ads you take out in the affinity magazines for state troopers, police, firefighters, and other service agencies. Basically, anything that has your name and business information that's seen by any segment of the public is advertising.

Line 9: Car and truck expenses

If you plan to make an entry on this line, be sure to answer questions 43 through 47b in Part IV on page 2 of Schedule C.

When you use your car for business, the expenses of operating your car are deductible. But keep in mind that "using it for business" is the key phrase. You compute this deduction by using a flat rate per business mile or by keeping track of actual expenses (gas, oil, repairs, insurance, depreciation, and so on). Regardless of which method you use, you're supposed to keep a log to record the mileage and the business purpose of your trips. You also have to record the odometer reading at the beginning and end of the year. You need all this information to be able to divide your expenses into personal and business use.

TIP

You don't have to write down the miles that you travel every time you get in and out of your car. Making entries in your log on a weekly basis meets the IRS requirement that you keep a record of your car's business use near or at the time of its use.

The following sections go into more detail on a few issues related to car and truck expenses.

STANDARD MILEAGE RATE OR ACTUAL EXPENSES?

You can deduct either the business portion of your actual expenses or use the standard mileage rate for your business miles. The standard mileage method relieves you of the task of keeping track of your expenses. It only requires that you track your miles. Deducting your actual expenses requires both. Whichever method you use, Part II of Form 2106 (although intended for employees who are deducting auto expenses) contains an excellent worksheet to help you compute your deduction. (Check out this form at www.irs.gov/pub/irs-pdf/f2106.pdf.)

Instead of figuring your actual expenses with those maddening depreciation computations, you can use a flat rate of 54.5 cents for every business mile you drive in tax year 2018. You can use the standard mileage rate whether you own or lease a vehicle.

When you're calculating your business mileage deduction on Form 2106, if you were reimbursed for any of your car expenses that weren't included in box 1 of your W-2 as taxable wages, a code L appears next to the amount of the reimbursement in box 12 of your W-2. You must deduct this amount from your total auto expenses (whether you use actual numbers or base it on the flat-rate mileage calculation) and enter it on line 7 of Form 2106.

REMEMBER

If you choose the flat-rate method, you can't claim any of your actual expenses, such as depreciation, gas, oil, insurance, and so on. If you want to use this method, you must choose it the first year that you start using your car for business. If you don't use the standard mileage rate in the first year, you can't use the standard mileage rate in a subsequent year. But if you use the standard mileage rate the first year, you can switch to deducting your actual expenses, but you probably won't want to after you take a look at the rules in IRS Publication 463 ("Travel, Entertainment, Gift, and Car Expenses").

Should you consider deducting your actual auto expenses instead of going the flat-rate route? You can deduct the business portion of the following: depreciation, leasing and rental fees, garage rent, licenses, repairs, gas, oil, tires, insurance, parking, and tolls. (You deduct the cost for leasing, which I don't generally recommend due to its relative costs, on line 20a of Schedule C).

Self-employed individuals may deduct the business portion of car loan interest, but employees may not. Fines for traffic violations aren't deductible for either — so slow down!

TIP

You can't separately deduct sales tax you pay when you purchase a car — it's added to the car's tax basis for the purposes of determining the amount of depreciation that you're entitled to claim. If you're an employee, you can deduct personal property tax on your car if you itemize your deductions on Schedule A of

Form 1040. If you're self-employed, you deduct the business portion of your personal property tax on line 23 of Schedule C and the personal part on Schedule A. (Flip to Chapter 9 for details on Schedule A.)

One auto expense that is always tricky to figure is depreciation. Still, if you feel you're going to have a better result using your actual car expenses instead of the flat rate, you're going to have to figure them out. Look at the "Line 13: Depreciation" section later in this chapter to find out which method of depreciation you're supposed to use for your car. Strangely enough, even though it relates directly to your car and is one of the valid car and truck expenses, all your auto depreciation gets lumped together on line 13 of Schedule C (and not line 9).

NO HELP FROM UNCLE SAM WITH COMMUTING EXPENSES

Commuting expenses between your home and office aren't deductible. These expenses are considered personal commuting expenses, no matter how far your home is from your office or place of work. And making telephone calls from your car while commuting or having a business discussion with a business associate who accompanies you doesn't turn your ride into a deductible expense. Using your car to display advertising material on your way to the office doesn't count as business use of your auto, either. Finally, the cost of parking at your place of business isn't deductible — but the cost of parking when you visit a customer or client is.

TIP

If you use your car to call on clients and don't have a regular office to go to, the mileage between your home and the first customer that you call on — and the mileage between the location of the last customer that you call on and your home — is considered commuting. If your office is in your home, you can deduct all your auto expenses for calling on customers. Use line 44 to split out your commuting and your business miles.

TRAVEL TO A SECOND JOB

You can deduct the cost of getting from one job to the other if you hold more than one job. But transportation expenses going from your home to a part-time job on a day off from your main job aren't deductible. A meeting of an Armed Forces Reserve unit is considered travel to a second job, however; if it's held on the same day as your regular job, it's deductible.

TRAVEL TO A TEMPORARY JOB SITE

If you have a regular place of business and commute to a temporary work location, you can deduct the cost of the daily round trip between your home and the temporary job site.

If you don't have a regular place of work (but ordinarily work at different locations in the general area where you live), you can't deduct the daily round trip between your home and your temporary job site. But if you travel to a job site outside your general area, your daily transportation is deductible. Sounds like a distinction without a difference, right? But if this exception applies to you, don't look a gift horse in the mouth.

Line 10: Commissions and fees

The fees that you paid to sell your merchandise or to bring in new clients (as in referral fees) go on this line.

REMEMBER

However, if you pay someone who isn't your employee $600 or more in a year, you have to file Form 1099-MISC with the IRS and send the person that you paid a copy of the form. IRS Publication 334 ("Tax Guide for Small Business") explains how to comply with this requirement.

Line 11: Contract labor

This line is meant to clearly identify businesses using independent contractors. The IRS zeroes in on businesses that pay workers as independent contractors instead of as employees where the employer is obligated to withhold and pay Social Security and Medicare taxes on their salaries. If someone works on your premises and under your control, she's probably your employee, and the rules about withholding taxes and Social Security apply (see Chapter 10 for more info).

However, if treating these types of workers as independent contractors is standard in your industry (that is, at least 25 percent of your industry treats them this way) and you issue these workers a Form 1099 at the end of the year, you may have an escape hatch. IRS Publication 1779 ("Independent Contractor or Employee Brochure") and IRS Publication 15-A ("Employer's Supplemental Tax Guide") address the independent contractor issue in greater detail.

Line 12: Depletion

This line applies if your business deals with properties such as mines, oil and gas wells, timber, or exhaustible natural deposits. You can compute depletion two ways, and, of course, you want to use the one that produces the larger deduction. Unlike depreciation, which measures the useful life of property (see the next section), depletion measures the actual reduction of a physical asset. To be on the safe side, take a look at IRS Publication 535 ("Business Expenses").

Line 13: Depreciation

Depreciation is the annual deduction that enables you to recover the cost of an investment (that has a useful life of more than one year) in business equipment or in income-producing real estate. Or, as an accountant explained (in a ten-words-or-less challenge), depreciation is "recovering an asset's value ratably over its useful economic life."

I know that the word *depreciation* is itself enough to send most readers to the next chapter, but just think of depreciation as a way of reducing your tax! Now, are you more excited about depreciation possibilities? Unless you elect the special provision that allows you to deduct up to $1,000,000 of equipment or furniture used in your business, you have to write off your purchase of these assets over their respective useful lives as established by the IRS. You can't depreciate land or works of art.

You should also know about 100 percent "bonus depreciation" on qualifying assets. The qualifying property must be new, have a recovery period of 20 years or less or be off-the-shelf computer software, water utility property (including municipal sewers and commercial water treatment facilities), or leasehold improvement property, including interior improvements to rented nonresidential property made more than three years after you first rented that piece of property.

TIP

If you're an employee claiming auto expenses, you claim the depreciation for the auto on Form 2106, "Employee Business Expenses"; Form 4562, "Depreciation and Amortization," isn't required. For rental income reported on Schedule E, use Form 4562.

You compute your depreciation deduction for business property that you started using on Form 4562 (found at www.irs.gov/pub/irs-pdf/f4562.pdf). Carry over the amount of depreciation that you calculate on this form to line 13 of Schedule C. The depreciation you normally can deduct every year is determined by an item's useful life. Based on that, you then take a percentage of the item's cost as a deduction. Before I get into explaining how that works, you need to know about a depreciation deduction that you can take right off the bat: the $1,000,000 deduction.

TIP

Calculating depreciation can be a headache, but doing so isn't impossible. Still, you may have questions along the way or want to check with someone else after you've finished to make sure you've done it right. Consider asking a tax professional to double-check your depreciation calculations after you're done to make sure they're correct.

THE $1,000,000 DEDUCTION (SECTION 179 DEPRECIATION)

Per section 179 of the Internal Revenue Code, you can deduct up to $1,000,000 of the cost of new or used business equipment that you purchased and started to use in 2018 (or the tax year in question). If you fall into this category, you don't have to fuss with the standard IRS depreciation tables to claim this depreciation deduction. Whether you purchased new or used equipment doesn't matter. You just have to use it more than 50 percent of the time in your business. If the equipment, machinery, or office furniture that you purchased for your company didn't exceed $1,000,000, simply deduct what you spent on Form 4562 and on line 13 of Schedule C.

Note that the $1,000,000 deduction can't produce a loss from all your business activities. If it does, the balance carries over to future year(s) until you can deduct it. But there is a pleasant surprise. You can count all your earned income to determine whether you pass the no-loss test.

IRS DEPRECIATION PERCENTAGES

If you're only depreciating property you started using prior to 2018, Form 4562 isn't required. On line 13 of Schedule C, you enter the amount to which you're entitled based on the useful life of the asset from the applicable IRS depreciation table (available at www.irs.gov/pub/irs-pdf/i4562.pdf). If you're depreciating cars, computers, cellular phones, or other so-called listed property, however, you must use Form 4562 because you can depreciate only the business portion of those kinds of items.

To calculate the amount of depreciation that you're entitled to claim, you must use relevant IRS depreciation tables. For business property other than real estate, you'll notice that each table has two categories: half-year convention and mid-quarter convention. Usually, you use the half-year convention because the mid-quarter convention comes into play when the business assets you acquired and started using in the last three months of the year exceed 40 percent of all business assets that you placed in service during the year. Got that?

WARNING

Real estate isn't eligible for the special $1,000,000 depreciation deduction described in the preceding section. You depreciate residential real estate over 27½ years. You depreciate nonresidential real estate (a factory or office building, for example) placed in use after May 12, 1993, over 39 years. If you placed it in service (that's the IRS term for when you started using it) after 1986 and before May 13, 1993, you depreciate it over 31½ years. You can get the depreciation rates for these two periods from IRS Publication 946 ("How to Depreciate Property"). For prior periods, you have to use the rates in IRS Publication 534 ("Depreciating Property Placed in Service before 1987").

Line 14: Employee benefit programs

Enter here the premiums you paid for your employees' accident, health, and group term life insurance coverage — but not those you paid for your own health insurance. See Chapter 7 to find out how to deduct your personal health insurance premiums.

Line 15: Insurance (other than health)

Enter on this line the premiums that you paid for business insurance, such as fire, theft, robbery, and general liability coverage on your business property.

Line 16a: Mortgage interest

If you own the building in which you operate your company, deduct any mortgage interest you paid on line 16a. If you're claiming a deduction for the portion of your home that you use for business, you deduct the mortgage interest you paid on line 10 of Form 8829, "Expenses for Business Use of Your Home" (see Chapter 9 for details). The amount of the deduction is stated on Form 1098, "Mortgage Interest Statement," which you should receive in January from your bank.

Line 16b: Other interest

You can deduct interest on business loans here. If you took out a mortgage on your house and used the proceeds of the loan to finance your business, deduct the interest here — and not on Schedule A. If you borrowed money for your company from other sources, such as a bank or even your credit card, deduct the interest on those loans here as well.

TIP

You can't deduct the interest you paid on the taxes you owed on your personal tax returns. You can, however, deduct late interest paid on employment taxes (Social Security, Medicare, and withholding taxes) that you paid as an employer. However, you're better off paying those taxes on time and avoiding late interest charges.

Line 17: Legal and professional services

On this line, enter any fees that you paid for tax advice, for preparing tax forms related to your business, and for legal fees regarding business matters. Professional services include fees for accounting and engineering work that you pay for. You enter general consulting work on line 11 (see the section earlier in the chapter).

REMEMBER

If you pay someone more than $600 (your accountant, for example), you have to provide him with Form 1099-MISC by January 31.

The exemption that allows you not to report payments made to corporations to the IRS on Form 1099 doesn't apply to lawyers. You must report all payments that you made to your lawyer — even for the reimbursement of expenses that you were billed.

Line 18: Office expense

Enter your costs for stationery, paper supplies, postage, printer toner, and other consumable items that you use in the operation of your office or business.

Line 19: Pension and profit-sharing plans

Enter your contribution to your employees' SIMPLE, or SEP account(s). As for your own SEP, enter that amount on Form 1040 (line 28).

Note: Employers with fewer than 100 employees may establish what's known as SIMPLE retirement plans. These plans have none of the mind-numbing rules to follow or forms to file that regular retirement plans have. A SIMPLE plan can also cover the owner(s) of a farm. See Chapter 3 for more about small business retirement plans.

Lines 20a and b: Rent or lease

If you rented or leased an auto, machinery, or equipment, enter the business portion of the rental payments on line 20a. But if you leased a car for more than 30 days, you may have to reduce your deduction by an amount called the *inclusion amount* if your leased car's value exceeded particular amounts when you started leasing it.

WARNING

Whether you enter your car lease payments here or on Form 2106, "Employee Business Expenses," you aren't allowed to deduct the full amount of the lease payments on pricey cars! Just as there are luxury car rules for calculating depreciation, there are essentially luxury car rules for leased cars, as well (only the IRS refers to inclusion amounts for leased cars, or the amount by which your lease payments must be reduced, as opposed to luxury car rules). The inclusion amounts and luxury car rules do the same thing — they both effectively limit your deduction.

You can find charts with the lease inclusion amounts for cars, SUVs, vans, light trucks, and electric cars in IRS Publication 463 ("Travel, Entertainment, Gift, and Car Expenses"). These numbers are adjusted annually for inflation, so you do need to check every year. Obtain IRS Publication 463 by calling 800-829-3676 or on the Internet at www.irs.gov.

Even though you reduce your rental payments by the lease-inclusion amount, leasing may still provide you with a larger deduction than purchasing. But note that lease payments that are payments toward the purchase price of a car aren't deductible. The IRS considers such leases a purchase contract because you end up owning the jalopy at the end of the lease. If you have such an agreement, you must depreciate the car based on its value, and doing so sends you right back to the annual limit that you can claim for auto depreciation.

On line 20b, enter rent or lease payments for other business property — your office rent, for example.

Line 21: Repairs and maintenance

Enter the cost of routine repairs — such as fixing your computer — on this line. But adding a new hard disk isn't a repair; you must depreciate that cost over five years unless it qualifies for the special election to write off the first $1,000,000 of business assets (described earlier in this chapter).

A repair (as opposed to an improvement) keeps your equipment or property in good operating condition. You must depreciate a repair that also prolongs the life of your equipment, so make the most of the $1,000,000 deduction instead of depreciating the cost over its useful life.

TIP

If you're confused about what qualifies as a repair and what qualifies as an improvement, you're not alone. Through the years, the Tax Court has been clogged with cases dealing with repairs as current write-offs versus improvements that have to be depreciated. If in doubt, contact a tax advisor to evaluate your specific situation.

Line 22: Supplies

If your company manufactures a product, you report factory supplies here. In other words, you deduct the cost of supplies that contribute to the operation of the equipment that you use in your office or business. For example, if you operate a retail store, you enter the cost of mannequins, trim, packaging, and other such items on this line.

Line 23: Taxes and licenses

On this line you deduct your business taxes, such as Social Security and unemployment insurance taxes for your employees. Also enter the costs of permits and business licenses. *Note:* Don't deduct the Social Security tax that you pay because you're self-employed here; instead, you can deduct half of this tax on line 27 of IRS Form 1040, Schedule 1 (covered in Chapter 7).

Lines 24a and b: Travel and meals

You can deduct 100 percent of the money you spent on airfare and hotels on line 24a for business trips. But be careful — money you spend on room service is limited to 50 percent, unless you work in the transportation industry. Because you can deduct only 50 percent of your meal expenses, only enter the 50 percent you're allowed to deduct on line 24b. The 2017 Tax Cuts and Jobs Act (TCJA) further limited meal deductions as follows:

> "The 2017 TCJA eliminated the deduction for any expenses related to activities generally considered entertainment, amusement or recreation. Taxpayers may continue to deduct 50 percent of the cost of business meals if the taxpayer (or an employee of the taxpayer) is present and the food or beverages are not considered lavish or extravagant. The meals may be provided to a current or potential business customer, client, consultant or similar business contact."

If you're in the transportation industry and are subject to the Department of Transportation restrictions on the number of hours you can work, you're allowed to deduct 80 percent of your meals and entertainment, so deduct them here, on line 24b.

If you don't have all your receipts but you still want to take this deduction, see Schedule A of Form 1040 for the per diem rules and regulations.

Line 25: Utilities

Can you imagine what this line is for? If you're thinking of electric and telephone bills, for example, you hit the nail on the head. However, if you claim a home office deduction (discussed in Chapter 9), your utility costs belong on Form 8829, "Expenses for Business Use of Your Home," and not here.

Line 26: Wages

Enter here the wages that you paid your employees. However, make sure you deduct payments to independent contractors on line 11 (described earlier in this chapter).

Line 27: Other expenses

On page 2 of Schedule C is Part V, a schedule where you list your expenses that don't fit into the neat categories of lines 8–26. Here you can enter dues, subscriptions to related business periodicals, messenger services, overnight express fees, and so on. If you have more than nine items in the other expense category, just add another Part V page, but enter the grand total on line 48 of only one of the forms; add it to line 27a, too.

After you wrap up line 27a, add together lines 8 through 27a and enter the total on line 28. Subtract line 7 from line 28 and enter the total on line 29.

Line 30: Form 8829

You must use Form 8829, "Expenses for Business Use of Your Home," to claim the deduction for the portion that you use for business. You can find detailed instructions for filling it out and other rules you must follow in Chapter 9.

You can't take a loss because of the home office deduction. You can, however, carry over an excess deduction amount to another year's tax return.

REMEMBER

Because you deduct only a portion of your total mortgage interest and real estate taxes as part of your home office expenses, don't forget to deduct the balance of your total mortgage interest and real estate taxes that you entered on Form 8829. The rest of your mortgage interest balance and real estate taxes goes on Schedule A. These two amounts represent your mortgage interest and taxes related to the portion of the house you live in.

Don't forget to subtract line 30 from line 29 and then enter the total on line 31.

Lines 32a and b: At-risk rules

Suppose that you borrow money to go into business. The at-risk rules limit the amount of business losses that you can deduct on borrowed money that you're personally not liable to repay. For example, you need $20,000 to go into business. You invest $10,000, and your rich uncle gives you $10,000. You lose the entire $20,000. You can deduct only the $10,000 that you personally invested in your business.

Basically, if you're personally responsible for all the liabilities of your business, check box 32a. If you are, you can deduct all your losses. If you're not at risk for all the investment that was made in your business, check 32b. Guess what? You have to fill out Form 6198, "At-Risk Limitations." This form (found at www.irs. gov/pub/irs-pdf/f6198.pdf) determines how much of your loss you're allowed to deduct.

TIP

If you aren't personally responsible, see a tax professional, because the rules in this area are anything but clear or simple.

The following sections describe start-up expenses and operating loss, both of which are related to at-risk rules.

START-UP EXPENSES

Start-up expenses are the expenses incurred in getting into business before the business actually begins operating. The types of expenses usually incurred during this period are market studies, consulting and professional services, and travel in securing prospective suppliers, customers, and feasibility studies. Whether you can deduct these expenses depends on whether you actually start the business.

TIP

If you go into business, you can elect to deduct these expenses over 60 months. You make the election in the year that you start the business by attaching a statement to your return describing the expenditures, the dates incurred, the month the business opened, and the number of months you're electing to deduct the expenditures. You can elect more than 60 months but not less. You compute the deduction in Part VI of Form 4562, "Depreciation and Amortization."

If you don't go into business, you can deduct some of your start-up expenses in the year that your attempt to go into business failed. Which expenses qualify? The answer isn't all that clear. You can deduct your business start-up expenses but not investigatory expenses. What's the difference, you ask? Here's what the IRS says the difference is:

>> *Investigatory expenses* are costs incurred in reviewing a prospective business prior to reaching a final decision to acquire or enter the business.

>> *Start-up expenses* are costs incurred after you decide to go into business but prior to the time the business actually begins to operate.

If you guessed that some taxpayers end up in audits as the result of how they decided to separate the two, you're right. You deduct start-up expenses on Schedule C.

OPERATING LOSS

Suppose that you start a business and it produces an *operating loss,* where your costs — not just equipment, but rent, salaries, and other expenses — exceed your income. You may write off that loss against any other income that you and your spouse made that year.

TIP

If the loss is greater than your combined income in the current year, you have what's known in IRS jargon as a *net operating loss* (NOL). Effective 2018, NOLs can no longer be carried back for two years. However, NOLs may now be carried forward indefinitely until they are used up. Previously the carry-forward limit was 20 years. NOLs are limited each year to 80 percent of taxable income.

REMEMBER

Keep in mind, however, that you can't operate a part-time business, for example, that continually loses money. This situation is known as a *hobby loss.* If you don't show a profit in at least three of every five consecutive years, you may have a fight with the IRS on your hands. You must show a profit in at least three of every five consecutive years or the IRS can declare your business a hobby and disallow your losses. The IRS doesn't consider your enterprise a business when you have continuing losses. No business, no business deductions. Some taxpayers have challenged this rule in Tax Court and won. They were able to prove that they ran their enterprises like a business and anticipated making a profit but didn't. The three-out-of-five-year rule was established to keep the IRS off your back. If you meet this requirement, the IRS can't claim that the losses in the two other years can't be deducted because the business is a hobby. Not making a profit in three out of five years doesn't automatically make the venture a hobby, but it's a strong indication that it may be.

And, here's a little more bad news, which took effect in 2018, if you engage in a hobby and realize a small profit from the efforts. If what you're doing is deemed a hobby, you do have to declare the income from your activity but aren't allowed to claim any deductions for it.

Chapter **9**

The Business Use of Your Home

Everybody who runs a small business needs a place to work. Even if your business is a laptop computer and your office is wherever you choose to locate your posterior, you should think through the decisions of where to work and how much space you need. In Chapter 4, I discuss these "real estate" decisions for your small business.

In this chapter, I explain how the home office deduction tax rules work, including the recent and simplified home office deduction. I detail what deductions you may and may not take for using your home for your business. I also discuss the downsides to home office deductions, including audit risks and issues that crop up when you go to sell your home.

The New, Simplified Home Office Deduction

To claim expenses for the business use of your home — or the so-called *home office deduction* — you have to complete a fairly complicated form: Form 8829, "Expenses for Business Use of Your Home," to be exact. Form 8829 weighs in at

43 lines (see the 2018 version in Figure 9-1; the most recent version is available at www.irs.gov/pub/irs-pdf/f8829.pdf, and the Introduction has the username and password you need).

Form **8829**

Department of the Treasury
Internal Revenue Service (99)

Expenses for Business Use of Your Home

▶ File only with Schedule C (Form 1040). Use a separate Form 8829 for each home you used for business during the year.
▶ Go to *www.irs.gov/Form8829* for instructions and the latest information.

OMB No. 1545-0074

20**18**

Attachment
Sequence No. **176**

Name(s) of proprietor(s)

Your social security number

Part I   Part of Your Home Used for Business

1 Area used regularly and exclusively for business, regularly for daycare, or for storage of inventory or product samples (see instructions) **1**

2 Total area of home **2**

3 Divide line 1 by line 2. Enter the result as a percentage . . . . **3**   %

For daycare facilities not used exclusively for business, go to line 4. All others, go to line 7.

4 Multiply days used for daycare during year by hours used per day **4**   hr.

5 Total hours available for use during the year (365 days x 24 hours) (see instructions) **5**   8,760 hr.

6 Divide line 4 by line 5. Enter the result as a decimal amount . . . **6** .

7 Business percentage. For daycare facilities not used exclusively for business, multiply line 6 by line 3 (enter the result as a percentage). All others, enter the amount from line 3 . . . . . ▶ **7**   %

Part II   Figure Your Allowable Deduction

8 Enter the amount from Schedule C, line 29, **plus** any gain derived from the business use of your home, **minus** any loss from the trade or business not derived from the business use of your home (see instructions) **8**

See instructions for columns (a) and (b) before completing lines 9–22.

	(a) Direct expenses	(b) Indirect expenses
9 Casualty losses (see instructions) **9**		
10 Deductible mortgage interest (see instructions) **10**		
11 Real estate taxes (see instructions) **11**		
12 Add lines 9, 10, and 11 . . . . **12**		

13 Multiply line 12, column (b), by line 7. . . . **13**

14 Add line 12, column (a), and line 13 . . . . **14**

15 Subtract line 14 from line 8. If zero or less, enter -0- **15**

16 Excess mortgage interest (see instructions) . **16**		
17 Excess real estate taxes (see instructions) . . **17**		
18 Insurance **18**		
19 Rent **19**		
20 Repairs and maintenance **20**		
21 Utilities **21**		
22 Other expenses (see instructions). **22**		
23 Add lines 16 through 22 . . . . **23**		

24 Multiply line 23, column (b), by line 7. . . . . **24**

25 Carryover of prior year operating expenses (see instructions) . . **25**

26 Add line 23, column (a), line 24, and line 25 . . . . **26**

27 Allowable operating expenses. Enter the **smaller** of line 15 or line 26 . . . . **27**

28 Limit on excess casualty losses and depreciation. Subtract line 27 from line 15 . . . . . . **28**

29 Excess casualty losses (see instructions) **29**

30 Depreciation of your home from line 42 below **30**

31 Carryover of prior year excess casualty losses and depreciation (see instructions) **31**

32 Add lines 29 through 31 . . . . **32**

33 Allowable excess casualty losses and depreciation. Enter the **smaller** of line 28 or line 32 . . **33**

34 Add lines 14, 27, and 33. . . . . **34**

35 Casualty loss portion, if any, from lines 14 and 33. Carry amount to **Form 4684** (see instructions) **35**

36 **Allowable expenses for business use of your home.** Subtract line 35 from line 34. Enter here and on Schedule C, line 30. If your home was used for more than one business, see instructions ▶ **36**

Part III   Depreciation of Your Home

37 Enter the **smaller** of your home's adjusted basis or its fair market value (see instructions) . . **37**

38 Value of land included on line 37 . . . . **38**

39 Basis of building. Subtract line 38 from line 37 . . . . **39**

40 Business basis of building. Multiply line 39 by line 7. . . . . **40**

41 Depreciation percentage (see instructions). . . . . **41**   %

42 Depreciation allowable (see instructions). Multiply line 40 by line 41. Enter here and on line 30 above **42**

Part IV   Carryover of Unallowed Expenses to 2019

43 Operating expenses. Subtract line 27 from line 26. If less than zero, enter -0- **43**

44 Excess casualty losses and depreciation. Subtract line 33 from line 32. If less than zero, enter -0- **44**

For Paperwork Reduction Act Notice, see your tax return instructions.   Cat. No. 13232M   Form **8829** (2018)

FIGURE 9-1:
Form 8829,
"Expenses for
Business Use of
Your Home."

Courtesy of the Internal Revenue Service

The IRS may be slow, but it eventually finds ways to simplify the tax code. And it often chooses to simplify tax laws by making them more complicated! For example, rather than simplifying Form 8829, the IRS has created a new filing option for some tax filers.

Folks who qualify for claiming a home office deduction (which I explain in the next section) can now do so with the simplified home office deduction. Here are the details of this newer option:

>> Your deduction is limited to $1,500 per year, which is based on a deduction of $5 per square foot for up to a 300-square-foot home office.

>> No depreciation deduction is allowed.

>> You claim your mortgage interest and property tax deductions on Schedule A of Form 1040 (which you can access at www.irs.gov/pub/irs-pdf/f1040sa.pdf).

>> You can't deduct any other actual expenses related to your home.

>> You can't carry forward a loss.

>> You may use either the simplified method or the regular method for any taxable year.

>> You choose a method by using that method on your timely filed, original federal income tax return for the taxable year.

>> After you choose a method for a taxable year, you can't later change to the other method for that same year.

>> If you use the simplified method for one year and use the regular method for any subsequent year, you must calculate the depreciation deduction for the subsequent year using the appropriate optional depreciation table. This is true regardless of whether you used an optional depreciation table for the first year the property was used in business. (See Chapter 8.)

TIP

With the tax bill that took effect in 2018, know that you may only deduct up to $10,000 in state and local taxes including property taxes on Schedule A. And, you may only deduct mortgage interest on new mortgages of up $750,000 of debt. So, if you have more than these amounts, that would argue for you to consider using the "Regular Method."

Every now and then, the IRS actually produces a table or summary that's useful. Table 9-1 is its summary comparing the simplified and regular home office deduction.

TABLE 9-1   The Simplified Option versus the Regular Method

Simplified Option	Regular Method
Deduction for home office use of a portion of a residence allowed only if that portion is *exclusively* used on a *regular basis* for business purposes	Same
Allowable square footage of home used for business (not to exceed 300 square feet)	Percentage of home used for business
Standard $5 per square foot used to determine home business deduction	Actual expenses determined and records maintained
Home-related itemized deductions claimed in full on Schedule A	Home-related itemized deductions apportioned between Schedule A and business schedule (Schedule C or Schedule F)
No depreciation deduction	Depreciation deduction for portion of home used for business
No recapture of depreciation upon sale of home	Recapture of depreciation on gain upon sale of home
Deduction can't exceed gross income from business use of home less business expenses	Same
Amount in excess of gross income limitation may *not* be carried over	Amount in excess of gross income limitation may be carried over
Loss carryover from use of regular method in prior year may *not* be claimed	Loss carryover from use of regular method in prior year may be claimed if gross income test is met in current year

Source: www.irs.gov

Filling Out Form 8829, "Expenses for Business Use of Your Home"

The rule allowing taxpayers to claim a deduction for the portion of their home that they use to perform administrative and management activities was originally designed to help doctors who perform their primary duties in hospitals, salespeople who spend most of their time calling at their customers' offices, and house painters and other tradespeople who spend their time at job sites but use an office (space) in their home to do all their paperwork. Use Form 8829, "Expenses for Business Use of Your Home," to claim the deduction. The following sections explain who can use the form, compare the simplified and original deduction methods, and walk you through the different parts of the form.

Recognizing who can use Form 8829

REMEMBER

You're entitled to claim a home office deduction if you have a dedicated space in your house that you use for your business, even if you use it only to conduct administrative or management activities for your company, provided you have no other office or other place of business where you can perform the same tasks. To qualify as a "home office" for tax purposes, your home office doesn't have to be the place where you meet customers or the principal place where you conduct business.

So a person who simply brings work home is out of luck. So is the person who spreads out work over the dining room table. So long as you eat there, that table isn't dedicated solely to the pursuit of your business.

A carpenter who sets up his computer and desk in a corner of that dining room so he can price jobs and bill his clients has a valid deduction. The reason: because that corner of his dining room is set aside solely for his company's administrative and management activities.

If you use a portion of your home to store inventory or samples, you're also entitled to deduct your home office expenses. Say that you sell cosmetics and use part of your study to store samples. You can deduct expenses related to the portion of your study that you use to store the cosmetics, even if you use the study for other purposes.

You can use Form 8829 whether you're a renter or a homeowner:

>> If you're a renter, filling out Form 8829 correctly means that you first determine your total rent — including insurance, cleaning, and utilities. Then you deduct the portion you use for business. For example, if you rent four rooms and use one room for business, you're entitled to deduct 25 percent of the total. (If the rooms are the same size, you can use this method. If not, you have to figure out the percentage on a square-footage basis.)

>> For homeowners, you compute the total cost of maintaining your home, including depreciation, mortgage interest, taxes, insurance, repairs, and so on. Don't forget to deduct the cost of your cleaning service if your office is cleaned in addition to the rest of the house. Then deduct the percentage you use for business.

Measuring the part of your home used for business

Complete lines 1 through 7 on Form 8829 to determine what portion of your home you used exclusively for your business.

>> **Line 1:** Enter the area, in square feet, of the part of your home that you used for business (for example, 500 square feet).

>> **Line 2:** Enter the total area, in square feet, of your home (for example, 2,500 square feet).

>> **Line 3:** To determine the percentage of your home that you used for business, divide line 1 by line 2 and enter the result as a percentage here. In the preceding example, you'd enter 20 percent (500 ÷ 2,500). Keep this percentage handy; it's the percentage of the expenses for the whole house — such as interest, real estate taxes, depreciation, utility costs, and repairs — that you use on Form 8829 to determine your deduction.

>> **Line 7:** Unless you use your home as a day-care facility, you can skip lines 4 through 6 (which calculate the percentage of your home that you use for your day care) and enter your deduction percentage from line 3 on line 7. If you use your home to provide day-care services, multiply the result from line 6 by the number on line 3 and enter the result here.

Figuring your allowable home office deduction

Lines 8 onward on Form 8829 get into some pretty involved calculations, much more than space allows in this book to fully detail. In this section, I walk you through the basics that apply to most people. (Take a look at IRS Publication 587, "Business Use of Your Home," for additional information.)

>> **Line 8:** Enter the amount from line 29 of your Schedule C (this amount is what you earned after expenses), plus any net gain or loss shown on Form 1040's Schedule D or Form 4797, "Sales of Business Property," that derives from your business. Your home office deduction can't exceed this amount.

>> **Lines 9 through 22, column (a):** Expenses that apply exclusively to your office go in this column. Repairs and maintenance, such as painting your office, are two such items.

>> **Lines 9 through 22, column (b):** Enter your expenses that apply to the entire house on these lines. The IRS refers to them as indirect expenses.

Note: If you rent, the rent that you paid goes on line 18, column (b).

>> **Lines 23 through 35:** It's number-crunching time — enough to make us wonder who came up with this form!

>> **Line 36:** This is your allowable deduction. Carry it over to line 30 on Schedule C.

TIP

If you use part of your residence for business, you can deduct the mortgage interest, real estate taxes, depreciation, insurance, utilities, and repairs related to that part of your house. (You deduct the remainder of your mortgage interest and property taxes, subject to the tax law limits, on Schedule A.) Renters get to deduct their business portion of the rental expenses.

REMEMBER

If you had more home office expenses than you could use last year, don't forget to add the amount you had left over from your prior year's Form 8829, onto line 25 of this year's Form 8829. The same goes for excess casualty losses from your prior year's Form 8829. Enter that amount on line 31.

Determining your home office's depreciation allowance

If you own your home, you also have to apply your home office deduction percentage (from line 7 of Form 8829) to your home's depreciation allowance. This section includes a line-by-line breakdown of the appropriate part on Form 8829.

Line 37: Your home's value

Here's where you compute your depreciation deduction. You get to write off the percentage of your home that you claim as a home office (20 percent in my example from the earlier section "Measuring the part of your home used for business") depending on when you set up your office (see the later section on line 40 instructions). Residential property usually is written off over 27½ years, but because the office is used for business, it's considered business property and has a longer life.

On line 37, enter the smaller of what you paid for your home (including the original and closing costs, as well as any improvements you've made to the property) or its fair market value at the time you first started to use it for business. You don't have to make this comparison every year — only when you started claiming a home office deduction.

Line 38: Land not included

TIP

Because you can't depreciate land, you have to subtract the value of the land that your home sits on from your home's cost so that you calculate the house's net cost. A value of 15 percent for the land is a safe subtraction unless you know for certain what you paid for your building lot, although a higher percentage may make sense in high-cost areas.

Line 39: Basis of building

Subtract line 38 from line 37. This amount is your home's basis after subtracting the value of the land that you can't depreciate.

Line 40: Business portion of your home

Multiply line 39 by your home office deduction percentage from line 7. In my earlier example, that's the 20 percent of the house used for business that you can write off.

Line 41: Depreciation percentage

The depreciation percentage you take for your home office depends on when you established your home office. If you set up your office before May 12, 1993, it's a 31½-year write-off. If you set up your office after May 12, 1993, the write-off is over 39 years. Use Table 9-2 to determine your depreciation percentage. (See Publication 946, "How to Depreciate Property," for more details.)

TABLE 9-2 **Depreciation Percentage for Business Use of Home**

If you first used your home for business . . .	Then the percentage to enter on line 41 is . . .
after May 12, 1993, and before 2012 (except as noted in the following exception),	2.564%.*
after May 12, 1993, and before 1994, and you either started construction or had a binding contract to buy or build that home before May 13, 1993,	the percentage given in Publication 946.
after May 12, 1993, and you stopped using your home for business before the end of the year,	the percentage given in Publication 946 as adjusted by the instructions under *Sale or Other Disposition Before the Recovery Period Ends* in that publication.
after 1986 and before May 13, 1993,	the percentage given in Publication 946.
before 1987,	the percentage given in Publication 534, "Depreciating Property Placed in Service Before 1987."

*__Exception:__ *If the business part of your home is qualified Indian reservation property (as defined in section 168(j)(4), see Publication 946 to figure the depreciation.*

Now, in the very first year you set up your home office, you don't take the full percentage in Table 9-2. See the depreciation tables at www.irs.gov/pub/irs-pdf/i4562.pdf (see the Introduction for the username and password you need).

Line 42: Depreciation allowable

Multiply line 40 by line 41. This number is your depreciation deduction, based on the business use of your home. Enter this amount on lines 42 and 30 of Form 8829.

WARNING

Many people avoid taking depreciation on their homes for a variety of reasons. Some may not understand how depreciation works. For others, the idea of trying to figure out their home's adjusted basis leaves them in tears. Yet others think that, if they depreciate now, they'll have a hard time calculating their gain or loss on the sale of that home down the road. What you may fail to realize is that the IRS deems that your home's value has depreciated whether or not you deduct the depreciation to which you're entitled. When you go to sell that home, you may be required to recapture that depreciation, even if you didn't actually take the deduction as part of your home office deductions on your tax return. (This admittedly esoteric example could occur if you qualify for and take other home office deduction costs on your tax return but don't take the depreciation.)

Carrying over what's left

Keep in mind that you can't take a loss because of the home office deduction. You can, however, carry over an excess deduction amount to another year's tax return.

On lines 43 and 44, compute the amount of your home office deduction that you couldn't deduct. You get to deduct it in future years, provided that you have enough income.

REMEMBER

On Schedule A, don't forget to deduct the balance (in my earlier example, 80 percent) of your total mortgage interest from line 10(b) of Form 8829, and the balance of your total real estate taxes from line 11(b). Your mortgage interest balance goes on line 8 of Schedule A; the real estate taxes balance goes on line 5 of Schedule A.

WARNING

A home office deduction can't produce a loss (exception: you can create a loss to the extent of mortgage interest, property tax, casualty loss, and qualified mortgage insurance premiums). For example, suppose that your business income is $6,000. You have $5,000 in business expenses and $1,500 in home office expenses ($1,000 of which is for the portion of your mortgage interest and real estate tax allocated for the use of the office). First, you deduct the interest and taxes of $1,000, which leaves a balance of $5,000 for possible deductions. Then you deduct $5,000 of business expenses, which brings your business income to zero. You can't deduct the remaining $500 of your home office expenses, but you can carry it over to the next year. If you don't have sufficient income to deduct the $500 next year, you can carry it over again.

Understanding the Downsides to Home Office Deductions

Because taking home office deductions can lower your tax bill, why would you not want to take them? Well, assuming that you may legally take home office deductions and that they actually lower your tax bill, by all means take them. But just be aware that taking these deductions can have some real drawbacks.

In this section, I discuss the increased audit risks for home-based businesses, especially those that regularly lose money, at least on paper for tax purposes. Also, I discuss the arcane-sounding topic of depreciation recapture, which can lead to a larger tax bill when you sell a home for which you've previously taken a home office deduction.

Audit risk and rejection of repeated business losses

According to the IRS, a sideline activity that generates a loss year in and year out isn't a business but a hobby. Specifically, an activity is considered a hobby if it shows a loss for at least three of the past five tax years. (Horse racing, breeding, and so on are considered hobbies if they show losses in at least five of the past seven tax years.)

Certainly, some businesses lose money. But a real business can't afford to do so year after year and still remain in business. Who likes losing money unless the losses are really just a tax deduction front for a hobby?

When the hobby loss rules indicate that you're engaging in a hobby, the IRS will disallow your claiming of the losses. To challenge this ruling, you must convince the IRS that you're seriously attempting to make a profit and run a legitimate business. The IRS will want to see that you're actively marketing your services, building your skills, and accounting for income and expenses. The IRS also will want to see that you aren't having too much fun! When you derive too much pleasure from an activity, in the eyes of the IRS, the activity must not be a real business.

The Tax Cuts and Jobs Act bill, which took effect in 2018, toughened the hobby loss rules further. Specifically, the IRS now requires you to report your revenue from a hobby, but you may not deduct any expenses from that hobby.

WARNING

Unfortunately, some self-anointed financial gurus claim that you can slash or even completely eliminate your tax bill by setting up a sideline business. They say that you can sell your services while doing something you enjoy. The problem, they argue, is that — as a regular wage earner who receives a paycheck from an employer — you can't write off many of your other (that is, personal) expenses. These hucksters usually promise to show you the secrets of tax reduction if you shell out far too many bucks for their audiotapes and notebooks of inside information.

"Start a small business for fun, profit, and huge tax deductions," one financial book trumpets, adding that, "The tax benefits alone are worth starting a small business." A seminar company that offers a course on "How to Write a Book on Anything in 2 Weeks . . . or Less!" also offers a tax course titled "How to Have Zero Taxes Deducted from Your Paycheck." This tax seminar tells you how to solve your tax problems: "If you have a sideline business or would like to start one, you're eligible to have little or no taxes taken from your pay".

Suppose that you're interested in photography. You like to take pictures when you go on vacation. These supposed tax experts tell you to set up a photography business and start deducting all your photography-related expenses: airfare, film, utility bills, rent for your "home darkroom," and restaurant meals with potential clients (that is, your friends). Before you know it, you've wiped out most of your taxes.

Sounds too good to be true, right? It is. Your business spending must be for the legitimate purpose of generating an income.

REMEMBER

What's the bottom line? You need to operate a legitimate business for the purpose of generating income and profits — not tax deductions. If you're thinking that it's worth the risk of taking tax losses for your hobby, year after year, because you won't get caught unless you're audited, better think again. The IRS audits an extraordinarily large number of small businesses that show regular losses.

Depreciation recapture when selling a home with previous home office deductions

If you've taken depreciation for your home office deduction after May 6, 1997, when you go to sell your home, you'll have to pay tax through *depreciation recapture.* Specifically, you'll owe tax at the rate of 25 percent on the amount of depreciation taken for your home office.

But if you qualify for the home office deduction, this shouldn't be a bad thing to have happen to you because the value of those deductions over the years should far exceed the cost of the depreciation recapture.

Chapter **10**

Estimated Taxes, Self-Employment Taxes, and Other Common Forms

I f you're self-employed or running a small business, you have plenty to keep you busy each day, week, month, and year. Adding employees to the mix increases the complexity of what you're doing.

For tax purposes, when you're running your own show, you need to submit estimated income taxes each quarter during the year. When you hire employees, you need to submit the taxes that you're required to withhold from their paychecks. This chapter tackles both of these issues.

Likewise, when it comes time to file your annual income tax return, you need to file forms to calculate your self-employment taxes (for Social Security and Medicare, for example). And you may want to contribute to a health savings account (HSA) for yourself, your employees, or simply to allow your employees to tap into this valuable benefit. Both of these topics are addressed here as well.

Form 1040-ES: Estimated Tax for Individuals

The U.S. tax system actually has a simple rule that most people don't think about: It's a pay-as-you-owe system, not a pay-at-the-end-of-the-year one. That's why *withholdings* (having your taxes deducted from your paycheck and sent directly to the government) are great — what you don't see, you don't miss, and your tax payments are periodically withheld and submitted for you throughout the tax year.

If you're self-employed or have taxable income, such as retirement benefits, that isn't subject to withholding, you need to make quarterly estimated tax payments on Form 1040-ES (which you can find at www.irs.gov/pub/irs-pdf/f1040es.pdf).

WARNING

When you don't pay your taxes on your income as you earn it, you may get hit with penalties and interest when you do pay them, on or before April 15 of the following year. Some small business owners are constantly taking current year's cash flow to pay last year's taxes and never quite catch up. In some cases, it can help to make payments more often than quarterly. Some business owners take a fixed percentage out of cash receipts and transfer that money to a separate account to make sure they have the money needed for their estimated tax payments.

You can avoid paying a penalty on tax underpayments if you follow these guidelines: You must pay in at least 90 percent of your current year's tax, either in withholdings or in estimated tax payments, as you earn your income, or you can use the safe harbor method (see the next section).

Comparing the safe harbor method to the 90 percent rule

If your income isn't constant or regular, you may choose to follow the so-called *safe harbor rule* and pay 100 percent of last year's tax on an equal and regular basis during this current tax year. This method is simpler than it sounds. If, for example, you have a $3,000 tax liability showing on your most recent year's Form 1040, you may make four quarterly payments of $750 during this current tax year. Provided that you do that, you won't owe any penalty for a current year tax underpayment, even if your current year's tax liability is substantially more — such as $15,000.

Because the safe harbor rule is so easy, you can simply choose to only use that when calculating your estimated taxes. Note, though, you do still have to pay the balance of tax due by the return filing date (April 15) to avoid late payment penalties and interest.

In comparison to the safe harbor rule, the 90 percent rule is tricky to calculate. In paying 90 percent of your current year's tax, you need to adjust your payment amounts every quarter during the year that your income rises or falls. Using this method leads to increased paperwork. Still, because it's one of your tax payment options, I explain how to calculate your estimated taxes using the 90 percent rule in the following section.

WARNING

If your current (prior) year's income is (was) more than $150,000, you have to make estimated tax payments equal to 110 percent of your previous year's tax to escape an underestimating penalty if your current year's total federal income tax bill turns out to be substantially more than your previous year's bill. So long as you do this, even if you end up paying a sizable tax bill on April 15, you won't have to pay any penalty or interest on the remaining balance due, despite the fact that your estimated tax payments were less than 90 percent of your tax. (*Note:* This rule doesn't apply to farmers or fishermen.)

Completing and filing your Form 1040-ES

You need to accompany your estimated tax payments with Form 1040-ES (payment voucher), "Estimated Tax for Individuals." This small form requires only your name, address, Social Security number, and the amount that you're paying. For your current year estimated federal income tax payments, make sure that you use the current tax year's 1040-ES.

When mailing in payment with your form 1040-ES, make your checks payable to the "United States Treasury," making sure your name, Social Security number, and the words "2019 Form 1040-ES" (or whatever the current tax year is) are clearly written on the face of the check, and then mail to the relevant address listed in the Form 1040-ES booklet.

TIP

For each tax year, quarterly estimated tax payments are due on April 15, June 15, and September 15 of the current calendar year and January 15 of the next calendar year. (If the 15th falls on a weekend, the actual due date is the next business day, which could be the 16th or 17th of a month.) If you file your completed current year's tax return and pay any taxes due by January 31, you can choose not to pay your fourth quarter estimate (which is due January 15) without incurring any penalty.

If you're not sure how much you need to pay in estimates, Form 1040-ES also contains instructions and a worksheet to help you calculate your current year's estimated tax payments. If you're using the safe harbor method to calculate your estimated tax requirements (see the preceding section) and you have nothing withheld from any source, you can skip the worksheet, take the total taxes from your last year's Form 1040, divide it by 4, and drop that number into each of the vouchers. You're done! Now you just need to remember to pay your quarterly bills.

If, on the other hand, some, but not all, of your income has taxes withheld on it or you want to only pay 90 percent of your current year's tax liability upfront (maybe because your income this tax year is going to be considerably less than it was in the previous tax year), you have to complete the worksheet that comes in the Form 1040-ES packet to calculate your estimated payment amounts.

The Estimated Tax Worksheet contained in the Form 1040-ES packet is a preview of your upcoming year's tax return, or what you think that tax return will show. On it you include your adjusted gross income (AGI), your deductions, whether you itemize or take the standard deduction, any credits you're entitled to, and any additional taxes you may be subject to. The worksheet can help you calculate the minimum amount you must pay during the current tax year to avoid paying penalties and interest when it comes time to file your annual tax return.

REMEMBER

You're only estimating when you're making these quarterly tax payments. If your circumstances change and your income rises or falls, you can adjust any payments you haven't yet made. After you make a payment, though, you're stuck with it, and you need to wait until you file your income tax return for the year before you can claim a refund.

WARNING

Don't include your first estimated tax payment for a new tax year with your previous year's Form 1040 or Form 1040A. Instead, mail it separately to the address shown in the instructions for Form 1040-ES. The IRS routes different types of payments to different post office boxes to help eliminate confusion on its end, and a payment sent to the wrong address may be more likely to be credited against the wrong year.

TIP

If you need an extension of time to file your most recent tax year's Form 1040 and you ordinarily make estimated tax payments, you can skip making a separate first quarter estimated tax payment for the next (upcoming) tax year. In-stead, add the amount of your first quarter estimate to what you think you still owe on your tax return, and then pay that resulting balance due with your extension. Place the total of your projected most recent tax year's liability and your first quarter estimate on line 4 of Form 4868, "Application for Automatic Extension of Time to File U.S. Individual Income Tax Return," and pay the balance shown on line 6. (Find this form at `www.irs.gov/pub/irs-pdf/f4868.pdf`.) If your most recent tax year's projections are correct, apply the overpayment (which should equal what you would have paid with your first quarter Form 1040-ES) to your next year's tax return. If your projections are off, though, and your most recent year's tax liability is higher than you thought it would be, you've protected yourself from owing penalties and interest on the underpayment of your tax. Although you may owe a small penalty for underpaying your next year's estimates, it will be minor compared to the penalty and interest you'd owe on your most recent year's tax return.

Keeping Current on Your Employees' (and Your Own) Tax Withholding

When you're self-employed, you're responsible for the accurate and timely filing of all your income taxes. Without an employer and a payroll department to handle the paperwork for withholding taxes on a regular schedule, you need to make estimated tax payments on a quarterly basis (I discuss how to do so earlier in this chapter).

When you have employees, you also need to withhold taxes on their incomes from each paycheck they receive. And you must make timely payments to the IRS and the appropriate state authorities.

In this section, I cover what you need to do for yourself and your employees.

TIP

Falling behind in paying taxes ruins some small businesses. When you hire employees, for example, you're particularly vulnerable to tax land mines. If you aren't going to keep current on taxes for yourself and your employees, hire a payroll company or tax advisor who can help you jump through the necessary tax hoops. Payroll companies and tax advisors are there for a reason, so use them selectively. They take care of all the tax filings for you, and if they mess up, you can hold them accountable. Check with a tax advisor you trust for the names of reputable payroll companies in your area (flip to Chapter 13 for info on finding and interviewing tax advisors).

Form W-4 for employee withholding

If an employee owes a bundle to the IRS when it comes time to complete his annual federal income tax return, chances are he isn't withholding enough tax from his salary and regular paychecks. Unless that employee doesn't mind paying a lot on April 15, he needs to adjust his withholding to avoid interest and penalties if he can't pay what he owes when it's due.

TIP

Relying on the worksheet on Form W-4 to accurately calculate the correct number of exemptions an employee should be claiming would be easy, but it's not that simple. Instead, employees should check out the IRS website (www.irs.gov), which has a nifty W-4 calculator that they can use at any time during the year to make sure they're having enough tax withheld from their paychecks. The calculator is easy to use and gives a reasonably accurate picture of how much they'll owe (or have refunded) next April 15. To access this calculator, click the Tools tab, and then click "IRS Withholding Calculator" on the next page. It's that easy!

Tax withholding and filings for employees

In addition to federal and state income taxes, you must withhold and send in Social Security and any state or locally mandated payroll taxes. You must also annually issue W-2s for each employee and 1099-MISCs for each independent contractor paid $600 or more.

To discover all the rules and regulations of withholding and submitting taxes from employees' paychecks, ask the IRS for Form 941, "Employer's Quarterly Federal Tax Return." Once a year, you also need to complete Form 940, "Employer's Annual Federal Unemployment (FUTA) Tax Return," for unemployment insurance payments to the feds. Also check to see whether your state has its own annual or quarterly unemployment insurance reporting requirements. And, unless you're lucky enough to live in a state with no income taxes, don't forget to get your state's estimated income tax package.

TIP

If your business has a part-time or seasonal employee and the additional burden of filing Form 941 quarterly, the IRS has just made the paperwork a tad easier. Now, you may be able to file Form 944, "Employer's Annual Federal Tax Return," if your tax withholding on behalf of employees doesn't exceed $1,000 for the year (which translates to about $4,000 in wages). If you qualify, you need to file only once each year. If you think you may qualify, call the IRS at 800-829-0115 or visit www.irs.gov. If you do qualify, the IRS will send you something in writing.

HOUSEHOLD EMPLOYMENT TAXES: SCHEDULE H

If you have household workers (including housekeepers, baby sitters, yard-care workers, and nannies) who earned more than $2,100 from you in 2018, you may be required to pay employment taxes for them — that's the employer's half of the Social Security and Medicare taxes, plus federal unemployment (FUTA) taxes. If your workers meet the employee test, fortunately, you don't need to figure out the ordinary employment tax forms, which need to be filed either monthly or quarterly; instead, if you qualify, you may use Schedule H to calculate what you owe.

Prior to the so-called *nanny tax,* which is retroactive to January 1, 1994, household employers had to file quarterly reports and pay Social Security taxes if they paid household help more than $50 in a quarter. Now you don't have to withhold and pay Social Security taxes unless you pay a domestic worker more than $2,100 during the year.

Here are two important provisions of the nanny tax that you should be aware of:

- You're not required to pay Social Security tax for domestic employees under the age of 18 (for any portion of the year), regardless of how much you pay them. The exemption doesn't apply if the principal occupation of the employee is household employment. So, you're off the hook for payroll taxes for your 12-year-old mother's helper, or the 16-year-old down the street who babysits occasionally.

- You don't have to file quarterly payroll tax forms. You can pay any Social Security, Medicare, or federal unemployment (FUTA) taxes, and income taxes that you choose to withhold, when you file your return in April.

If your withholding or estimated tax payments aren't enough to cover the Social Security, Medicare, and FUTA taxes that you owe, the IRS assesses a penalty. So, make sure that you pay in enough.

Although the nanny tax simplifies your IRS filings, you still have to keep filing quarterly state unemployment tax returns, unless your state elects to conform to the IRS method of filing annually.

Schedule H looks more formidable than it really is. Here's the lowdown on what it's really about:

- If you paid your household help less than $2,100 in 2018 and didn't withhold any income tax, you don't have to file this form.

(continued)

(continued)

- If you paid any one household employee less than $2,100 during 2018 but you withheld federal income tax, you need to fill out only Part I, beginning with line 5. Note that you also have to furnish your employee with a W-2 stating the amount that you paid and the amount of Social Security, Medicare, and income tax that you withheld. Withholding income tax is optional on your part. One further chore: You have to file a copy of the W-2 and Form W-3 (if more than one W-2 is being filed) with the Social Security Administration by February 29 (online filing deadline is March 31). Your employees must get their W-2s by January 31.

- If you had one or more household employees in 2018 and paid wages totaling $1,000 or more in any calendar quarter to all of your household employees, you have to fill out Parts II and III of Schedule H. Not only do you owe Social Security and Medicare taxes, you also have to pay FUTA tax.

Check with your state tax department to find out whether you have to register and pay state unemployment tax on a quarterly basis. Also check with your insurance broker to see whether your homeowner's insurance covers domestic employees or whether you need a separate workers' compensation policy. Don't play fast and loose in this area. If your household worker gets hurt or injured, you may have to pay a bundle if you don't have insurance coverage.

The immigration law requires that you verify that every new employee is eligible to work in the United States. You do this by completing Form I-9, "Employment Eligibility Verification." You can get this form from the U.S. Citizenship and Immigration Services' website at www.uscis.gov. You don't file this form — just hang on to it in case someone from Immigration Services comes calling.

Schedule SE: Self-Employment Tax

If you earn part or all of your income from being self-employed, use Schedule SE to figure another tax that you owe — the Social Security tax and Medicare tax.

>> The first $128,400 of your self-employment earnings is taxed at 12.4 percent (this is the Social Security tax part) for tax year 2018.

>> The Medicare tax doesn't have any limit; it's 2.9 percent of your total self-employment earnings. For amounts of $128,400 or less, the combined rate is 15.3 percent (adding the two taxes together), and for amounts above $128,400, the rate is 2.9 percent (see the exception in the following paragraph).

If your self-employment earnings are under $400, you aren't subject to self-employment tax.

> **Note:** Effective with tax year 2013, to help pay for federally mandated health insurance, higher income earners pay a greater Medicare tax rate. The additional Medicare tax amount is 0.9 percent on earned individual income of more than $200,000 (married couples filing jointly pay the additional tax on amounts above $250,000).

Your self-employment earnings may be your earnings reported on the following:

>> Schedule C

>> Schedule C-EZ; I discuss Schedules C and C-EZ in Chapter 8

>> Schedule K-1, Form 1065 (box 14, code A) or Form 1065-B (box 9, code J1); use Form 1065-B if you're a partner in a firm

>> Schedule F or Schedule K-1, box 14, code A (Form 1065) if you're a farmer

>> Form 1040; your self-employment income that you reported as miscellaneous income (see Chapter 7 for more about Form 1040)

The following sections explain how to use Schedule SE to pay self-employment tax for Social Security and Medicare. Check out the 2018 version of this form in Figure 10-1 (and find the most recent version at www.irs.gov/pub/irs-pdf/f1040sse.pdf).

Choosing a version of Schedule SE: Short or long?

Wouldn't it be nice if Schedule SE simply said, "If you're self-employed, use this form to compute how much Social Security and Medicare tax you have to pay"? Paying this tax ensures that you'll be entitled to Social Security and Medicare when you're old and gray.

You have three choices when filling out this form:

>> **Section A — Short Schedule SE:** This section is the shortest and easiest one to complete — six lines. But if you were also employed on a salaried basis and had Social Security tax withheld from your wages, you'll pay more self-employment tax than required if you use the short schedule. Moonlighters beware.

>> **Section B — Long Schedule SE:** Use this part of the form if you received wages and are self-employed on the side. Suppose that you have wages of $40,000 and have $90,000 in earnings from your own small business. If you use the

Short Schedule SE, you'll end up paying Social Security tax on $145,000 when the maximum amount of combined earnings that you're required to pay on is only $128,400. You pay Medicare tax, however, on the entire $145,000.

This section isn't all that formidable. Make use of it so you don't end up paying more Social Security tax than you have to.

REMEMBER

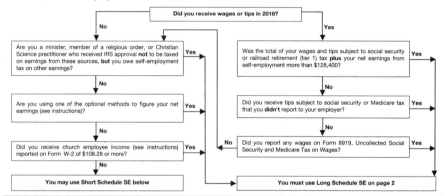

FIGURE 10-1:
Schedule SE.

Name of person with **self-employment** income (as shown on Form 1040 or Form 1040NR)	Social security number of person with **self-employment** income ▶

Section B—Long Schedule SE

Part I   **Self-Employment Tax**

Note: If your only income subject to self-employment tax is **church employee income**, see instructions. Also see instructions for the definition of church employee income.

A   If you are a minister, member of a religious order, or Christian Science practitioner **and** you filed Form 4361, but you had $400 or more of **other** net earnings from self-employment, check here and continue with Part I . . . . ▶ ☐

1a	Net farm profit or (loss) from Schedule F, line 34, and farm partnerships, Schedule K-1 (Form 1065), box 14, code A. **Note:** Skip lines 1a and 1b if you use the farm optional method (see instructions)	**1a**	
b	If you received social security retirement or disability benefits, enter the amount of Conservation Reserve Program payments included on Schedule F, line 4b, or listed on Schedule K-1 (Form 1065), box 20, code AH	**1b**	( )
2	Net profit or (loss) from Schedule C, line 31; Schedule C-EZ, line 3; Schedule K-1 (Form 1065), box 14, code A (other than farming); and Schedule K-1 (Form 1065-B), box 9, code J1. Ministers and members of religious orders, see instructions for types of income to report on this line. See instructions for other income to report. **Note:** Skip this line if you use the nonfarm optional method (see instructions)	**2**	
3	Combine lines 1a, 1b, and 2	**3**	
4a	If line 3 is more than zero, multiply line 3 by 92.35% (0.9235). Otherwise, enter amount from line 3	**4a**	
	Note: If line 4a is less than $400 due to Conservation Reserve Program payments on line 1b, see instructions.		
b	If you elect one or both of the optional methods, enter the total of lines 15 and 17 here . .	**4b**	
c	Combine lines 4a and 4b. If less than $400, **stop;** you don't owe self-employment tax. **Exception:** If less than $400 and you had **church employee income**, enter -0- and continue ▶	**4c**	
5a	Enter your **church employee income** from Form W-2. See instructions for definition of church employee income **5a**		
b	Multiply line 5a by 92.35% (0.9235). If less than $100, enter -0-	**5b**	
6	Add lines 4c and 5b	**6**	
7	Maximum amount of combined wages and self-employment earnings subject to social security tax or the 6.2% portion of the 7.65% railroad retirement (tier 1) tax for 2018	**7**	128,400 00
8a	Total social security wages and tips (total of boxes 3 and 7 on Form(s) W-2) and railroad retirement (tier 1) compensation. If $128,400 or more, skip lines 8b through 10, and go to line 11 **8a**		
b	Unreported tips subject to social security tax (from Form 4137, line 10) **8b**		
c	Wages subject to social security tax (from Form 8919, line 10) **8c**		
d	Add lines 8a, 8b, and 8c	**8d**	
9	Subtract line 8d from line 7. If zero or less, enter -0- here and on line 10 and go to line 11 ▶	**9**	
10	Multiply the **smaller** of line 6 or line 9 by 12.4% (0.124)	**10**	
11	Multiply line 6 by 2.9% (0.029)	**11**	
12	**Self-employment tax.** Add lines 10 and 11. Enter here and on **Schedule 4 (Form 1040), line 57,** or **Form 1040NR, line 55**	**12**	
13	**Deduction for one-half of self-employment tax.** Multiply line 12 by 50% (0.50). Enter the result here and on **Schedule 1 (Form 1040), line 27,** or **Form 1040NR, line 27** . **13**		

Part II   **Optional Methods To Figure Net Earnings** (see instructions)

Farm Optional Method. You may use this method **only** if **(a)** your gross farm income[1] wasn't more than $7,920, **or (b)** your net farm profits[2] were less than $5,717.

14	Maximum income for optional methods	**14**	5,280 00
15	Enter the **smaller** of: two-thirds (2/3) of gross farm income[1] (not less than zero) or $5,280. Also include this amount on line 4b above	**15**	

Nonfarm Optional Method. You may use this method **only** if **(a)** your net nonfarm profits[3] were less than $5,717 and also less than 72.189% of your gross nonfarm income,[4] **and (b)** you had net earnings from self-employment of at least $400 in 2 of the prior 3 years. **Caution:** You may use this method no more than five times.

16	Subtract line 15 from line 14	**16**	
17	Enter the **smaller** of: two-thirds (2/3) of gross nonfarm income[4] (not less than zero) **or** the amount on line 16. Also include this amount on line 4b above	**17**	

[1] From Sch. F, line 9, and Sch. K-1 (Form 1065), box 14, code B.
[2] From Sch. F, line 34, and Sch. K-1 (Form 1065), box 14, code A—minus the amount you would have entered on line 1b had you not used the optional method.
[3] From Sch. C, line 31; Sch. C-EZ, line 3; Sch. K-1 (Form 1065), box 14, code A; and Sch. K-1 (Form 1065-B), box 9, code J1.
[4] From Sch. C, line 7; Sch. C-EZ, line 1; Sch. K-1 (Form 1065), box 14, code C; and Sch. K-1 (Form 1065-B), box 9, code J2.

FIGURE 10-1: continued

Schedule SE (Form 1040) 2018

Courtesy of the Internal Revenue Service

>> **Part II — Optional methods to figure net earnings:** If your self-employment earnings are less than $5,280 (for 2018), you can elect to pay Social Security tax on at least $5,280, so you'll build up Social Security (and Medicare) credit for when you reach retirement age. You may do this for up to five years.

You may be able to use Section A of Schedule SE (the short schedule) if your only income subject to Social Security and Medicare tax is self-employment income. If you're self-employed and also are employed by someone else, you have to use the long form (Section B); otherwise, you may end up paying more Social Security than you're required to because Social Security tax has already been withheld from your salary. To prevent this disaster, enter the total of the amounts from boxes 3 and 7 of your W-2 on line 8a of page 2 of Schedule SE. (And if you file Form 4137, "Social Security and Medicare Tax on Unreported Tip Income," enter the amount from line 9 of that form on line 8b of Schedule SE.)

Half of your self-employment tax is deductible. Complete Schedule SE and note the following: The amount on line 5 of Schedule SE is the amount of tax that you have to pay (on the long form, it's line 12); you carry it over to Form 1040 (line 56) and add it to your income tax that's due. Enter half of what you have to pay — the amount on line 6 of Schedule SE (that's line 13 of the long form) — on Form 1040 (line 27).

Completing the Short Schedule SE

Here's the lowdown on completing Section A — Short Schedule SE:

>> **Line 1:** If you're not a farmer, you can skip this line. If farming is your game, enter the amount from line 34 of Schedule F or box 14, Code A, Form 1065, Schedule K-1 for farm partnerships.

>> **Line 2:** Enter the total of the amounts from line 31, Schedule C (line 3, Schedule C-EZ) and box 9, Code J1, Form 1065-B, Schedule K-1 (for partnerships). This is how each partner pays his or her Social Security and Medicare tax. You may also have to pay Social Security and Medicare tax on the miscellaneous income reported on line 21 of Form 1040. This would include income such as from directors' fees, finders' fees, and commissions.

Note: The following aren't subject to self-employment tax: jury duty, notary public fees, forgiveness of a debt even if you owe tax on it, rental income, executor's fees (only if you're an ordinary person, and not an attorney, an accountant, or a banker, who may ordinarily act in this capacity), prizes and awards, lottery winnings, and gambling winnings — unless gambling is your occupation.

>> **Line 3:** A breeze. Add lines 1 and 2.

>> **Line 4:** Multiply line 3 by 92.35 percent (0.9235). Why? If you were employed, your employer would get to deduct its share of the Social Security tax that it would have to pay, and so do you.

>> **Line 5:** If line 4 is $128,400 or less (for tax year 2018), multiply line 4 by 15.3 percent (0.153) and enter that amount on line 56 of Form 1040. For example, if line 4 is $10,000, multiply it by 15.3 percent, and you get $1,530.

If line 4 is more than $128,400, multiply that amount by 2.9 percent (0.029) and add that amount to $15,922. (This is the maximum Social Security tax that you're required to pay.) For example, if line 4 is $140,000, multiply that amount by 0.029 (2.9 percent is your Medicare tax), which comes to $4,060. Now add your Medicare tax ($4,060) to your Social Security tax ($15,922) for a grand total of $19,982. Enter $19,982 on line 56 of Form 1040. (**Note:** You get to use cents on Schedule SE if you so desire, but the IRS wants you to use the whole dollar method on Form 1040.)

>> **Line 6:** Multiply line 5 by 50 percent (0.5). You can deduct this amount on line 27 of your 1040.

Form 8889: Health Savings Accounts (HSAs)

Health savings accounts (HSAs) allow people to put money away on a tax-advantaged basis to pay for healthcare-related expenses. This section explains how they work and the tax form — Form 8889 — that you must file with the IRS to claim an HSA deduction for contributions. (Check out the most recent version of this form at www.irs.gov/pub/irs-pdf/f8889.pdf.)

Understanding how HSAs work and who can use them

Money contributed to an HSA is tax-deductible, and investment earnings compound without tax and aren't taxed upon withdrawal so long as you use the funds to pay for eligible healthcare costs. So, unlike a retirement account, HSAs are actually triple tax-free!

The list of eligible expenses is generally quite broad — surprisingly so in fact. You can use HSA money to pay for out-of-pocket medical costs not covered by insurance, prescription drugs, dental care (including braces), vision care, vitamins, psychologist fees, and smoking cessation programs, among other expenses. IRS Publication 502 details permissible expenses.

Now, some folks think that it's not worth contributing to an HSA if the money won't be left in the account for long because of current medical expenses. I strongly disagree with this perspective because simply passing money through the account before paying medical expenses gains you the highly valuable upfront tax break. For example, suppose you have $1,000 in medical expenses currently (for an office visit and diagnostic test). By contributing the $1,000 to your HSA, if you're in a moderate tax bracket, you could easily save yourself about $300 in income taxes.

Most insurance premiums aren't eligible for being paid with HSA money, but some are. According to the IRS, you may "treat premiums for long-term care coverage, healthcare coverage while you receive unemployment benefits, or healthcare continuation coverage required under any federal law as qualified medical expenses for HSAs." Also, if you have a balance in your account at age 65, you can use that money to reimburse for Medicare costs.

To be eligible to contribute to an HSA, you must participate in a high-deductible health plan that has a deductible of at least $1,350 for individuals and $2,700 for families for tax year 2018. The plan must have a maximum out-of-pocket limit of no more than $6,650 for individuals and $13,300 for families for 2018. Ask health insurers which policies they offer are HSA-compatible.

The maximum amount that you may contribute to an HSA is $3,450 for singles and $6,900 for families in 2018. (Those age 55 or older may make an additional $1,000 "catch-up contribution.") All these dollar limits and amounts increase annually with the rate of medical inflation.

Employers with fewer than 50 employees can offer HSAs. Self-employed folks can use them as well. Anyone (so long as you aren't covered by Medicare) who has an HAS-compatible policy may have an HSA.

Most HSAs require that some amount of money ($1,000, for example) be invested in a safe option like a money fund or savings account that is accessed with a debit card or checks that enable you to pay for medical expenses. Many HSAs offer a menu of investments — typically mutual funds. So, when comparing HSAs, you should compare the quality of those offerings.

Also, be sure to examine fees, which can really add up on some HSAs. In addition to the fees of the offered funds, beware of load fees and maintenance fees of about $5 per month (which may be waived for regular automatic investments or once you meet a certain minimum).

TIP

So far, mostly banks and brokerages linked with banks are offering HSAs. Among the HSAs that I've examined, ones worth considering are offered by UMB Bank (866-520-4472) and HealthEquity (866-346-5800).

Investment companies have held off on offering HSAs themselves until they're convinced that the market for them is large enough to make it worth their while. HSAs have also found themselves in the political cross hairs in Congressional debates and possible regulatory changes. So long as there's a division in power in Congress, an erosion of HSA tax benefits is unlikely.

Completing Form 8889

Form 8889, "Health Savings Accounts," is one of those IRS forms that looks much worse than it actually is, at least from the standpoint of the actual experience of most folks who get stuck filling it out. That said, for a minority of folks, Form 8889 can be cumbersome and time consuming.

If you're contributing to an HSA, you generally need only concern yourself with Part I of the form. Here are the primary issues you need to address in this part of the form:

>> **Line 1:** This is where you indicate whether your health insurance covers just you or your family.

>> **Line 2:** Enter the amount of your HSA contributions (and those made on your behalf).

>> **Line 3:** This is where you enter your maximum allowable HSA contribution. Note that the maximum is more for those age 55 and older at the end of the most recent tax year (see line 7).

>> **Line 4:** If you have one of the older Archer MSAs, you need to enter the amount, if any, that you and your employer contributed to said account during the tax year, as that will reduce your allowable HSA contribution.

If you took any distributions from an HSA during the tax year, you address that in Part II of this form. You must track and report your distributions so that the IRS gets the taxes owed on them.

Finally, in Part III, if you failed to maintain a high-deductible health plan for the entire tax year, you may owe additional tax, which is determined and calculated here.

3 Getting Help

Dealing with audits and notices isn't pleasant, but it's important! Understand the IRS notice process, study different types of notices, get a handle on audits, and figure out how to correct mistakes — both yours and those made by the IRS.

Use tax software and advice guides, among other resources, to research tax strategies and rules.

Distinguish the different tax advisors and preparers you can hire — such as enrolled agents and certified public accountants — and prepare a list of questions to ask in interviews.

IN THIS CHAPTER

» **Deciphering IRS notices**

» **Understanding the different types of assessment and non-assessment notices**

» **Dealing with audits successfully**

» **Fixing IRS errors that affect you**

» **Righting mistakes that you've made**

Chapter **11**

Dealing with Notices and Audits

very year the Internal Revenue Service (IRS) issues millions of notices, the majority of which claim that the taxpayer receiving said notice owes the IRS more money. Sometimes, the IRS even notifies that you actually overpaid and that it found a change in your return that's in your favor!

In this chapter, I explain what's on an IRS notice and help you make sense of assessment and non-assessment notices you may have received. I also discuss the dreaded IRS audit, including how to best handle one. Finally, I discuss how to fix errors that the IRS makes and those that you've made.

REMEMBER

One of the biggest headaches in dealing with the IRS is that the agency can be big and impersonal. When you're dealing with the IRS, remember the three P's — promptness, persistence, and patience! Don't become discouraged when matters move more slowly than you'd like. Keep in mind that although you may feel like the IRS is a huge, unfriendly bureaucracy, it's actually filled with individuals who may be able to help you, if you let them. "I shall overcome" should be your motto.

Understanding the Basics You'll Find on an IRS Notice

If you're like most taxpayers, you'll look at an IRS notice, see a dollar figure, and decide it's too painful to look at again. Don't panic! Do yourself a favor and take a peek at it again; the dollar figure may be a refund — but it isn't likely.

REMEMBER

Don't think you can ignore the folks at the IRS. The IRS can and will use any and all means within its extensive arsenal to collect the tax it determines you owe. If you disregard the IRS, don't expect the IRS just to go away. The computers at the service centers won't tolerate being ignored. Maybe they hooked you by error, but there's no satisfying them until they reel you in, or until you convince the IRS that the computer made an error. To do so, you must respond promptly and courteously to a notice; robots or monsters aren't on the other end of the telephone, just IRS employees trying to do their jobs. Otherwise, you severely prejudice your appeal rights and end up with no recourse but to pay the tax and forget the whole thing — or to pay the tax and then try to get your money back.

Every notice contains the following:

>> Date of the notice

>> Taxpayer identification number — your Social Security number or employer identification number for your business (make sure that it's yours)

>> The form number you filed — 1040, 1040A, or 1040EZ (all described in Chapter 7, by the way)

>> Tax period — the year

>> A control number (evidently your name, address, and Social Security number aren't enough)

>> Penalties charged

>> Interest charged

>> Amount owed

>> Tax payments you made

Both you and the IRS can track any missing tax payment made by check by a long series of numbers printed on the back of your check. The first 14 numbers make up the IRS's control or tracking number; the next 9 numbers are your Social Security number, followed by a 4-letter abbreviation of your name. The next 4 numbers are the year the payment was applied (1812 means the year ending December 2018), and the last 6 digits record the date on which the IRS received your payment.

Unfortunately, not every notice provides all the information necessary to precisely determine what went wrong — IRS notices are famous for their lack of clarity. All is not lost if you receive an IRS notice and, after careful inspection, you still don't understand it. Call the IRS at the telephone number indicated on the notice or at 800-829-1040 and request a record of your tax account information, which takes about seven to ten days to arrive. This printout lists every transaction posted to your account. With this additional information, you should be able to understand why you were sent the notice. If the transcript of your tax account fails to clarify why you received the notice in the first place, contact the IRS and ask it to provide a better or more exact explanation.

Assessing Assessment Notices

Assessment notices usually inform you of one of the following situations:

>> You weren't given credit for all the tax payments that you claim you made.

>> You made a math error or used the wrong tax table or form.

>> You filed a return but neglected to pay what you owed.

>> You agreed to the results of a tax examination.

>> You owe a penalty.

The IRS uses one of the CP series forms to inform you that your refund is being reduced or eliminated. This may be the case if your refund is being applied to other taxes you owe, which is announced on Form CP49, for example. Or it may be the result of one of the reasons from the preceding list. The IRS also intercepts refunds to pay nontax governmental debts, such as defaults on student loans and nonpayment of child support.

In addition to the CP series notices, you may receive other correspondence from the IRS. If you've failed to pay your income taxes in the past or you haven't given your correct Social Security number to your bank, brokerage, partnership, trust or estate, or any other entity that is paying you income, the IRS may require these payers to withhold income tax from any payments they make to you (I describe this notice later in this chapter).

The IRS also sends a general assessment notice to assess a penalty for filing or paying late, failing to make timely estimated tax payments, failing to report all your income, or overstating credits or deductions on your return. I discuss some of these situations in the following sections.

Income verification and proposed changes to your tax return: Forms CP2501 and CP2000

The IRS sends you a Form CP2501 when information on your income tax returns doesn't match information it has received about you from a third party on either a Form W-2 (wages and tips), Form 1098 (mortgage interest), or Form 1099 of any variety (which covers most other types of income). Don't believe that just because the notice comes from the IRS that it's necessarily correct.

Income verification notices ask you to explain differences between the income and deductions you claim on your return and the income and deductions reported to the IRS by banks, your employer, and brokerage firms. The IRS assumes that the information it collects from these third parties is correct and that you've made a mistake on your return.

Often, the IRS doesn't bother sending an income verification notice; it simply assumes that the information about you in its computer system is correct and sends Form CP2000, "Notice of Proposed Adjustment for Underpayment/Overpayment." This form cuts right to the chase; it assumes the information that the government received regarding your income and that doesn't appear on your return is correct, no questions asked. The IRS bills you for penalties, interest, and additional tax. (You also get this notice when you ignore an income verification request.) CP2000 proposes changes but includes a response form where you can explain why the notice is incorrect.

REMEMBER

One of the quickest ways to become separated from your money is to ignore one of these nice little notices. If the notice you receive is wrong or unclear, you need to notify the IRS, as I explain in the earlier section "Understanding the Basics You'll Find on an IRS Notice."

Request for your tax return: Forms CP515 and CP518

Form CP515, "Request for Your Tax Return," and Form CP518, "You Didn't Respond Regarding Your Tax Return," are reserved as the non-filers' first notice and then final notice of overdue returns. These notices go to million people each year, asking why they didn't file a tax return.

The fact that the IRS expects you to file a return doesn't mean that you're actually required to. For example, you should verify whether your income falls below certain limits, which means you don't need to file a return. Still, if the IRS comes calling, looking for that return, you need to be able to answer.

Here are some of the reasons the IRS may be looking for a return from you when you don't feel you need to file one:

>> The income that the IRS says you didn't report is exempt from tax (for example, the interest received on municipal bonds).

>> The income that the IRS says you failed to report isn't yours. For example, you opened a bank account for your child or a relative, and you inadvertently gave the bank your own Social Security number.

>> The IRS counted the income twice. Perhaps you reported interest income on the wrong schedule. Or your broker reported your total dividends to the IRS as having been paid by the broker, while you reported those dividends on your return according to the names of the corporations that paid them.

>> You reported income in the wrong year. Maybe someone paid you at the end of the year, but you didn't receive this income until the beginning of the next year — and you reported it in that year.

>> You made a payment to the IRS for which you weren't given credit.

If you think that the IRS's conclusions about your return are wrong, see the section "Correcting IRS Errors" later in this chapter.

WHY SOME TAX ADVISORS FILE A RETURN WHEN IT'S NOT REQUIRED

Some tax preparers and advisors that I know struggle with the concept of not needing to file a federal income tax return because a particular person didn't meet certain thresholds, especially for very low income individuals. It is completely acceptable for them to not file a federal income tax return if there is no tax liability. But, the concern is that if such a person doesn't file a return (even a "zero" return) then the statute of limitations remains open forever.

So, some tax preparation practices file the return, even if it is a zero tax re-turn. That way, the statute of limitation's clock starts running and they avoid a notice requesting "why" a return wasn't filed and then having to "prove" at a much later date why there was no filing requirement for that period.

Backup withholding notice

As a trade-off for repeal of the short-lived mandatory withholding on interest and dividends, Congress enacted a system of backup withholding if you fail to furnish a payer of taxable income with your Social Security number. The IRS also notifies the payer that backup withholding should be started if you fail to report interest and dividend income on your tax return.

If the IRS determines that backup withholding is required, the payer is informed to withhold tax at the rate of 24 percent (it was 28 percent prior to tax cuts which began in 2018). What type of income most often gets hit for this type of withholding? The IRS usually targets interest and dividends, payments of more than $600 per year to independent contractors, sales of stocks and bonds, and royalties.

Backup withholding usually applies only to interest and dividend income. Other payments, however, are subject to withholding if you fail to provide the payer with your Social Security number. The IRS doesn't notify you that you're subject to backup withholding — it instead notifies the payer, who is required by law to notify you.

TIP

By notifying your local *taxpayer advocate* — the IRS problem-solving official that I discuss in detail later in this chapter — you can stop backup withholding under certain circumstances:

>> You didn't underreport your income.

>> You did underreport, but you paid the tax, interest, and penalties on the unreported income.

>> The backup withholding will cause you undue hardship, and the underreporting probably won't happen again.

If you get hit with backup withholding, file all your returns for delinquent years, start reporting all your income, or pay what you owe. If you do this, the IRS automatically stops backup withholding on January 1 if everything is in order by the preceding October 15.

Federal tax lien notice: Form 668(F)

A *statutory lien* automatically goes into effect when you neglect or refuse to pay the tax the IRS demands. This type of lien attaches to all property that you own. A statutory lien is sometimes referred to as a *secret lien* because its validity doesn't depend on its being filed as a matter of public record. *Statutory* simply means that, under the law, the IRS has the right to do it. The IRS doesn't have to prove that you failed to pay what you owe before it files a lien. Guilty unless proven innocent!

Because a statutory lien places the rights of only the IRS ahead of yours, the IRS usually files Form 668(F), "Notice of Lien," so that it places itself first in line before your other creditors. A federal tax lien covers all of a taxpayer's property, including real estate, cars, bank accounts, and personal property. These liens are filed in accordance with state law, usually with the county clerk, town hall, or court where the taxpayer lives.

WARNING

You should be aware that credit agencies routinely pick up liens that have been filed against you. After a credit agency has this information, your credit is marked as lousy. Even if paid, a lien stays on your credit history for 7 years. If you're unable to pay the taxes you owe, the unpaid lien remains on your credit report for up to 15 years!

Although the law requires that the IRS release a lien within 30 days after you pay it, the IRS doesn't always comply. Upon paying the tax, you can obtain a release of the lien by either contacting the revenue officer who filed the lien or following the procedure in IRS Publication 1450, "Certificate of Release of Federal Tax Lien."

TIP

Always keep copies of any correspondence you have with the IRS. If you have phone conversations with the IRS, be sure to get the name and ID number of each IRS employee you speak with. Also, ask the IRS employee whether the conversation will be logged in, so if you have to call again, there will be a record of the earlier conversation.

Handling Non-Assessment Notices

The IRS usually issues a *non-assessment notice* to inform you of one of the following situations:

>> You forgot to sign a return.

>> You failed to attach a W-2.

>> You omitted a form or schedule.

>> You didn't indicate your filing status.

If you receive a non-assessment notice, simply write across it in bold lettering: "Information requested is attached." Then attach the requested information to the notice and return it to the IRS in the envelope provided. After you provide the IRS with the requested information, the matter usually is closed — unless the information you submit conflicts with information previously reported on your return. If this situation occurs, the IRS sends a notice that assesses additional tax, interest, and possibly a penalty, or that instructs you to contact a particular person at the IRS.

Don't view a notice correcting a refund due to you (usually made on Form CP49) as a non-assessment notice. Just because a notice doesn't demand that you write a check, don't think that the IRS isn't billing you for something. Quite often, the IRS reduces a refund when it assesses additional tax or penalties.

Paying interest on additional tax

The IRS must send a notice of additional tax due within 36 months of the date when you file your return. If it doesn't send a notice before the 36 months are up, it can't charge interest after this 36-month period. Nor can the IRS resume charging interest until 21 days after it gets around to sending a notice.

This provision doesn't cover all notices, so here's what you should know about this 36-month rule:

» Your return has to be filed on time; otherwise, you're not entitled to this suspension of interest.

» The rule doesn't cover a failure to file or to pay penalties.

» Additional tax due as a result of an audit isn't covered.

Receiving a delinquent tax return notice

WARNING

You should treat a *delinquent tax return notice* as seriously as it sounds. If your tax return is delinquent, the IRS will always contact you by mail and will never demand payment over the phone (see the sidebar, "Beware of IRS phone scams"). Note that the IRS has the right to issue a summons commanding you to appear with your tax records and explain why you didn't file a tax return. Any taxpayer who receives a delinquent tax return notice should consider seeking the services of a qualified tax advisor.

Failure to file a required tax return is a criminal violation of the Internal Revenue Code and can result in jail time. Usually, the IRS isn't terribly interested in prosecuting the small fry who don't owe a huge amount of tax and saves its prosecutorial dollars for the big fish who owe the farm. These cases make big headlines, serving as lessons for people who wonder what would happen if, just once, they "forgot" to file.

If you file late returns — even in response to an IRS inquiry — and don't owe a substantial amount of tax (what's considered substantial is known only to the

IRS), the IRS probably will accept the return and assess a penalty for late payment and possibly fraud instead of trying to send you to prison (although the IRS does have that option).

If you don't reply to a delinquent tax return notice, the IRS can take one of the following steps:

>> Refer the case to its criminal investigation unit

>> Issue a summons to appear

>> Refer you to the audit division

>> Prepare a "substitute" return

If the IRS decides to prepare a substitute return for you, it uses the information that it has on you in its master file, using the married-filing-separately or filing-as-single tax table, the standard deduction, and one exemption. Having the IRS prepare your return is the quickest way to become separated from your money. Although no fee is involved, you're likely to pay more tax. Remember, the IRS isn't interested in saving you money.

Why not beat the IRS to the punch? The IRS has an official policy of usually not prosecuting anyone who files a return prior to being contacted and who makes arrangements to pay what's owed. Penalties and interest, however, are assessed. This procedure is called a *voluntary disclosure.*

Begin sidebar

BEWARE OF IRS PHONE SCAMS

Phone scammers, posing as IRS agents are all over the place. I myself have received such calls numerous times. Please keep in mind that the real IRS will never call you by phone and demand payments. Following is some valuable information from the IRS on these scams and what you need to know.

"There are clear warning signs about these scams, which continue at high levels throughout the nation," says IRS Commissioner John Koskinen. "Taxpayers should remember their first contact with the IRS will not be a call from out of the blue, but through official correspondence sent through the mail. A big red flag for these scams are angry, threatening calls from people who say they are from the IRS and urging immediate payment. This is not how we operate. People should hang up immediately and contact TIGTA (Treasury Inspector General for Tax Administration) or the IRS."

(continued)

(continued)

Additionally, it is important for taxpayers to know that the IRS:

- Never asks for credit card, debit card, or prepaid card information over the telephone.

- Never insists that taxpayers use a specific payment method to pay tax obligations

- Never requests immediate payment over the telephone and will not take enforcement action immediately following a phone conversation. Taxpayers usually receive prior notification of IRS enforcement action involving IRS tax liens or levies.

Potential phone scam victims may be told that they owe money that must be paid immediately to the IRS or they are entitled to big refunds. When unsuccessful the first time, sometimes phone scammers call back trying a new strategy.

Other characteristics of these scams include:

- Scammers use fake names and IRS badge numbers. They generally use common names and surnames to identify themselves.

- Scammers may be able to recite the last four digits of a victim's Social Security number.

- Scammers spoof the IRS toll-free number on caller ID to make it appear that it's the IRS calling.

- Scammers sometimes send bogus IRS emails to some victims to support their bogus calls.

- Victims hear background noise of other calls being conducted to mimic a call site.

- After threatening victims with jail time or driver's license revocation, scammers hang up and others soon call back pretending to be from the local police or DMV, and the caller ID supports their claim.

If you get a phone call from someone claiming to be from the IRS, here's what you should do:

- If you know you owe taxes or you think you may owe taxes, call the IRS at 1-800-829-1040. The IRS employees at that line can help you with a payment issue, if there really is such an issue.

- If you know you don't owe taxes or have no reason to think that you owe any taxes (for example, you've never received a bill or the caller made some bogus threats as described previously), then call and report the incident to TIGTA at 1-800-366-4484.

- You can file a complaint using the FTC Complaint Assistant; choose "Other" and then "Imposter Scams." If the complaint involves someone impersonating the IRS, include the words "IRS Telephone Scam" in the notes.

What You Should Know about Audits

On a list of real-life nightmares, most people would rank tax audits right up there with having a tooth pulled without Novocain. The primary trauma of an audit is that it makes many people feel like they're on trial and are being accused of a crime. Don't panic.

You may be audited for many reasons, and not necessarily because the IRS thinks you're a crook. You may receive that audit notice because some of the information on your return doesn't match up with information from third parties, because an IRS data entry operator added (or subtracted) a zero off a number on your return, or because your return deviates greatly from average returns in your neighborhood or your income range. Finally, some returns are plucked at random, and searching for a reason will just make you crazy!

About 15 percent of audited returns are left unchanged by the audit — that is, the taxpayers don't end up owing more money. In fact, if you're the lucky sort, you may be one of the rare individuals who actually get a refund because the audit finds a mistake in your favor! Unfortunately, you'll more likely be one of the roughly 85 percent of audit survivors who end up owing more tax money, plus interest. How much money hinges on how your audit goes.

REMEMBER

Most people would agree that not knowing what to expect in a situation is what's most terrifying about it. This is even truer when dealing with the IRS. Here's what you need to know about audits:

>> You needn't attend your audit. An enrolled agent (EA), a certified public accountant (CPA), or your attorney can go in your place.

>> If at any time during the audit you realize that you're in over your head, you can ask that the audit or interview be suspended until you can speak to a tax advisor of your choosing. When you make this request, the IRS must stop asking questions and adjourn the meeting so you can seek help and advice.

>> You should make the best effort to determine whether you can handle yourself early on. Although most people can handle themselves, if you have to have an audit suspended for professional advice, it will delay things and can make it more difficult for the professional who takes over. If the audit involves any unreported income/large unsubstantiated deductions, you should seek the advice of a tax attorney.

>> The burden of proof is on you. You're considered guilty until proven innocent. Unfortunately, that's how the tax system operates. However, if you and the IRS end up in court, the burden of proof switches to the IRS, provided you meet the IRS's substantiation and record-keeping requirements and present

credible evidence. What all this means is that you can't just sit in court and say "Prove it" to the IRS.

>> Although the number of people who are audited isn't great, the IRS's computers constantly compare the information received from employers, banks, and brokers with the information reported on people's returns. Because of these constant comparisons, the IRS sends bills totaling billions of dollars to millions of taxpayers each year.

The following sections describe types of audits, show you how to prepare for (and do well during) an audit, and explain the statute of limitations on audits.

Surviving the four types of audits

Four types of audits exist: correspondence audits, office audits, field audits, and random statistical audits, more commonly referred to as the audits from hell. With all four types of audits, maintaining good records is the key to survival. If you haven't already taken out the trash and lost all your evidence, you can refer to Chapter 6 for help filing and organizing the documents you may need.

Correspondence audits

Correspondence audits are exactly what the name suggests. The IRS conducts correspondence audits completely by mail and limits them to a few key areas of individual returns, such as itemized deductions, casualty or theft losses, employee business expenses, IRA plan payments, dependency exemptions, child-care and earned income credits, deductions for forfeited interest on early withdrawals from savings accounts, and exclusion from income of disability payments. A correspondence audit may also examine income items.

If you're ever the proud subject of a correspondence audit, the IRS gives you a return envelope in which to submit your documents, canceled checks, bills, and statements to substantiate the items the IRS questions. Never send original documents — only copies. Retaining the originals is crucial in case you have to stare down further inquiries or if the IRS does the unthinkable and loses your documentation.

When it comes to substantiating any deduction, the burden of proof is on you. If what you must substantiate is complex or requires a detailed explanation, you can ask for an interview to explain the circumstances in person.

Office audits

An *office audit* takes place at an IRS office. The IRS informs a taxpayer that it's scheduling an office audit by sending Notice 904. The front of this notice lists the date, time, and place of the audit, and the back lists the items that the IRS wants to examine.

The audit date isn't chiseled in granite. If you can't gather the information necessary to substantiate the items the IRS is questioning, or the date they chose simply won't work with your work and personal schedule, you can request a postponement by contacting the IRS. As a general rule, the IRS grants only two postponements unless you can demonstrate a compelling reason for an additional delay, such as an illness or the unavailability of certain tax records.

If you need more time but can't get an additional postponement, go to the audit with the records you have, put on your most confident face, and calmly inform the tax examiner that you need more time to secure the documents you need so that you can substantiate the remaining items the IRS is questioning. The tax examiner then prepares a list of the additional items the IRS needs to complete the audit, together with a mailing envelope so you can mail copies of the requested documents to the IRS.

REMEMBER

Never, ever mail original documents to the IRS (or any other tax authority for that matter). If the additional documents don't lend themselves to easy explanation through correspondence, then schedule a second appointment to complete the audit.

Most office audits are concerned with employee business expenses, itemized deductions such as medical expenses, charitable contributions, tax and interest expense deductions, and issues related to small business tax returns. Office audits also include income from rental property, and income from tips and capital gains.

If the IRS is trying to verify your income, it may want to know about your lifestyle. How does the IRS find out about your lifestyle? You tell it, that's how. Auditors are trained to control the interview (and they scour your social media accounts and other data sources). They feign ignorance, use appropriate small talk, use silence and humor appropriately, pay attention to a taxpayer's nonverbal communication, and avoid overtly taking notes so as not to distract the taxpayer. The IRS even has a form to flush out lifestyle information — Form 4822, "Statement of Annual Estimated Personal and Family Expenses" — which it can spring on you when a routine examination establishes the likelihood of unreported income. The form asks all about your expenses, from groceries to insurance — anything you and your family would spend money on as consumers. However, most people are unaware that you're under no obligation to fill out this form. The law only requires you to fill out and file a tax return.

REMEMBER

Statistical research has revealed that the IRS can collect more tax by examining sources of income than by examining deductions. If you operate a small business or have rental income, be prepared to explain where every deposit into your bank account came from.

Field audits

Field audits are conducted at a taxpayer's place of business. (This audit can also generally be done at the office of your tax advisor or attorney.) These audits focus on business returns and complex individual returns. If you file Form 1040, Schedule C (see Chapter 8), you're a likely candidate for a field audit.

Be prepared to verify the source of every deposit into your bank account. Field agents are required to survey both your preceding and subsequent years' tax returns to determine whether you treated similar items in a consistent manner. If an audit results in a significant increase in tax, you're now suspect, and the tax examiner will audit your subsequent years' tax returns (which normally are only surveyed).

An office audit specifies what items are examined from the very beginning of the process. Not so with a field audit — tax examiners have a great deal of discretion as to what items they review and to what depth they review them. Count on having to verify your total income, travel and entertainment expenses, gifts, automobile expenses, commissions, payments to independent contractors, and any expenses that appear large in relation to the size of your business.

A tax examiner may examine each and every deduction or merely select a month or two of expenses and examine them on a sample basis. If the examiner doesn't discover any discrepancies, he'll accept the rest of the expenses for that category as correct.

Random statistical audits

Although it's extremely unlikely, your return may be selected at random for an audit, just because the IRS can. The IRS uses these *random statistical audits* to gather information to determine pockets of tax cheating and errors. The IRS, however, never uses those words. It refers to failing to report income or inflating deductions as "noncompliance."

Under its research program, the IRS annually selects certain types of taxpayers' returns so it can measure the degree of tax compliance for particular industries, trades, or professions. On the basis of these audits, the IRS National Office determines which areas require stricter or greater enforcement efforts.

If you're selected for a random statistical audit, the IRS may review your return in the following ways: computer checking, correspondence, and face-to-face. Everything is subject to verification, but in most cases, only certain lines are checked. Be prepared, though, to provide your children's birth certificates to prove you're entitled to claim your kids as dependents. If something smells fishy or doesn't look right, you can count on being questioned in detail about the matter. The IRS looks under every rock, including matching up cash settlements you may have received in a personal injury lawsuit, for example.

Prepping for an audit

Preparing for an audit is sort of like preparing for a test in school: The IRS informs you which sections of your tax return it wants to examine so that you know what to "study." The first decision you face when you get an audit notice is whether to handle it yourself or to turn to a tax advisor to represent you. Hiring representation costs money but saves you time, stress, and possibly money. (*Note:* You may of course still attend the audit if you hire a tax advisor to represent you. Ask the advisor his/her opinion as to whether you should attend the audit or not.)

If you normally prepare your own return and are comfortable with your understanding of the areas being audited, represent yourself. If the IRS is merely asking you to substantiate deductions, you'll probably do all right on your own. What constitutes substantiation may at times involve a somewhat complicated interpretation of the law and its accompanying regulations. If the amount of tax money in question is small compared to the fee you'd pay a tax advisor to represent you, self-representation is probably the answer. However, if you're likely to turn into a babbling, intimidated fool and you're unsure of how to present your situation, hire a tax advisor to represent you.

The IRS permits three types of individuals to represent taxpayers: enrolled agents (EAs), certified public accountants (CPAs), and attorneys. All three are bound by IRS rules of practice. EAs become enrolled to practice before the IRS by passing a two-day written examination administered by the IRS in which their knowledge of the tax code is tested. Alternatively, they must have at least five years of experience as an IRS tax auditor. CPAs and attorneys are also permitted to represent taxpayers before the IRS. Many states have continuing education requirements for CPAs and attorneys. The IRS requires that EAs also meet continuing education requirements.

TIP

Probably the best way to find a qualified tax professional is to ask relatives or friends for a recommendation of someone whose level of service and performance they're more than satisfied with. To figure out which of these tax practitioners may be best suited to help you in an audit, see Chapter 13.

Changing your mind regarding representation partway through an audit is okay. At any time during the examination, such as when you feel a dizzy sensation and before you throw up in the examiner's lap, the Taxpayer Bill of Rights allows you to request that the audit be suspended until you have time to consult with an EA, a CPA, or an attorney. After you make this request, the IRS agent must stop asking questions or requesting documents until you're properly represented. (You can see the Taxpayer Bill of Rights at www.irs.gov/taxpayer-bill-of-rights.)

But if you decide to handle the audit yourself, get your act together sooner rather than later. Don't wait until the night before to start gathering receipts and other documentation. You may discover, for example, that you can't find certain documents.

You need to document and be ready to speak with the auditor about the areas the audit notice says are being investigated. Organize the various documents and receipts in folders. Being organized for the items requested in the audit letter is critical both to establish credibility and to avoid prolonging the exam. Don't show up, dump shopping bags full of receipts and paperwork on the auditor's desk, and say, "Here ya go. . . ."

Don't bring documentation for parts of your return that aren't being audited, either. Besides creating more work for yourself, you're required to discuss only those areas mentioned in the audit letter.

Whatever you do, don't ignore your audit request letter. The IRS is the ultimate bill-collection agency. And if you end up owing more money (the unhappy result of most audits), the sooner you pay, the less interest and penalties you'll owe.

Winning your audit

Two people with identical situations can walk into an audit and come out with very different results. The loser can end up owing more in taxes and having the audit expanded to include other parts of the return. Here's how to be a winner:

>> **Treat the auditor as a human being.** Although this seems like obvious advice, your anger and resentment at being audited won't win you any points. The examiner is just doing her job and knows you're busy and don't want to be at an audit. Ranting and raving in front of her is likely to make her search extra hard for places where your return may be dicey. Treating the examiner with respect and courtesy makes the audit a much easier experience for everyone concerned.

>> **Stick to the knitting.** You're there to discuss only the sections of your tax return in question. Don't volunteer other information unless you want the examiner to look at those areas as well.

- » **Discuss and don't argue.** If the auditor wants to disallow a deduction or otherwise increase the tax you owe and you don't agree, state once why you don't agree. Don't get into a knockdown, drag-out confrontation. The auditor may not want to lose face and will only feel inclined to find additional tax money — that's her job. Keep in mind that you can plead your case with several layers of people above your auditor during an appeals process. If that course fails and you still feel wronged, you can take your case to Tax Court.

- » **Don't be intimidated.** Just because IRS auditors have the authority of the government behind them, that doesn't make them right or all-knowing. The audit is only round one. If you disagree with the results, you have the right to appeal.

- » **Go to Tax Court.** If you receive a Statutory Notice of Deficiency (this notice comes after you've exhausted all your appeals within the IRS or if you don't respond to a notice that the IRS wants to audit your return), you have 90 days to appeal your case to the U.S. Tax Court. If you don't appeal, the IRS can enforce collection on the 91st day. A good tax advisor can help you at Tax Court; see Chapter 13 for details on finding one.

Understanding the statute of limitations on audits

The IRS must make any assessment of tax, penalties, or interest within three years from the due date for filing a tax return. If the IRS grants you an extension of the filing deadline, the statute of limitations is extended to include the extension period. If the due date falls on a legal holiday or a Saturday or Sunday, the due date is postponed to the next business day.

If you omit from your return more than 25 percent of the income that you're required to report, the statute of limitations extends to six years. No statute of limitations runs on a false or fraudulent return. Thus, if you filed a false or fraudulent return, there's no time limit on when the government can assess additional tax. The same goes for not filing a return; there's no time limit.

Correcting IRS Errors

Although the IRS is reluctant to admit it, it does make mistakes. In fairness to the IRS, collecting taxes from well over 140 million individuals (not to mention all the returns from corporations, partnerships, trusts, estates, and other assorted entities) under an extraordinarily complex tax system is, to say the least, difficult. The number of errors can appear to be limitless, but most errors occur for simple reasons.

The following is a long list of the types of flubs the IRS can make:

>> **Misapplied payments:** The IRS may not have posted tax payments that you made to your tax account (under your Social Security number). The IRS sometimes posts payments to the wrong year or type of tax. Perhaps the IRS didn't properly post overpayments from a preceding or subsequent year.

>> **Misunderstood date:** The IRS may claim that you didn't file or pay tax on time. Computers at a service center may not acknowledge that the due date for filing or paying fell on a legal holiday or on a Saturday or Sunday and may therefore blame you for filing late, when in fact you filed on the first business day following a legal holiday or a Saturday or Sunday. Or perhaps you had a valid extension of time to file, but the IRS said that you filed your return late.

>> **Wrong Social Security/ID number:** A data processing clerk may incorrectly input your Social Security number, or you may have been assigned two numbers. Because all data on a joint return is recorded under the Social Security number of the spouse whose name is listed first, any payments or credits that the other spouse made may not be posted under the first spouse's number. This situation frequently occurs when taxpayers file jointly for the first time or when a taxpayer files separately after having filed jointly in a prior year.

>> **Wrong income:** Income earned by another person may be inadvertently reported under your Social Security number. This often happens when a taxpayer opens a bank account for a child or another relative.

>> **Exempt income:** Money you earned on your IRA or other retirement account, or from municipal bond investments may have been reported to the IRS as being taxable.

>> **Double-counted income:** Income earned from your business or profession may be recorded as income from wages, or vice versa, and the IRS moved the income to the line or schedule on your return where it correctly belongs. That's okay, but sometimes the IRS moves the income without removing it from the line or schedule where it first was incorrectly entered!

>> **Lost return:** The IRS or the U.S. Postal Service (or another approved private delivery service such as FedEx or UPS) may have lost your return and payment, leaving you in the unenviable position of having to prove the timely filing of the return. Hopefully you made a copy and sent the original by an approved method, via either certified mail from the post office or an approved private delivery service!

>> **Partially corrected error:** The IRS may have corrected only one of the errors that were previously made. For example, an IRS error may be corrected, but the penalties and interest that were incorrectly charged were not removed.

>> **Data processing error:** A computer bug or another unexplained phenomenon may have caused a notice to be issued stating that a math error on your return was made where no error exists. Or someone may have failed to input all the data from the schedules attached to your return into the IRS computer. Data processing errors are common with Form 2210, "Underpayment of Estimated Tax by Individuals, Estates, and Trusts," where a taxpayer claims an exemption from the penalty for underestimating the amount of his required estimated tax payments. This type of error usually causes the IRS either to assess a penalty when it shouldn't or to issue a refund for the underestimating penalty that the taxpayer has paid.

>> **Incorrect 1099:** The IRS may have received an incorrect Form 1099 from a bank or brokerage firm. Either the amount of income reported on the form is wrong or the income isn't yours. Even if you correct it (and file the correction with the IRS), the correction may never make it into the IRS computer. Don't you just hate it when that happens?

The following sections explain how to correspond with the IRS when you discover an error, how to answer a balance due notice, and how to reach out to a taxpayer advocate.

Keeping your correspondence short and sweet

TIP

There's elegance in simplicity when corresponding with the IRS. Keep to the point. Letters should be no longer than one page. A clearly written and concise half page should get even quicker results. Note that the tax examiner reviewing your inquiry could have little experience in the area you're writing about. Such people are, however, extremely conscientious in performing their duties. You stand a better chance of achieving the results you want by making their jobs as easy as possible. Don't succumb to the temptation to go into a narrative on how unfair the tax system is or how you're paying more than your fair share. Save that stuff for your representative in Congress or pals you chat with about politics.

Your letter to the IRS should contain the following items — and nothing more:

>> Vital facts: name, mailing address, Social Security number on the tax return, and the year of the disputed tax return.

>> The control number from the notice, type of tax, and a copy of the notice you received.

>> The type of mistake the IRS made.

>> The action you want the IRS to take.

>> Copies of the documents necessary to prove your case — canceled checks, corrected Form 1099s, mailing receipts, and so on — but never the originals.

Address your letter to the Adjustments/Correspondence (A/C) branch at the service center that issued the notice. You should note the type of request you're making at the extreme top of the letter — "Request to Adjust Form [form number]." Use the bar-coded envelope that was sent with the notice to mail your letter.

Include a simple thank-you and the telephone number where you can be reached in case the clerk at the IRS service center has any questions. Telephone contact between you and an IRS employee can take weeks off the adjustments/correspondence process.

TIP

Always keep copies of any documents you send to the IRS. It's also a good idea to keep a log of all of your interactions with the IRS, such as received original notice on this date, called IRS on this date, sent written response on this date, and so on. Note that the IRS has been affected by the recent congressional action (or inaction) and is taking longer to process responses. If you send correspondence and receive no response, you can call to see whether the IRS received it. Consider sending documents via certified mail so you know when the IRS receives them.

Sending a simple response to a balance due notice

TIP

If you receive a balance due notice for a tax that you've already paid, it's time to dig out the proof you kept that shows when and how much you paid. With proof in hand, it's a simple matter to write on the front of the notice:

"This balance has been paid. Enclosed is a copy of proof of payment of taxes that you have failed to credit to my account. Please remove all penalties and interest charges that were assessed."

If you paid by check, you need to send a copy, front and back, of the canceled check. For credit card payments, a copy of your credit card bill, with the payment to the IRS and the date and amount highlighted, should suffice. If you transferred the funds directly from your bank account through an electronic funds transfer, send a highlighted copy of your bank statement that shows the amount taken from your account and the date. And if you're enrolled in the Electronic Federal Tax Payment System (EFTPS), include a copy of the electronic funds transfer (EFT) acknowledgment number you received as a receipt.

Getting attention when the IRS ignores you with the help of a taxpayer advocate

At times, it seems that a black hole ravages every IRS service center, devouring loads of taxpayer correspondence. Naturally, the IRS won't respond right away in these cases. If you don't get a response, the IRS has a special office that handles these problems: the office of your local taxpayer advocate.

Understanding what your local taxpayer advocate does

The local taxpayer advocate office is the IRS's complaint department. Every state has at least one local taxpayer advocate office; in addition, each of the ten IRS service centers has one, too. An advocate's function is to resolve taxpayer problems that can't be resolved through normal channels.

The National Taxpayer Advocate, who is appointed by the Secretary of the Treasury, oversees all functions of the local taxpayer advocates and their employees. The national and local advocates operate independently from the IRS and report directly to Congress. The purpose behind this independence is to provide taxpayers with a "customer-friendly" problem-solving office. Being independent of all other IRS offices enables the office of the local advocate to cut through red tape.

Local taxpayer advocates don't interpret tax law, give tax advice, or provide assistance in preparing tax returns. They resolve procedural, refund, notice, billing, and other problems that couldn't be fixed after one or more attempts by a taxpayer. A local advocate can abate penalties, trace missing tax payments, and credit them to a taxpayer's account. An advocate also can approve replacement refund checks for originals that were either lost or stolen, release a lien, and, of greatest importance, stop IRS collection action.

Meeting the criteria for a taxpayer advocate case

Under the Problem Resolution Program, caseworkers working under the local taxpayer advocate are the folks who do the actual problem solving. They accept cases for a variety of reasons. The following are common types of cases with which they can assist:

>> You call or write the IRS about a problem. After 30 days, you contact the IRS again, but the IRS still ignores you.

>> You file your return expecting a nice refund, but after 60 days, you're still waiting. You contact the IRS, but nothing happens.

>> You receive a letter from the IRS promising to respond to your particular inquiry by a certain date, but the IRS fails to respond by the promised date.

>> You're suffering a hardship or are about to suffer one, such as the loss of your credit or livelihood.

Advocates are experts at cutting through red tape. If the advocate won't take your case, she'll refer it to the IRS office that should have handled it from the start.

Knowing what happens if the taxpayer advocate takes your case

Taxpayer advocate caseworkers are committed to resolving your problem in seven working days. If they can't, you'll be informed, usually by phone, when you can expect the problem to be resolved. Most cases are closed in 30 days or fewer.

If an advocate asks for certain information and it isn't sent or you fail to contact the advocate to request additional time to comply, the case isn't held open indefinitely; after two weeks, it's closed, in which case you must make a new taxpayer advocate contact. A caseworker closes a case by writing to the taxpayer and explaining what corrective action has been taken, if any. If no corrective action can be taken, the advocate's letter explains that.

Contacting your local taxpayer advocate

Except in emergency cases, such as when a levy has been filed and the taxpayer owes no money, taxpayers should write to the advocate in the district where they reside. Your letter should contain the following:

>> A complete but concise description of the problem

>> Copies of the fronts and backs of canceled checks (if applicable)

>> A signed copy of your tax return (if applicable)

>> Copies of all notices received from the IRS

>> Copies of your previous letters written to the IRS regarding the problem

>> A summary of phone calls you made to the IRS, whom you spoke with, the dates, and what was discussed

>> Any other documents or information that may help the advocate expedite the resolution of this problem

>> A telephone number where you can be reached during the day

In emergency situations, contact the taxpayer advocate by phone. The advocate can immediately take a variety of actions. For example, the advocate can issue a Taxpayer Assistance Order (TAO) if a notice of levy has been incorrectly issued. A TAO stops the original IRS action that the IRS never should have undertaken. The taxpayer advocate toll-free phone number (877-777-4778) can direct you to the office of your local advocate, or you can find that information at www.irs.gov by plugging "taxpayer advocate" into the keyword search.

Amending a Return

If you discover that you forgot to claim a deduction, and the statute of limitations hasn't expired, you have to file an amended return. Similarly, if you discover that you improperly claimed a deduction, you must file an amended return and pay any additional tax plus interest.

If you forgot to claim a deduction in a prior year, you must file an amended return within three years from the date of filing your original return, or within two years from the time the tax was paid, whichever is later. (You have up to seven years for worthless securities and bad debts.) You use Form 1040X, "Amended U.S. Individual Income Tax Return," to correct a prior year's tax return.

Note: This three-year rule is suspended for anyone suffering from a serious disability that renders him unable to manage his financial affairs. However, when a taxpayer's spouse or another person such as a guardian is authorized to act on the disabled taxpayer's behalf, this waiver of the rule doesn't apply.

The following sections provide details on a couple of situations related to amended returns.

More expenses than income (net operating losses)

Before the tax reform that took effect in 2018, an amended return was permitted whenever you incurred a *net operating loss* (NOL). You have an NOL if the amount of money you lost (in a business or profession) exceeds all your other income. In the past, you could carry back an NOL to offset your taxable income in the two previous years. Tax reform eliminated the NOL carryback provision. The new laws did however somewhat open up the carrying forward of NOLs, which are now allowed for an unlimited number of years, up from the previous limit of 20 years until it's used up. One final detail: NOLs are limited to 80 percent of taxable income in any given tax year.

The tax benefit rule

Whenever you deduct an expense in one year and part or all of that expense is reimbursed in a subsequent year, you usually have to report the reimbursement as income. For example, suppose that you deducted $10,000 in medical expenses in 2018 and were reimbursed $3,000 by your insurance company in 2019. You have to report the $3,000 as income in 2019.

However, if the original deduction didn't result in a tax savings, you don't have to report the reimbursement. For example, if you receive a state tax refund for a year in which you claimed the standard deduction instead of itemizing your deductions, you don't have to report the refund.

Taking Action Even When You Can't Pay Your Taxes

"If you can't pay," goes the old saw, "you can owe." That's certainly the way the IRS looks at things. Every year, the IRS receives millions of returns from taxpayers who can't pay what they owe before the April 15 deadline, and that amounts to tens of billions of dollars of taxes due each year.

If you find yourself among the millions of Americans who can't pay all or any part of what they owe, you have four options:

>> You can pay off the tax in installments, which millions of taxpayers currently are doing. You can request to pay in installments by attaching Form 9465, "Installment Agreement Request," to your return or to any of the notices you receive. (Find this form at www.irs.gov/pub/irs-pdf/f9465.pdf.) Then send it to the IRS service center where you file or to the center that issued the notice. You also can request an installment agreement by calling the IRS taxpayer services office at 800-829-1040.

>> You can put off paying the tax until you have more money. Contact the IRS so that you can temporarily delay collections.

>> You can try to persuade the IRS to take less than it wants. The IRS doesn't accept every offer that's made, but it is fairly pragmatic. From where the IRS sits, receiving some of what it's owed is better than receiving nothing.

>> You can file for bankruptcy in the absolute worst-case scenario. Please note, however, if the IRS recorded a tax lien on your property before you file for bankruptcy, the lien will remain on the property.

Whatever you do, don't confuse filing with paying. More people get into hot water because they mistakenly believe that they need to put off filing until they can pay. If you're one of the approximately 2 million non-filers that the IRS currently is looking for, file your return as soon as possible, even if you can pay only part of what you owe. Owing the IRS money is expensive, but owing money and tax returns is far worse! Although the interest rates the IRS charges are lower than what you get on your credit card, interest compounds daily on the balance you owe, in addition to a late-payment penalty of half a percentage point per month. If you haven't filed your tax return, though, the IRS tacks on additional non-filing penalties of 5 percent per month, up to a maximum of 25 percent. Ouch!

At first, the IRS comes after you through the mail. If you owe money, either from the findings of an audit or because you simply couldn't pay it all on April 15, you get four notices from the IRS at five-week intervals. If you don't pay everything you owe on April 15, the fourth and last letter arrives by certified mail around Labor Day. That's when things start to get ugly.

Many taxpayers freeze when they receive one of these notices and then place the unopened envelope in a pile to be dealt with when the cows come home or hell freezes over. Bad idea! Whether or not you actually open the envelope, you're still responsible to respond to the requests inside, even if to tell the IRS that you can't pay right now. If you fail to respond, your account is considered delinquent and is forwarded to the IRS automated collection system (ACS), which means you'll start getting phone calls at home demanding payment and, if the IRS can't reach you at home, at work, at your club, or anywhere the IRS has a number for you. If the ACS isn't successful in getting you to pay up, your account may be transferred to an IRS revenue officer who will contact you in person.

Because the IRS usually has what it refers to as *levy source information* about you in its files, it has the option to place a levy on your assets or salary or to simply seize your property. IRS collection agents can have your cars seized. Keep in mind that from the return you filed, the IRS already knows where your income comes from and how much you make, and it has the right to get additional information about you from credit and governmental agencies, such as the department of motor vehicles, passport agencies, and the U.S. Postal Service. It can make you pay in numerous ways. And every time you make a payment, the IRS makes a permanent record of your bank account.

To avoid that hassle, if there's any way that you can get the money together, send a partial payment to the IRS when filing your return; a partial payment with the first, second, and third notices; and the balance (including interest and penalties) with the fourth notice.

The IRS must notify you of your right to protest a levy of your salary or property. You have 30 days from the date the IRS sends you a levy notice by certified mail to request what's known as a *collection due process hearing.*

Reducing Your Chances of Being Audited

If you've never been audited, you probably fall into one of these categories: You're still young, you haven't made gobs of money, or you're just plain lucky. The fact is that many taxpayers are audited during their adult lives. It's just a matter of time and probability.

Most people assume that an IRS audit involves going to an IRS office or having an auditor come to your place of business or home. In reality, most audits are actually correspondence audits handled through the mail and often cover only one or a few issues. Recent IRS statistics show that correspondence audits occur at double the number of field audits.

You can take some common-sense steps (honesty being the star of the show) to reduce your chances of facing an audit. This section details my top tips for lessening your chances of being audited and avoiding all the time and associated costs of an audit.

Declare all your income

When you prepare your return, you may be tempted to shave off a little of that consulting income you received. Who will miss it, right? The IRS, that's who.

Thanks largely to computer cross-checking, the IRS has many ways of finding unreported income. Probably the most common cause of IRS correspondence audits is omitting interest, dividends, wages, pension, or other kinds of income that is reported to the IRS. Be particularly careful if you're self-employed; anyone who pays you more than $600 in a year is required to file a Form 1099, which tells the IRS how much you received.

When you knowingly hide income, you face substantial penalties and, depending on the amount, criminal prosecution. That wouldn't be a picnic, especially if you can't afford to hire a good defense attorney.

Don't itemize

People who itemize their deductions on Schedule A of Form 1040 (discussed in Chapter 9) are far more likely to be audited because they have more opportunity and temptation to cheat. By all means, if you can legally claim more total deductions by using Schedule A than you can with the standard deduction, then itemize. Just don't try to artificially inflate your deductions.

On the other hand, if it's basically a tossup between Schedule A and your standard deduction, taking the standard deduction is safer, easier, quicker, and the IRS can't challenge it.

Earn less money

At first glance, earning less money may seem like an odd suggestion, but there really are costs associated with affluence. One of the costs of a high income — besides higher taxes — is a dramatic increase in the probability of being audited. If your income is more than $100,000, you have about a 1 in 20 chance each year of being audited. But your chance is less than 1 in 100 if your income is less than $50,000. You see, besides being subjected to lower income tax rates, earning less has additional advantages!

WARNING

If you manage to pile up a lot of assets and don't enjoy them in retirement, your estate tax return — your final tax return — is at great risk of being audited. Do you think a 1 in 20 or 1 in 100 chance is bad in the audit lottery? Uncle Sam audits about 1 in 7 estate tax returns. The IRS collects an average of more than $100,000 for each estate tax return it audits! So enjoy your money while you're alive or pass it along to your heirs in the here and now. Otherwise, your heirs may have trouble getting it in the there and later!

Don't cheat

It may have taken the IRS a while to wise up, but now the government is methodically figuring out the different ways that people cheat. The next step for the IRS — after it figures out how people cheat — is to come up with ways to catch the cheaters. Cheaters beware!

The IRS also offers rewards for informants. If you're brazen enough to cheat and the IRS doesn't catch you, you may not be home-free yet. Someone else may turn you in. So be honest — not only because it's the right thing to do but also because you'll probably sleep better at night knowing that you aren't breaking the law.

Tax protesters, take note. The IRS may flag returns that are accompanied by protest notes. Threats are bad, too — even if they're meant in fun (humor isn't rife at the IRS). The commandment to follow is: Thou shalt not draw attention to thyself.

The protest issue is interesting. During congressional hearings, tax protesters stand up and tell members of Congress that the income tax is unconstitutional. They say they have proof. (If I can get my hands on the proof, I'll include it in the next edition of this book.) In the meantime, pay your taxes and resist the temptation to send along a cranky letter with your tax returns and payments. To read the IRS's "The Truth About Frivolous Tax Arguments," point your web browser to `www.irs.gov/pub/irs-utl/friv_tax.pdf` for 60-plus action-packed pages, including legal citations.

Don't cut corners if you're self-employed

People who are self-employed have more opportunities to make mistakes on their taxes — or to creatively take deductions — than company-payroll wage earners. As a business owner, you're responsible for self-reporting not only your income but also your expenses. You have to be even more honest when dealing with the tax authorities because the likelihood of being audited is higher than average.

Don't disguise employees as independent contractors. Remember the old barb: You can't put a sign around the neck of a cow that says, "This is a horse." You don't have a horse — you have a cow with a sign around its neck. Just because you call someone an independent contractor doesn't mean that person isn't your employee. If you aren't sure about the relationship, consult a tax advisor.

Other audit triggers for small businesses cited by tax advisors include:

>> Cash businesses

>> Businesses with relatively high expenses

>> Relatively high charitable and medical deductions

>> 100 percent business use of vehicle

Nothing is wrong with being self-employed, but resist the temptation to cheat, because you're far more likely to be scrutinized and caught as a self-employed worker.

Double-check your return for accuracy

Review your own return before you send it in. If the IRS finds mistakes through its increasingly sophisticated computer-checking equipment, you're more likely to be audited. The IRS figures that if it finds obvious errors, some not-so-obvious ones lurk beneath the surface.

Have you included all your income? Think about the different accounts you had during the tax year. Do you have interest and dividend statements for all your accounts? Finding these statements is easier if you keep your financial records in one place. Check your W-2s and 1099s against your tax form to make sure that you wrote the numbers down correctly.

Don't forget to check your math. Have you added, subtracted, multiplied, and divided correctly? Are your Social Security number and address correct on the return? Did you sign and date your return?

Such infractions won't, on their own, trigger an audit. In some cases, the IRS simply writes you a letter requesting your signature or the additional tax you owe (if the math mistake isn't too fishy or too big). In some rare instances, the IRS even sends a refund if the mistake it uncovers is in the taxpayer's favor. Regardless of how the IRS handles the mistake, it can be a headache for you to clear up, and, more important, it can cost you extra money.

Stay away from back-street refund mills

WARNING

Although this advice doesn't apply to the majority of tax-preparation firms, unfortunately, some firms out there fabricate deductions. Run away fast from tax preparers who tell you, after winking, that they have creative ways to reduce your tax bill, or those who base their fees on how many tax dollars they can save you. Also beware of any preparer who promises you a refund without first thoroughly reviewing your situation.

The IRS is actively going after fly-by-night preparers, who promise you the moon and the stars but may end up landing you in the muck. When the IRS audits a preparer, it looks at many (and sometimes all) of the returns the preparer has worked on and filed for taxpayers. If it finds problems in how that preparer runs his or her business, you can expect the IRS to also look more closely at all the returns that preparer prepared.

TIP

With any preparer you should review the return. Questionable preparers often overstate charitable, business, and medical deductions. A quick check will show whether these amounts agree with the information you provided to the preparer.

Chapter **12**

Keeping Up with and Researching Tax Strategies and Rules

y the time you actually get around to filing your annual income tax return, it's too late to take advantage of many tax-reduction strategies for that tax year. And what can be more aggravating than — late in the evening on April 14, when you're already stressed out and unhappily working on your return — finding a golden nugget of tax advice that works great, if only you'd known about it last December!

REMEMBER

Be sure to review all the important tax-planning issues discussed throughout this book that you need to take advantage of in future years. In the event that you've waited until the last minute to complete your return this year, be sure to thoroughly read this book after you file your return so you don't miss out next year.

Whether you're now faced with the daunting task of preparing your return or you're simply trying to increase your tax intelligence during the year, you're probably trying to decide how to do it with a minimum of pain and taxes owed. As you find out in this chapter, you have several options for completing your return and gaining knowledge. The best choice for you depends on the complexity of your tax situation, your knowledge about taxes, and the amount of time you're willing to invest.

REMEMBER

Privately published tax-preparation and advice books such as this one are invaluable when they highlight tax-reduction strategies and possible pitfalls in clear, simple English. Such books help you complete your return accurately and save you big money. The amount of money invested in a book or two is significantly smaller than the annual cost of a tax expert. This book covers the important tax-preparation and planning issues that affect the vast majority of taxpayers. A minority of taxpayers may run into some nitpicky tax issues caused by unusual events in their lives or extraordinary changes in their incomes or assets. This book may not be enough for those folks. In such cases, you need to consider hiring a tax advisor, which I explain how to do in Chapter 13.

The Benefits of Preparing Your Own Return

You already do many things for yourself. Maybe you cook for yourself, do some basic car maintenance or home repairs, clean your own home, and so on. You may do these tasks because you enjoy them, because you save money by doing them, or because you want to develop a particular skill or have control over these issues.

Sometimes, however, you hire others to help you do work for you. Occasionally, you may buy a meal out, do more involved maintenance on your car or hire someone to make a home improvement. And so it can be with your annual income tax return — you may want to hire help, but you may end up, like many people, preparing your own return.

REMEMBER

Doing your own income tax return is an especially good option if your financial situation doesn't change much from year to year. You can use last year's return as a guide. You may need to do some reading to keep up with the small number of changes in the tax system and laws that affect your situation (and this book can help). Given the constant changes to various parts of the tax laws, you can't simply assume that the tax laws that apply to your situation are the same from one year to the next just because your situation is the same.

Another benefit of preparing your own return is the better financial decisions that you make in the future by using the tax knowledge you gain from learning about the tax system. Most tax preparers are so busy preparing returns that you probably won't get much of their time to discuss tax laws and how they may apply to your future financial decisions. Even if you can schedule time with a preparer, you may rightfully worry about paying for the personal tutorial you're sitting through.

Doing your own return should be your lowest-cost tax-return-preparation option. Of course, this assumes that you don't make costly mistakes and oversights and that the leisure time you forgo when preparing your return isn't too valuable!

TIP

You don't have to go all or nothing in terms of preparing your own return. Consider having a tax professional prepare your return every few years as a sort of second opinion to verify that you're preparing it correctly and not missing out on any tax savings strategies. Or if you have concerns, you can schedule an out-of-tax-season consultation with a professional.

Using IRS Publications

In addition to the instructions that come with the annual tax forms that the good old IRS prints every year, the IRS also produces hundreds of publications that explain how to complete the myriad tax forms various taxpayers must tackle. These free materials provide more detail than the basic IRS publications and are available in printed form by mail if you simply call and order them from the IRS (800-829-3676) or digitally through the IRS's website (www.irs.gov; see the later section "The Internal Revenue Service" for more on what the site has to offer). Examples of these pamphlets include

>> Publication 17: "Your Federal Income Tax" is designed for individual tax-return preparation.

>> Publication 334: "Tax Guide for Small Business" is for (you guessed it) small-business tax-return preparation for individuals who use Schedule C or C-EZ.

>> Publication 583: "Starting a Business and Keeping Records" is also an excellent resource.

Additionally, the IRS provides answers to common questions through its automated phone system and through live representatives.

If you have a simple, straightforward tax return, completing it on your own using only the IRS instructions may be fine. This approach is as cheap as you can get, costing only your time, patience, photocopying expenses, and postage to mail the completed tax return (unless you choose to file electronically). Unfortunately (for you), IRS publications and employees don't generally offer the direct, helpful advice provided in this book. For example, here's something you don't see in an IRS publication:

> STOP! One of the most commonly overlooked deductions is . . . . You still have time to . . . and whack off hundreds — maybe thousands — of dollars from your tax bill! HURRY!

WARNING

Another danger in relying on the IRS staff for assistance is that it has been known to give wrong information and answers. When you call the IRS with a question, be sure to take notes about your phone conversation, thus protecting yourself in the event of an audit. Date your notes and include the IRS employee's name you spoke with, employee number, office location, what you asked, and the employee's responses. File your notes in a folder with a copy of your completed return.

The IRS also offers more in-depth booklets focusing on specific tax issues. However, if your tax situation is so complex that this book (and Publications 17 and 334) can't address it, you need to think long and hard about getting help from a tax advisor; see Chapter 13 for details.

REMEMBER

IRS publications present plenty of rules and facts, but they don't make finding the information and advice you really need easy. The best way to use IRS publications is to confirm facts that you already think you know or to check the little details. Don't expect IRS publications and representatives to show you how to cut your tax bill.

Buying Software

If you don't want to slog through dozens of pages of tedious IRS instructions or pay a tax preparer hundreds of dollars to complete your return, you may be interested in computer software that can help you finish your IRS Form 1040 (see Chapter 7) and supplemental schedules. If you have access to a computer and printer (unless you choose to file electronically), tax-preparation software can be a helpful tool.

Tax-preparation software also gives you the advantage of automatically recalculating all the appropriate numbers on your return if one number changes. Tax programs can be helpful in doing complex calculations such as determining whether you're subject to the alternative minimum tax or calculating allowable real estate passive losses. The best tax-preparation software is easy to install and use on your computer, provides help when you get stuck, and highlights deductions you may overlook.

WARNING

Before plunking down your hard-earned cash for some tax-preparation software, know that it has potential drawbacks.

>> A tax return prepared by a software program is only as good as the quality of the data you enter into it. (Of course, this drawback exists no matter who actually fills out the forms; some human tax preparers don't probe and clarify to make sure that you've provided all the right details, either.)

>> Subpar tax software programs may contain glitches that can lead to incorrect calculating or reporting of some aspect of your tax return.

TIP

TurboTax is a leading program and does a solid job of helping you through the federal tax forms. TurboTax Home & Business is designed for sole proprietors and single owner LLCs, and TurboTax Business is intended for S corporations, partnerships, C corporations, and multiple-owner LLCs.

Accessing Internet Tax Resources

In addition to using your computer to prepare your income tax return, you can do an increasing number of other tax activities via the Internet. The better online tax resources are geared more to tax practitioners and tax-savvy taxpayers. But in your battle to legally minimize your taxes, you may want all the help you can get! Use the Internet for what it's best at doing — possibly saving you time tracking down factual information or forms. The following sections describe some of the better websites out there.

WARNING

On the Internet, many websites provide information and discussions about tax issues. Take advice and counsel from other Net users at your peril. Don't rely on the accuracy of the answers to tax questions that you ask in online forums. The problem: In many cases, you can't be sure of the background, expertise, or identity of the person with whom you're trading messages. However, if you want to liven up your life, and taxes make you mad, a number of political forums enable you to converse and debate with others. You can complain about recent tax hikes or explain why you think that the wealthy still don't pay enough taxes!

The Internal Revenue Service

When you think of the Internal Revenue Service — the U.S. Treasury Department office charged with overseeing the collection of federal income taxes — you probably think of a bureaucratic, humorless, and stodgy agency. Difficult as it is to believe, the IRS website (www.irs.gov) is well organized and relatively user-friendly.

The IRS site also has links to state tax organizations, convenient access to IRS forms (including those from prior tax years), and instructions. To be able to read and print the forms, you need Adobe Acrobat Reader, which you can download for free from many Internet sites, including the IRS site or the Adobe website at `www.adobe.com`. To download forms from the IRS site, start browsing at `www.irs.gov/forms-instructions`.

You can complete your tax forms online at the IRS site using Adobe Acrobat Reader. The IRS site even features a place for you to submit comments on proposed tax regulations, with a promise that the comments are "fully considered." Is this the IRS we know and love?

Tax preparation sites

A number of websites enable you to prepare federal and state tax forms and then file them electronically. Many of these sites allow you to prepare and file your federal forms for free if you access their site through the IRS website. Just go to `www.irs.gov` and click the "File" and then the "Free File" links to see whether you qualify. If you access a tax-preparation site directly instead, you may have to pay a fee for a service that would be free through the Free File program.

If you don't want to use Free File, a reasonably priced alternative worth your consideration can be found at CCH's eSmart Tax website (`www.esmarttax.com`), where you enter data on interview forms and calculate your tax. The premium edition, for $58.95, is designed for small business owners and self-employed folks. (State tax filing is an additional $39.95.) The service also includes tax support from professional tax advisors.

TIP

Keep in mind that if you're simply after the tax forms, plenty of the sites mentioned in this chapter offer such documents for free, as do some public libraries.

TaxTopics.net

A number of sites on the Internet claim to be directories — collections of all the best stuff on the Internet on a particular topic. However, many of these sites lack objectivity and expertise. The worst of these sites simply provide links to other sites that are willing to pay them a referral fee.

TaxTopics.net is a comprehensive Internet tax resource compendium organized with links by topic. It appears to be run by a California CPA and is the best tax directory resource I've found online.

Research sites

For true tax junkies, the U.S. Tax Code On-Line (`www.fourmilab.ch/ustax/ustax.html`) is a search engine that enables you to check out the complete text of the U.S. Internal Revenue Code. Hyperlinks embedded in the text provide cross-references between sections at the click of a mouse. And, if you really have nothing better to do with your time, check out the government sites with updated information on tax bills in Congress:

>> `www.jct.gov/`

>> `www.waysandmeans.house.gov`

Wolters Kluwer Tax & Accounting (`https://taxna.wolterskluwer.com/`) is geared toward tax and legal professionals who need to keep up with and research the tax laws. Access to most of the site's resources comes by subscription only.

Hiring Help

Because they lack the time, interest, energy, or skill to do it themselves, some people hire a contractor to handle a home-remodeling project. And most people who hire a contractor do so because they think that they can afford to hire a contractor. (Although sometimes this last part isn't true, and they wind up with more debt than they can afford!)

For some of the same reasons, some people choose to hire a tax preparer and advisor. By identifying tax-reduction strategies that you may overlook, competent tax practitioners can save you money — sometimes more than enough to pay their fees. They may also reduce the likelihood of an audit, which can be triggered by blunders that you may make. Like some building contractors, however, some tax preparers take longer, charging you more and not delivering the high-quality work you expect. See Chapter 13 for how to proceed in hiring tax help.

Chapter **13**

Paying for Tax Help

Throughout this book, I discuss the many ways the nation's tax code is complicated and confusing. So it should come as no surprise that legions of tax preparers and advisors stand ready to be hired by you to assist you with your tax quandaries and tasks.

You can hire various types of tax pros, with varying credentials and qualifications. You want to identify possible folks to hire through trusted sources, and then you should ask them some tough questions. In this chapter, I help you make sense of your options and give you pointers on whom to hire for what tax jobs. I also suggest how to find possible candidates and list key questions that you should ask them before hiring them.

REMEMBER

Because you've gone to the trouble and expense of tracking down this book, please make use of it. The more you know before you seek a tax advisor's services, the better able you'll be to make an informed decision and reduce your expenditures on tax preparers.

Deciding to Hire Tax Help

Odds are quite good that you can successfully prepare your own return. Most people's returns don't vary that much from year to year, so you have a head start and can hit the ground running if you get out last year's return — which, of course, you kept a copy of, right? However, preparing your own return may not work as well whenever your situation has changed in some significant way — if you bought your first home or started your own business, for example.

Don't give up and hire a preparer just because you can't bear to open your tax-preparation booklet and get your background data organized. Even if you hire a tax preparer, you still need to get your stuff organized before a consultation.

TIP

As hard and as painful as it is, confront preparing your return as far in advance of April 15 as you can so that, if you feel uncomfortable with your level of knowledge, you have enough time to seek help. The more organizing you do before hiring a preparer, the less having your return prepared should cost you. If an annual compilation of tax records is too daunting, try monthly or quarterly. A more frequent effort can help if you have lots of business expenses, auto use, and charitable deductions. Avoid waiting until the last minute to hire an advisor — you won't do as thorough a job of selecting a competent person, and you'll probably pay more for the rush job. If you get stuck preparing your own return, you can get a second opinion from one of the resources I discuss in this chapter.

If you decide to seek out the services of a tax preparer/advisor, know that tax practitioners come with various backgrounds, training, and credentials. One type of professional isn't necessarily better than another. Think of them as different types of specialists who are appropriate for different circumstances. The four main types of tax practitioners, which I discuss in the next few sections, are preparers, enrolled agents, certified public accountants, and tax attorneys.

Unenrolled preparers

Among all the tax practitioners, *unenrolled preparers* generally have the least amount of training, and more of them work part time. H&R Block is the largest and most well-known tax-preparation firm in the country. In addition, other national firms and plenty of mom and pop shops are in the tax-preparation business.

The appeal of preparers is that they're tend to be relatively less costly than the other major categories — they can do basic returns for $150 or so. The drawback is that you may hire a preparer who doesn't know much more than you do! As with financial planners, no national regulations apply to tax-return preparers, and no licensing is required, although this may change in the future. Several states (for example, California, Maryland, New York, and Oregon) require licensing of such tax preparers. In most states, almost anybody can hang a tax-preparation shingle and start preparing. Most preparers, however, complete some sort of training program before working with clients.

TIP

Preparers make the most sense for folks who don't have complicated financial lives, who are budget-minded, and who dislike doing their own taxes. If you aren't good about hanging on to receipts or don't want to keep your own files with background details about your taxes, you definitely need to shop around for a tax preparer who's going to be around for a few years. You may need all that paperwork someday for an audit, and some tax preparers keep and organize their clients' documentation rather than return everything each year. (Can you blame them for keeping your records after they go through the tedious task of sorting them all out?) Going with a firm that's open year-round may also be safer, in case tax questions or problems arise. (Some small shops are open only during tax season.)

Enrolled agents

A person must pass IRS scrutiny to be called an *enrolled agent* (EA). This license enables the agent to represent you before the IRS in the event of an audit. The training to become an EA is longer and more sophisticated than that of an unenrolled preparer. Continuing education also is required; EAs must complete at least 16 hours of continuing education each year (and 72 hours per three years) to maintain their licenses, which are renewed every three years. Some EAs offer bookkeeping and payroll tax services, and some even do financial planning.

Enrolled agents' fees tend to fall between those of a preparer and a certified public accountant (I discuss CPAs in the next section). If you require tax return preparation and related advice and representation, and nothing more (no corporate audits or production of financial reports), an EA can provide the expertise you need for a reasonable cost.

TIP

The main difference between enrolled agents and CPAs and tax attorneys is that EAs work exclusively in the field of taxation. Not all CPAs and attorneys do. In addition to preparing your return (including simple to complex forms), good EAs can help with tax planning, represent you at tax audits, and keep the IRS off your back. You can find names and telephone numbers of EAs in your area by contacting the National Association of Enrolled Agents (toll-free 855-880-6232; www.naea.org).

Certified public accountants

Certified public accountants (CPAs) go through significant training and examination to receive the CPA credential. To maintain this designation, a CPA must complete 40 hours of continuing education classes per year.

As with any other professional service you purchase, CPA fees can vary tremendously. Expect to pay more if you live in an area with a high cost of living, if you use the services of a large accounting firm, or if your needs are involved and specialized.

TIP

Competent CPAs are of greatest value to people completing some of the more unusual and less user-friendly schedules, such as Schedule K-1 of Form 1065 for partnerships. CPAs also are helpful for people who had a major or first-time tax event during the year, such as the child-care tax-credit determination. (Good EAs and other preparers can handle these issues as well.) CPA firms are often a good choice for business owners because they're usually larger than EA firms and can offer software services beyond tax and bookkeeping, such as computer consulting.

WARNING

Whenever your return is uncomplicated and your financial situation is stable, hiring a high-priced CPA year after year to fill in the blanks on your tax returns is a waste of money. A CPA once bragged to me that he was effectively making more than $500 per hour from some of his clients' returns that required only 20 minutes of an assistant's time to complete.

However, paying for the additional cost of a CPA on an ongoing basis makes sense if you can afford it and if your financial situation is reasonably complex or dynamic. If you're self-employed and/or you file many other schedules, hiring a CPA may be worth it. But you needn't do so year after year. If your situation grows more complex one year and then stabilizes, consider getting help for the perplexing year and then using other preparation resources discussed in this chapter or a lower-cost preparer or enrolled agent in the future.

TIP

If you desire more information about CPAs in your area, use the "For the Public" link on the American Institute of Certified Public Accountants' website at www.aicpa.org/forthepublic/findacpa.html. If you're considering hiring a CPA, be sure to ask how much of his or her time is spent preparing individual income tax returns and returns like yours.

Tax attorneys

Unless you're a super-high-income earner with a complex financial life, hiring a tax attorney to prepare your annual return is prohibitively expensive. In fact, many tax attorneys don't prepare returns as a normal practice. Because of their level of specialization and training, tax attorneys tend to have high hourly billing rates — $200 to $400-plus per hour isn't unusual, and rumor has it that some attorneys in a major metropolitan area have just crossed the $1,000-per-hour threshold.

Tax attorneys sometimes become involved in court cases dealing with tax problems, disagreements, or other complicated matters, such as the purchase or sale of a business. However, other good tax advisors also can help with these issues.

Who's best qualified?

Who is best qualified to prepare your return? That really depends on the individual you want to hire. The CPA credential is just that, a credential. Some people who have the credential try to persuade you not to hire someone without it.

Some tax-preparation books perpetuate the myth that only a CPA can do your taxes. In one such book, in a chapter about choosing a tax preparer, the authors warn that you shouldn't choose an accountant casually and note that there are more than 300,000 certified public accountants. These authors then recommend that you ask a potential preparer, "Are you a certified public accountant?" (As you may have guessed, the firm behind the book is a large CPA company.)

What about all the non-CPAs, such as EAs, who do a terrific job helping prepare their clients' returns and tax plans throughout the year?

If you can afford to and want to pay hundreds of dollars per hour, hiring a large CPA firm can make sense. But for the vast majority of taxpayers, spending that kind of money is unnecessary and wasteful. Many EAs and other tax preparers are out there doing outstanding work for less.

REMEMBER

The more training and specialization a tax practitioner has (and the more affluent the clients), generally the higher the hourly fee. Select the tax pro who best meets your needs. Fees and competence at all levels of the profession vary significantly. If you aren't sure of the quality of work performed and the soundness of the advice, get a second opinion.

Finding Tax Advisors

Your challenge is to locate a tax advisor who does terrific work, charges reasonable fees, and thus is too busy to bother calling to solicit you! Here are some resources to find those publicity-shy, competent, and affordable tax advisors:

>> **Friends and family:** Some of your friends and family members probably use tax advisors and can steer you to a decent one or two for an interview.

- **Coworkers:** Ask people in your field what tax advisors they use. This strategy can be especially useful if you're self-employed.

- **Other advisors:** Financial and legal advisors also can be helpful referral sources, but don't assume that they know more about the competence of a tax person than you do.

WARNING

Beware of a common problem: Financial or legal advisors may simply refer you to tax preparers who send them clients.

- **Associations:** Enrolled agents (EAs) and certified public accountants (CPAs) maintain professional associations that can refer you to members in your area. See the relevant earlier sections for EAs and CPAs.

REMEMBER

Never decide to hire a tax preparer or advisor solely on the basis of someone else's recommendation. To ensure that you hire a competent advisor with whom you'll work well, take the time to interview at least two or three candidates (with the help of the following section).

Interviewing Prospective Tax Advisors

When you believe that your tax situation warrants outside help, be sure to educate yourself as much as possible before searching for assistance. The more you know, the better able you'll be to evaluate the competence of someone you may hire. That's why you should read the portions of this book that apply to your tax situation even if you're determined to pay for help.

Make sure that you ask the right questions to find a competent tax practitioner whose skills match your tax needs. The following questions/issues are a great place to start.

REMEMBER

When all is said and done, make sure that you feel comfortable with a tax advisor. I'm not suggesting that you evaluate an advisor the way you would a potential friend or spouse! But if you're feeling uneasy and can't understand what your tax advisor says to you in the early stages of your relationship, trust your instincts and continue your search.

What tax services do you offer?

Most tax advisors prepare tax returns. I use the term *tax advisors* because most tax folks do more than simply prepare returns. Many advisors can help you plan and file other important tax documents throughout the year. Some firms can also assist your small business with bookkeeping and other financial reporting, such as income statements and balance sheets. These services can be useful when your business is in the market for a loan or if you need to give clients or investors detailed information about your company.

As a small business owner, you should seek out tax advisors who work with a large number of small businesses. This should comprise a significant portion of their practice.

TIP

Ask tax advisors to explain how they work with clients. You're hiring the tax advisor because you lack knowledge of the tax system. If your tax advisor doesn't explore your situation, you may experience "the blind leading the blind." A good tax advisor can help you make sure that you don't overlook deductions or make other costly mistakes that may lead to an audit, penalties, and interest. Beware of tax preparers who view their jobs as simply plugging your information into tax forms.

What are your particular areas of expertise?

This question is important because you want to find an advisor who's a good match for your situation. For example, if a tax preparer works mainly with people who receive regular paychecks from an employer, the preparer probably has little expertise in helping small business owners best complete the blizzard of paperwork that the IRS requires.

TIP

Find out what expertise the tax advisor has in handling whatever unusual financial events you're dealing with this year — or whatever events you expect in future years. For example, if you need help completing an estate tax return for a deceased relative, ask how many of these types of returns the tax preparer has completed in the past year. About 15 percent of estate tax returns are audited, so you don't want a novice preparing one for you.

What other services do you offer?

Ideally, you want to work with a professional who is 100 percent focused on taxes. I know it's difficult to imagine that some people choose to work at this full time, but they do — and lucky for you!

WARNING

A multitude of problems and conflicts of interest crop up when a person tries to prepare tax returns, sell investments, and appraise real estate all at the same time. That advisor may not be fully competent or current in any of those areas.

By virtue of their backgrounds and training, some tax preparers also offer consulting and financial planning services for business owners and other individuals. Because such preparers already know a great deal about your personal and tax situation, they may be able to help in these areas. Just make sure that this help is charged on an hourly consulting basis. Avoid tax advisors who sell financial products that pay them a commission — this situation inevitably creates conflicts of interest.

Who will prepare my return?

If you talk to a solo practitioner, the answer to this question should be simple — the person you're talking to should prepare your return. But if your tax advisor has assistants and other employees, make sure that you know what level of involvement these different people will have in the preparation of your return.

It isn't necessarily problematic if a junior-level person does the preliminary tax return preparation that your tax advisor reviews and finalizes. In fact, this procedure can save you money in tax-preparation fees if the firm bills you at a lower hourly rate for a junior-level person.

Be wary of firms that charge you a high hourly rate for a senior tax advisor who then delegates most of the work to a junior-level person.

How aggressive or conservative are you regarding interpreting tax laws?

Some tax preparers, unfortunately, view their role as enforcement agents for the IRS. This attitude often is a consequence of one too many seminars put on by local IRS folks, who admonish and sometimes intimidate preparers with threats of audits.

On the other hand, some preparers are too aggressive and try tax maneuvers that put their clients on thin ice — subjecting them to additional taxes, penalties, interest, and audits.

Assessing how aggressive a tax preparer is can be difficult. Start by asking what percentage of the preparer's clients gets audited (see the next question). You can also ask the tax advisor for references from clients for whom the advisor helped unearth overlooked opportunities to reduce tax bills.

What's your experience with audits?

As a benchmark, you need to know that the IRS audits about 1 percent of all taxpayer returns. Small business owners and more affluent clients can expect a higher audit rate — somewhere in the neighborhood of 2 percent to 4 percent.

WARNING

If a tax preparer proudly claims no audited clients, be wary. Among the possible explanations, any of which should cause you to be uncomfortable in hiring such a preparer: She isn't telling you the truth, she has prepared few returns, or she's afraid of taking some legal deductions, so you'll probably overpay your taxes.

A tax preparer who has been in business for at least a couple of years will have gone through audits. Ask the preparer to explain her recent audits, what happened, and why. This explanation sheds light not only on her work with clients but also on her ability to communicate with you in plain English.

How does your fee structure work?

Tax advisor fees, like attorney and financial planner fees, are all over the map — from about $50 to $300 or more per hour. Many preparers simply quote you a total fee for the preparation of your tax return.

Ultimately, the tax advisor charges you for time, so you should ask what the hourly billing rate is. Alternatively, you can ask him how many hours of work he is assuming it will take to complete your tax return. If the advisor balks at answering such questions, try asking what his fee is for a one-hour consultation. You may want a tax advisor to work on this basis if you've prepared your return yourself and want it reviewed as a quality-control check. You also may seek an hourly fee if you're on top of your tax preparation in general but have some specific questions about an unusual or one-time event, such as making some major purchases for your business or possibly selling your business.

Clarify whether the preparer's set fee includes follow-up questions that you may have during the year or covers IRS audits on the return. Some accountants include these functions in their set fee, but others charge for everything on an as-needed basis. The advantage of the all-inclusive fee is that it removes the psychological obstacle of your feeling that the meter's running every time you call with a question. The drawback can be that you pay for additional services (time) that you may not need or use.

What qualifies you to be a tax advisor?

REMEMBER

Tax advisors come with a variety of backgrounds. The more tax and business experience they have, usually the better. But don't be overly impressed with credentials. As I discuss earlier in this chapter, tax advisors can earn certifications such as CPAs and EAs. Although gaining credentials takes time and work, these certifications are no guarantee that you get quality, cost-effective tax assistance or that you won't be overcharged.

Generally speaking, more years of experience are better than fewer, but don't rule out a newer advisor who lacks gray hair or who hasn't yet slogged through thousands of returns. Intelligence and training can easily make up for less experience.

Newer advisors also may charge less to build up their practices. Be sure, though, that you don't just focus on each preparer's hourly rate (which of course can change over time). Ask each practitioner you interview how much total time she expects your tax return to take. Someone with a lower hourly fee can end up costing you more if she's slower than a more experienced and efficient preparer with a higher hourly rate.

Do you carry liability insurance?

If a tax advisor makes a major mistake or gives poor advice, it could cost you thousands of dollars. The greater your income, assets, and the importance of your financial decisions, the more financial harm that can be done.

Even my presuming that you're not a litigious person, your tax advisor needs to carry what's known as *errors and omissions* or *liability* insurance. You can, of course, simply sue an uninsured advisor and hope the advisor has enough personal assets to cover a loss, but don't count on it. Besides, you'll have a much more difficult time getting due compensation that way!

You may also ask the advisor whether he has ever been sued and how the lawsuit turned out. Asking this type of question doesn't occur to most people, so make sure that you tell your tax advisor that you're not out to strike it rich on a lawsuit!

INVESTIGATE

Another way to discover whether a tax advisor has gotten into hot water is by checking with appropriate professional organizations to which that preparer may belong. You can also check whether any complaints have been filed with your local Better Business Bureau (BBB), although this is far from a foolproof screening method. Most dissatisfied clients don't bother to register complaints with the BBB, and you should also know that the BBB is loath to retain complaints on file against companies that are members.

Can you provide references of clients similar to me?

You need to know that the tax advisor has handled cases and problems like yours. For example, if you're a small business owner (and I assume that by picking up this book, you either are or want to be), ask to speak with other small business owners. But don't be overly impressed by tax advisors who claim that they work mainly with one occupational group, such as retailers or physicians. Although there's value in understanding the nuances of a profession, tax advisors are ultimately generalists — as are the tax laws.

When speaking with a tax advisor's references, be sure to ask what work the advisor performed and what the client's satisfaction was with it.

4

The Part of Tens

Keep track of your business financials and taxes with software and apps.

Set your sights on overlooked tax-cutting opportunities. They fall into two categories: lowering your taxable income and taking a variety of deductions.

Discover a list of resources to consult after reading this book. You can find help for tax-related issues and get answers to general small business questions.

Chapter **14**

Ten (Almost) Useful Apps and Software Packages for Small Business Tax Issues

S mall business owners and managers have plenty to keep track of concerning their business' financials and taxes. So, using well designed technology to help with those tasks can be money well spent.

In this chapter, I highlight and discuss a variety of software programs and apps to help you with your small business' taxes.

Tracking Expenses with Expensify

Expensify (www.expensify.com/) as you may surmise from its name, is an expense-tracking app. You can capture pictures of receipts on your smartphone and classify by expense category as well as download transactions from your credit card.

Although its basic version is free for individual users, most users will find that they need to pay at least $4.99 per month to get the functionality that they desire. Expensify is also partnering with other companies like Lyft and Uber so that you can import expenses from those services, and Expensify can integrate with applications like QuickBooks.

Processing Sales with Square

Square (https://squareup.com/) is a point-of-sale service that allows business owners, especially those who want to process transactions in the field and on the go, to accept credit cards and other commonly used payment vehicles. The base transaction charge is 2.75 percent of the amount processed for swiped transactions. Manually entered transactions cost more — 3.5 percent fee plus a $0.15 surcharge. Link the service to your bank account and funds received on your transaction will be deposited there typically in one day.

PayPal (www.paypal.com/) and **Stripe** (https://stripe.com/) are other popular alternatives and charges similar fees. These platforms make more sense for businesses focused online.

Managing Transactions with EMS+

Electronic Merchant Systems' EMSplus is a lower cost alternative to Square at 2.25 percent transaction fee for swiped transactions. The parent company has been in business since 1987 and receives good reviews for its service. For more information, visit https://plusbyems.com/.

Marking Miles with MileIQ

MileIQ (www.mileiq.com/) is a smartphone-based app that easily allows you to track when you use your car for business purposes. The basic version is free (and covers you for 40 drives per month) whereas the Premium version costs $59.99 when paid annually ($5.99 per month if paid monthly). The Premium version is included in Microsoft's Office 365 Business Premium package.

Managing Your Accounting with QuickBooks

QuickBooks by Intuit (https://quickbooks.intuit.com/) has been a long-term player in the small business accounting marketplace. Their self-employed version for sole proprietors who file IRS Form 1040 Schedule C, which enables users to

» Track income and expenses

» Capture and organize receipts

» Estimate quarterly taxes

» Invoice and accept payments

» Run basic reports

» Track miles

Even though this package is a quality one, I don't care for the fact that rather than selling you the software for a fixed one-time fee, QuickBooks has moved to charging a monthly fee. The self-employed version, for example, costs $10 per month ($120 annually).

Intuit also offers **Payroll,** a cloud-based payroll service. This can be bought separately or in addition to QuickBooks. As you may expect, this service integrates well with Intuit's other offerings such as QuickBooks. For more information, visit https://payroll.intuit.com/.

Handling Accounting and Invoicing with FreshBooks

FreshBooks (www.freshbooks.com/) is an online small business accounting and invoicing tool. You can try it for free for 30 days, and after that the pricing is based upon how many clients you bill. The Lite plan, which lets you bill up to five clients, costs $15 per month. The Plus plan lets you bill 50 clients for $25 per month. The Premium plan enables you to bill up to 500 clients for $50 per month.

Preparing Taxes with TurboTax Self-Employed

TurboTax Self-Employed is a tax preparation software package for those who file Schedule C, which is what most self-employed people do. This program also includes industry specific tax tips costs $119.99 for the federal income tax return and $39.99 for the state version. (They also offer software for other types of small business entities.)

Made by Intuit, it integrates well with QuickBooks. Visit `https://turbotax.intuit.com/personal-taxes/online/self-employed.jsp` for more information.

Completing Taxes with H&R Block Tax Preparation and Filing Software

H&R Block offers a menu of tax software preparation options. For most people with modestly challenging returns, the Deluxe version, which costs $54.95 for the federal return plus your state return, handles the basic Form 1040 schedules although not Schedule C or Schedule C-EZ. If you're filing this latter schedule, you'll need the "Premium" version, which costs $74.95 for the federal return plus your state. You'll also need this version if you need to file Schedule D or Schedule E.

The "Premium and Business" version costs $89.95 for the federal return plus your state. Visit `www.hrblock.com/tax-software/` for more information.

Chapter **15**

(Almost) Ten Often Overlooked Tax Reduction Opportunities

Throughout this book, I present information and strategies to help you deal with and minimize the income taxes you're legally required to pay. The reality is that you may not read this whole book, retain all that is covered, or get around to doing everything that can benefit your situation.

This chapter presents some commonly overlooked opportunities to reduce your small business and individual income taxes that I want to be sure you don't miss. The income tax you pay is based on your taxable income minus your deductions. I start first with overlooked ways to minimize your taxable income and then move on to often-ignored deductions.

Invest in Wealth-Building Assets

During your working years, while you're earning employment income, you probably don't need or want taxable income from your investments because it can significantly increase your income tax bill. Real estate, stocks, and small business investments offer the best long-term growth potential, although you need to be able to withstand downturns in these markets.

Most of the return that you can earn with these wealth-building investments comes from appreciation in their value, making them tax-friendly because you're in control and can decide when to sell and realize your profit. Also, as long as you hold on to these investments for more than one year, your profit is taxed at the lower, long-term capital gains rate.

Fund Some Retirement Accounts

When you funnel your savings dollars into retirement accounts, such as a 401(k), 403(b), SEP-IRA, or SIMPLE-IRA, you can earn substantial upfront tax breaks on your contributions. If you think that saving for retirement is boring, consider the tens of thousands of tax dollars these accounts can save you during your working years.

If you don't use these accounts to save and invest, you may well have to work many more years to accumulate the reserves necessary to retire. See Chapter 3 to find out more about these accounts.

Contribute to a Health Savings Account

Health savings accounts (HSAs) hold promise for people to put money away on a tax-advantaged basis to pay for healthcare-related expenses. Money contributed to an HSA is tax-deductible, and investment earnings compound without tax and aren't taxed upon withdrawal so long as you use the funds to pay for eligible healthcare costs. So, unlike a retirement account, HSAs are actually triple tax-free!

The list of eligible expenses is generally quite broad — surprisingly so in fact. To qualify for an HSA, you need to maintain a so-called high-deductible healthcare plan. For more on HSAs, flip to Chapter 2.

Work Overseas

You've always wanted to travel overseas, right? When you go to work in a foreign country with low income taxes, you may be able to save big-time on income taxes. For tax year 2019, you can exclude $105,900 of foreign-earned income (whether working for a company or on a self-employed basis) from U.S. income taxes. To qualify for this income tax exclusion, you must work at least 330 days (about 11 months) of the year overseas or be a foreign resident. You claim this income tax exclusion on Form 2555, "Foreign Earned Income."

If you earn more than $105,900, don't worry about being double-taxed on the income above this amount. You get to claim credits for foreign taxes paid on your U.S. tax return on Form 1116, "Foreign Tax Credit." Perhaps to give you more time to fill out this form and others, the IRS gives Americans working abroad two extra months (until June 15) to file their tax returns.

As with many things in life that sound too good to be true, this pot of overseas gold has some catches.

» First, many of the places you've romanticized about traveling to and perhaps living in — such as England, France, Italy, Sweden, Germany, and Spain — have higher income tax rates than the ones in the United States.

» Also, this tax break isn't available to U.S. government workers overseas.

TIP

Investigate the whole package when deciding whether to work overseas. Some employers throw in a housing allowance and other benefits. Be sure to consider all costs and benefits of living overseas, both financial and emotional.

Calculate Whether a Deduction Is Worth Itemizing

Deductions are just what they sound like: You subtract them from your income before you calculate the tax you owe. So the more deductions you take, the smaller your taxable income — and the smaller your tax bill. The IRS gives you two methods of determining your total deductions. You get to pick the method that leads to the largest total deductions — and thus a lower tax bill. But sometimes the choice isn't so clear, so be prepared to do some figuring.

Taking the standard deduction usually makes sense if you have a pretty simple financial life — a regular paycheck, a rented apartment, and no large expenses, such as medical bills, moving expenses, or loss due to theft or catastrophe. The standard deductions almost doubled in 2018 thanks to the Tax Cuts and Jobs Act. In 2019, single folks qualify for a $12,200 standard deduction, and married couples filing jointly get a $24,400 standard deduction.

The other method of determining your allowable deductions is to itemize them on your tax return. This painstaking procedure is definitely more of a hassle, but if you can tally up more than the standard deduction amount, itemizing saves you money. Schedule A of Form 1040 is the page for summing up your itemized deductions, but you won't know whether you have enough itemized deductions unless you give this schedule a good examination (refer to Chapter 9).

If you currently don't itemize, you may be surprised to discover that your personal property and state income taxes are itemizable, subject to an annual cap of $10,000. If you pay a fee to the state to register and license your car, you can itemize the expenditure as a deduction (line 8, "Other Taxes," on Schedule A). The IRS allows you to deduct only the part of the fee that relates to the car's value, however. The state organization that collects the fee should be able to tell you what portion of the fee is deductible. If it's a user-friendly organization, it may even show this figure on your invoice.

When you total your itemized deductions on Schedule A and that amount is equal to or less than the standard deduction, take the standard deduction without fail (unless you're married filing separately and your spouse is itemizing — then you have to itemize). The total for your itemized deductions is worth checking every year, however, because you may have more deductions in some years than others, and you may occasionally be able to itemize.

TIP

Because you can control when you pay particular expenses for which you're eligible to itemize, you can shift or bunch more of them into selected years when you know that you'll have enough deductions to take full advantage of itemizing. For example, suppose that you're using the standard deduction this tax year because you just don't have many itemized deductions. Late in the tax year, though, you feel certain that you'll buy a home sometime during the next year. Thanks to the potential write-off of mortgage interest and property taxes, you also know that you'll be able to itemize next year. It makes sense, then, to shift as many deductible expenses as possible into the next year.

If you're near the threshold for itemizing, you could make several years' worth of charitable donations in one year. Also, in most cases, you can make an extra property tax payment near the year's end.

Trade Consumer Debt for Mortgage Debt

Suppose that you own real estate and haven't borrowed as much money as a mortgage lender currently allows (given your property's current market value and your financial situation). And further suppose that you've run up high-interest consumer debt. Well, you may be able to trade one debt for another. You probably can refinance your mortgage and pull out extra cash to pay off your credit card, auto loan, or other expensive consumer credit line. You usually can borrow at a lower interest rate for a mortgage, thus lowering your monthly interest bill. Plus, you may get a tax-deduction bonus because consumer debt — auto loans, credit cards, and credit lines — isn't tax-deductible, but mortgage debt generally is. Therefore, the effective borrowing rate on a mortgage is even lower than the quoted rate suggests.

Don't forget, however, that refinancing your mortgage and establishing home equity lines involve application fees and other charges (points, appraisals, credit reports, and so on). You must include these fees in the equation to see whether exchanging consumer debt for more mortgage debt makes sense.

WARNING

Swapping consumer debt for mortgage debt involves one big danger: Borrowing against the equity in your home can be an addictive habit. I've seen cases in which people run up significant consumer debt three or four distinct times and then refinance their homes the same number of times over the years so they can bail themselves out. At a minimum, continued expansion of your mortgage debt handicaps your ability to work toward other financial goals. In the worst case, easy access to borrowing encourages bad spending habits that can lead to bankruptcy or foreclosure on your debt-ridden home.

Consider Charitable Contributions and Expenses

When you itemize your deductions on Schedule A, you can deduct contributions made to charities. For example, most people already know that when they write a check for $50 to their favorite house of worship or college, they can deduct it. Yet many taxpayers overlook the fact that they can also deduct expenses while performing activities for charitable organizations. For example, when you go to a soup kitchen to help prepare and serve meals, you can deduct your transportation costs to get there. You just need to keep track of your bus fares or driving mileage.

You can also deduct the fair market value (determined from online sales, for example) of donations of clothing, household appliances, furniture, and other goods to charities. Many of these charities will even drive to your home to pick up the stuff. Just make sure to keep some documentation: Write a detailed list and get it signed by the charity. You can also take a picture of non-cash items you donate.

If you contribute money to your local schools, including for youth sports, you can deduct it as long as the money goes toward the overall program and team rather than being specifically earmarked for your child. If you drive kids to school events, you can deduct those costs as well. Finally, if a charitable organization selects you as a representative, for example, to attend its national convention, you should be able to deduct unreimbursed costs for the trip and event.

Scour for Self-Employment Expenses

If you're self-employed, you already deduct a variety of expenses from your income before calculating the tax that you owe. When you buy a computer or office furniture, you can deduct those expenses (sometimes you need to gradually deduct or depreciate them over time). Employee salaries, office supplies, rent or mortgage interest for your office space, and phone expenses are also generally deductible.

REMEMBER

Although more than a few business owners cheat on their taxes, some self-employed folks don't take all the deductions they should. In some cases, people simply aren't aware of the wonderful world of deductions. For others, large deductions raise the concern of an audit. Taking advantage of deductions for which you're eligible makes sense and saves you money. Hiring tax help is worth the money — by using a book like this one and/or by paying a tax professional to review your return one year (see Chapter 13 for details on getting tax help).

Married Couples Should Crunch the Numbers on Filing Separately

About five percent of married couples file their federal income tax returns under the status of "Married Filing Separately" rather "Married Filing Jointly." Most married couples that file separately do so to save money but there can be other reasons such as each spouse not wanting to be liable for their spouses' tax transgressions.

The only way that a couple can know if they may save money by filing separately is to run the numbers. Couples with the following characteristics are more likely to benefit:

>> If one spouse owns a pass-through business that is eligible for the 20 percent pass-through deduction but loses that deduction due to the combined income of their spouse.

>> If one spouse has high medical expenses, which can be written off when they exceed 7.5 percent of adjusted gross income but loses that deduction due to the higher combined income with their spouse.

>> If the couple lives in a state that has a tax code that may favor spouses that file separately.

If you have a tax preparer, be careful to understand their additional fee for filing separate returns as that cost may wipe out the potential tax savings.

Chapter **16**

Ten Resources to Turn to After Reading This Book

Throughout this book, I provide many suggested resources and tips. In this chapter, I cover some additional topics and resources that you may find useful in your travels. Suggested resources in this chapter are organized by the purpose that they help you accomplish.

To Develop a Good Business Plan and Improve Your Small Business

Though taxes are an important aspect and challenge in running your small business, you have many bigger topics to tackle as an entrepreneur or small business owner. How will you grow your business, gain new customers, manage costs, acquire the right equipment at the best price, hire and retain good employees, and so on?

TIP

Small Business For Dummies, which I co-wrote with small business veteran Jim Schell (and which is published by John Wiley & Sons, Inc.), answers all these questions and more.

To Whip Your Finances into Shape

Many small business owners and folks in general haven't optimized their personal finances. Don't you make that mistake! Running a business is hard enough, and if you aren't making the most of your money, you diminish your chances for business success.

TIP

Check out the latest edition of my bestselling book, *Personal Finance For Dummies* (published by John Wiley & Sons, Inc.), for a comprehensive review of your financial situation and a guide for what you need to do and when regarding your personal finances.

To Select the Best Business Entity

As I discuss in Chapter 2, the business entity you choose for your business will impact (among other issues) the taxes you owe, the types of liability you're exposed to, and the benefits you may offer or deduct for tax purposes.

For the best advice after reading what I have to say in this book, a tax advisor who specializes in small business work is ideal. (Chapter 13 has advice on how to find and interview prospective tax advisors.) Legal advisors who work mostly with small businesses can help you as well.

To Set Up an Accounting and Financial Management System

If you want to maximize your chances for small business success and stay on top of your business's financial situation, an accounting and financial management system is mandatory. It's your best way to "keep score" in your small business.

Although there are many systems, among the best are software packages like QuickBooks and Quicken. For more information on all your accounting options, please see Chapter 6.

To Hone Your Investment Savvy for Your (and Your Employees') Retirement Funds

Making money and then saving money requires your efforts and focus. After saving some money, you want to be sure to make the most of it. The investing universe includes plenty of land mines and pitfalls.

TIP

To maximize your chances for investing success, be sure to boost your investing intelligence. Check out the latest edition of my bestselling book *Investing For Dummies* (John Wiley & Sons, Inc.).

For Help with Payroll Regulations and Employee Tax Withholdings

Good luck keeping up with the continually changing rules and regulations surrounding the withholding and submission of various local, state, and federal income taxes for your employees (and yourself). It's a quagmire and a nightmare all rolled into one!

Though retaining the services of a payroll company costs money, it's money well spent because it ensures that tax withholdings are done correctly and on time, which saves you headaches and money. If you've been subject to IRS and/or state tax authority deposit penalties, having a payroll service take over your payroll can often cost less in the long run. Of course, you still have to have the money available for the payroll service to make deposits.

By all means, shop around and compare services from payroll processing companies. Don't select the cheapest or a company lacking a longer-term track record. Be sure to assess customer satisfaction and the competence of any company you may hire.

To Dig Deeper into IRS Rules and Regulations

You may need to delve into the intricacies of a particular set of tax laws and want to do some research on your own. After all, tax advisors don't come cheap, and even if you hire one to assist you, the more educated you are, the better decision you can make.

TIP

On the IRS website, you can check out the section "IRS News and Published Guidance," which as of the printing of this book is located at `www.irs.gov/government-entities/federal-state-local-governments/irs-news-and-published-guidance`. For additional resources, see Chapter 12.

To Deal with IRS Collection Efforts

Getting behind on some taxes is, unfortunately, an all too common problem among small business owners. This typically happens when an owner fails to hire a payroll processing company and neglects to do what he needs to on his own.

If you get in a pickle like this, by all means hire a tax pro or a payroll company to help you get out of the mess as soon as possible. To find out more about IRS collection efforts, IRS Publication 594, "The IRS Collection Process," is a concise and reasonably comprehendible missive for an IRS publication. You can find it online at `www.irs.gov/pub/irs-pdf/p594.pdf`.

For More Detailed Advice about All Aspects of Your Income Tax Return

This book provides a good overview of the most common tax quandaries faced by small business owners and taxpayers in general. But there's a limit, of course, to what I can cover in a book of this length.

TIP

J. K. Lasser's Your Income Tax (John Wiley & Sons, Inc.) is a detailed reference book you may want to consider. It weighs in at about 800 pages and goes into great detail on numerous topics, although it doesn't focus specifically on small business issues. This classic book was first published in 1937 and is updated annually.

For Assistance in Preparing Your Income Tax Return

In addition to using books, you have two main resources to assist you with preparing your annual income tax return.

» You can use a time-tested software program. TurboTax (https://turbotax.intuit.com) is one that I can recommend for its longevity and accuracy.

» You can hire a tax advisor. Check out Chapter 13 for my advice on how to find and interview prospective tax advisors.

Index

Numerics

A

C

C corporations, 26–32, 33
canceled debt, 124
capital gain (or loss), 122
capitalization (cap), 62–63
car expenses
  about, 109
  on IRS Form 1040 Schedule C, 143–146
cash accounting basis, 11
cash basis, 107
cash method of accounting, 139
cash-value life insurance, 95–97
certified public accountant (CPA), 197, 201,
  227–228, 230
CFA (Chartered Financial Analyst), 55
charitable contributions/expenses, 247–248
charitable lead trust, 99
charitable remainder trust, 98–99
charitable trusts, 98–99
Chartered Financial Analyst (CFA), 55
Cheat Sheet (website), 4
cheating, 213–214
child care expenses, 133
choosing
  business entities, 252
  investments for retirement accounts, 54–70
  stock funds, 62–65
Clifford, Denis (attorney)
  Plan Your Estate, 100
collection due process hearing, 212
collections, 254
commercial leases, 85–86
commissions, on IRS Form 1040 Schedule C, 146
commuting expenses, 145
compounding returns, 73–74
consumer debt, 247
continuity of life, 31
contract labor, on IRS Form 1040 Schedule C, 146
contributing to health savings accounts, 244
co-payments, for health insurance plans, 39–40
corporate taxes, 12, 20–21, 29–31
correspondence audits, 198

cost of goods sold, on IRS Form 1040 Schedule C,
  141–142
costs. *See also* accounting system
  about, 103
  for bonds, 67
  controlling with home office, 77
  ETFs and, 60
  of funds, 55
  minimizing for funds, 57–58
CPA (certified public accountant), 197, 201,
  227–228, 230
credit card expenses, 107
credit quality, for bonds, 67
Crumney trust, 94
custodian, 56

D

data processing errors, 205
date, misunderstood, 204
declaring all income, 212
deductibles, for health insurance plans,
  39–40
deductions
  interest, 14–15
  itemizing, 115, 120–121, 213, 245–246
  meal and entertainment, 15
  missing, 10
  for pass-through entities, 13–14
Delaware, incorporating in, 32
delinquent tax return notice, 194–195
dependent care
  as an employee benefit, 43
  expenses for, 133
depletion, on IRS Form 1040 Schedule C, 146
depreciation
  for automobiles, 14
  for cars, 145
  for home office, 163–165
  on IRS Form 1040 Schedule C, 147–148
  percentages for, 148
depreciation recapture, 168
discipline, home office and, 78

FreshBooks, 241

funding retirement accounts, 244

funds

balanced, 66

bond, 67–70

G

general partners (GPs), 34–35

generation-skipping transfer tax, 93

gifting, 93, 94

GPs (general partners), 34–35

Griswold, Robert (author)

Real Estate Investing For Dummies, 86

gross receipts, on IRS Form 1040 Schedule C, 141

group term life insurance, as an employee benefit, 43

growth stocks, value stocks *vs.,* 63

guaranteed renewability, for health insurance plans, 40

H

Harbor Capital Appreciation, 64

Harbor International, 65

Health Care and Education Reconciliation Act (2010), 40–41

health insurance agents, 41

health insurance mandate, 15

health insurance plans, as an employee benefit, 38–42

health savings account (HSA), 42, 127, 181–182, 244

healthcare provider choice, for health insurance plans, 39

healthcare reimbursement account, 42

HealthEquity, 182

hiring tax preparers, 223

hobby loss, 24, 155

home expenses, 109

home office

about, 11, 76, 157–160

controlling costs, 77

cost comparisons, 79

disadvantages of, 166–168

IRS Form 8829, "Expenses for Business Use of Your Home," 160–166

local ordinances, 76–77

separating work and personal life, 78

hotels, as an employee benefit, 43

household employment taxes, 175–176

H&R Block tax preparation and filing software, 242

HSA (health savings account), 42, 127, 181–182, 244

I

icons, explained, 3

ID number, incorrect, 204

income (loss). *See also* adjustments to income

about, 121–122

declaring all, 212

documenting, 105

double-counted, 204

exempt, 204

incorrect, 204

repeated, 166–167

taxable, 16–17

income tax, paying, 106–107

income verification notices, 190

incorporation, 26–32

index funds, 59

individual 401(k), 53

individual tax rates, 12–13

inheritance tax, 89–91

insurance (other than health), on IRS Form 1040 Schedule C, 149

interest

on additional tax, 194

deductions for, 14–15

on IRS Form 1040 Schedule C, 149

intermediate-term bond funds, 69

Internal Revenue Service (IRS), 106, 113, 116, 124, 136, 174, 195–196, 203–209, 219, 221–222

international stock funds, 64–65

About the Author

Eric Tyson, MBA, is an internationally acclaimed and bestselling personal finance book author, former financial advisor, and speaker. He has worked with and taught people from all financial situations, so he knows the financial concerns and questions of real folks just like you. Despite being handicapped by an MBA from the Stanford Graduate School of Business and a BS in economics and biology from Yale University, Eric remains a master of "keeping it simple."

An accomplished personal finance writer, he's an award-winning columnist and the author of numerous national bestselling financial books in the *For Dummies* series, on personal finance, investing, mutual funds, home buying and real estate investing (coauthor), small business (coauthor) and other topics. His *Personal Finance For Dummies* was awarded the Benjamin Franklin Award for best business book of the year.

Eric's work has been featured and quoted in hundreds of local and national publications and outlets, including the *Wall Street Journal, Los Angeles Times, Fox News, Chicago Tribune, Forbes, Kiplinger's Personal Finance, Parenting, Money,* and *Bottom Line/Personal*; on NBC's *Today Show,* ABC, CNBC, Fox Business Network, PBS's *Nightly Business Report,* CNN, and on CBS national radio, NPR's *Sound Money,* and Bloomberg Business Radio.

Eric's website is www.erictyson.com.

Author's Acknowledgments

A special shout-out and thank-you to the editorial folks at Wiley, who put countless hours and ideas into making this book what it is. First up is Tracy Boggier, whose guidance, wisdom, and patience are always valued and appreciated. Project editor Linda Brandon did an excellent job continually improving the book and making sure it stayed on track and on schedule. And a big thank-you to copy editor Chad Sievers for his tireless and intelligent editing of this book.

Last but not least, a big round of applause to technical reviewer and tax advisor Christopher De Penti. He made many helpful suggestions to make the book better.

Publisher's Acknowledgments

Acquisitions Editor: Tracy Boggier

Senior Project Editor: Linda Brandon

Copy Editor: Chad Sievers

Technical Editor: Christopher De Penti

Production Editor: Magesh Elangovan

Cover Image: © Jewelsy/iStock.com